THOREAU'S RELIGION

Thoreau's Religion presents a ground-breaking interpretation of Henry David Thoreau's most famous book, *Walden*. Rather than treating Walden Woods as a lonely wilderness, Balthrop-Lewis demonstrates that Thoreau's ascetic life was a form of religious practice dedicated to cultivating a just, multispecies community. The book makes an important contribution to scholarship in religious studies, political theory, English, environmental studies, and critical theory by offering the first sustained reading of Thoreau's religiously motivated politics. In Balthrop-Lewis's vision, practices of renunciation like Thoreau's can contribute to the reformation of social and political life.

In this, the book transforms Thoreau's image, making him a vital source for a world beset by inequality and climate change. Balthrop-Lewis argues for an environmental politics in which ecological flourishing is impossible without economic and social justice.

ALDA BALTHROP-LEWIS is a Research Fellow in the Institute for Religion and Critical Inquiry at Australian Catholic University. She holds a PhD in Religion from Princeton University and has taught Religious Studies at Brown University. Her research, which focuses on religious ethics and the circulation of ideas among theological, artistic, and popular idioms, has appeared in the *Journal of the American Academy of Religion* and the *Journal of Religious Ethics*.

"Here at last is a thoughtful and deeply informed reflection on Thoreau as a religious writer, a contemplative who went to Walden Pond to reorient his deepest values against a world gone mad with casual cruelty. As Balthrop-Lewis shows, Thoreau lived his ethical transformation not alone for himself but, as a writer, in partnership with us, toward a renewal of religious thought and action. She gives us *Walden* as scripture, a call to live a higher life by locating and reconnecting with all on whom we depend — human and nonhuman alike — so we might renounce the lures of domination and awaken the world to both environmental and political justice. *This* is the Thoreau we need now."

— Laura Dassow Walls, William P. and Hazel B. White Professor of English, University of Notre Dame, and author of Henry David Thoreau: A Life *(2017)*

"This book by Balthrop-Lewis is more than just a brilliantly conceived, wonderfully written, and thoroughly convincing reinterpretation of Thoreau. Much more broadly, in its implications for theology, politics, and environmental ethics, the book counters artificial separations between spiritual practice and efforts at political reform, between religiously inspired appreciation for the natural world and the struggle for justice. In every respect, it represents a groundbreaking achievement."

— Kathryn Tanner, Marquand Professor of Systematic Theology, Yale Divinity School

"This book is undoubtedly the best treatment of Thoreau in this generation. Alda Balthrop-Lewis is herself a profound philosopher-poet who captures the subtle and sublime genius of the great philosopher-poet Thoreau like no other. And in these bleak times of ecological catastrophe, we need them both!"

— Cornel West, Professor of the Practice of Public Philosophy, Harvard University

"New Cambridge Studies in Religion and Critical Thought" combines philosophical clarity, historical scholarship, and ethical inquiry into the study of religion, considering such questions as: What does a properly critical approach to "religion" or to particular religious traditions, practices, and ideas involve? What concepts might such an approach employ and how should these be understood? What are the political implications of taking such an approach – for religious studies and for the people studied therein? How should attention to race, class, gender, sexuality, capital, empire, and domination inform our assessment of religious traditions, institutions, and practices? The answers offered, while diverse in their methodologies, topics, and conclusions, are intended alike to be clear, precise, and historically attuned investigations of important subjects or figures in the study of religion and critical thought.

Thoreau's Religion

Walden Woods, Social Justice, and the Politics of Asceticism

Alda Balthrop-Lewis

CAMBRIDGE
UNIVERSITY PRESS

University Printing House, Cambridge CB2 8BS, United Kingdom

One Liberty Plaza, 20th Floor, New York, NY 10006, USA

477 Williamstown Road, Port Melbourne, VIC 3207, Australia

314–321, 3rd Floor, Plot 3, Splendor Forum, Jasola District Centre, New Delhi – 110025, India

79 Anson Road, #06–04/06, Singapore 079906

Cambridge University Press is part of the University of Cambridge.

It furthers the University's mission by disseminating knowledge in the pursuit of education, learning, and research at the highest international levels of excellence.

www.cambridge.org
Information on this title: www.cambridge.org/9781108835107
DOI: 10.1017/9781108891608

First published 2021

A catalogue record for this publication is available from the British Library.

Library of Congress Cataloging-in-Publication Data
Names: Balthrop-Lewis, Alda, author.
Title: Thoreau's religion : Walden woods, social justice, and the politics of asceticism / Alda Balthrop-Lewis.
Description: Cambridge, United Kingdom ; New York, NY, USA : Cambridge University Press, [2020] | Series: New Cambridge studies in religion and critical thought | Includes bibliographical references and index.
Identifiers: LCCN 2020040015 (print) | LCCN 2020040016 (ebook) | ISBN 9781108835107 (hardback) | ISBN 9781108799676 (paperback) | ISBN 9781108891608 (epub)
Subjects: LCSH: Thoreau, Henry David, 1817-1862–Religion.
Classification: LCC PS3057.R4 B35 2020 (print) | LCC PS3057.R4 (ebook) | DDC 818/.309–dc23
LC record available at https://lccn.loc.gov/2020040015
LC ebook record available at https://lccn.loc.gov/2020040016

ISBN 978-1-108-83510-7 Hardback

To Anat Benzvi

a writing partner
who provides wisdom and whimsy
in all the right measures

The reason why an ingenious soul shuns society, is to the end of finding society. It repudiates the false, out of love for the true.

Ralph Waldo Emerson, "Literary Ethics"

Contents

Preface

I care about people and their flourishing. I care about the places we live and the other things that live in those places, and about the relationship between us and the places we live. I care about growing things and making things. I care about walking, and trees. I want to follow Jesus and I think that the gospel teaches a preferential option for the poor, which just means that the poor have a special relationship to God, and that all people, but especially those with privileges, should prioritize the wellbeing of the poor. I care about communities, and about building communities in which people are supported, loved, and provided the freedom to live as they like. I care about building a future for humans in which our greatest goods are valued: our love for one another, our capacity for learning, our differences from one another.

And I also care about books. One of the books that I love is Henry David Thoreau's *Walden*.

I like it because it is funny, and beautiful, and weird. It is hard. I like it because it is about people and the places they live and the relationships they have to other people. I like that it doesn't hide how cranky it is. I like that it shows me something about how much is possible outside of what I expect. I like that it doesn't seem to hide its weird messy bits, its contradictions and vices.

One of the places in the world that I love most of all is a region on the Gulf of Mexico, on the Panhandle of Florida, where I grew up, where my mother now lives and where my father farmed clams. It is an extraordinary place, one of the biodiversity hotspots of North America, full of forests, rivers, marshes, and estuaries that host teeming ecosystems. It attracts people who care about and enjoy such things, and it is beautiful.

This place I love also has a fascinating, mostly forgotten, important history. Because of its geographical position, the British built a fort on the Apalachicola River in the last year of the war of 1812, in what was then Spanish Florida. They made alliances there with Indigenous people who lived in the region or had fled there from Alabama – especially Red Stick Creek and Seminole. They also collaborated with free Black people including some free citizens of Spanish Florida (where there was not slavery) and some formerly enslaved people who had fled to Spanish Florida from enslavement in the United States.[1] The British distributed arms and ammunitions

[1] As this manuscript is being copyedited, there is an important, ongoing debate about race and typography. The question is about whether to capitalize the words "black" and "white" when they are used to refer to a person's race or ethnicity. Until recently, many style guides have suggested they should be downcased. However, in 2020 several major style guides changed their practice in response to the Movement for Black Lives. Some people still argue that neither should be capitalized, because to do so would be to naturalize race, when racialization is a historical process that has often been used as a tool of domination. Others argue that Black (with a capital letter) as a racial and ethnic adjective is the appropriate way to describe Black Americans who identify as such, and whose longer ethnic histories were violently obscured by enslavement. Among those who capitalize Black, some think that "white" as a racial description should stay downcased, because it is not claimed as an ethnic identity in the same way except by white supremacists. Others argue that both Black and White should be capitalized, since Black is claimed as an identity by Black people, but is not a natural fact and was always in historical relationship to White identity. According to this view, capitalizing White shows up whiteness as a socially constructed racial identity, when it often otherwise remains normalized and invisible, conferring undue advantages on White people.

I want my typographical choices to show that I consider racialization a historical process that has been used as both a tool of domination and of resistance, that this historical process has real effects in social life and politics, and that I respect the self-identifications of Black people and admire their contributions to American life. With respect for many who disagree on this question and without a standardized consensus, I have chosen to capitalize "Black" and leave "white" downcased when

among their allies in the region, and when they withdrew in 1815, after learning of the end of the War of 1812, they left the fort under the control of their Indigenous and Black allies. Most of the Indigenous people returned to the places that they had lived before, but the Black British allies remained at the fort, cleared land along the river for farming, and established a growing community in freedom.[2] A Creek observer named William McGirt wrote, in the summer of 1815: "They Keep Sentry & the Negroes are Saucy & insolent, and say they are all Free."[3] I find these "saucy," "insolent" people deeply admirable. They enacted their own freedom.

This community of free Black people was only about 60 miles down the river from Georgia, where 105,218 people were reported enslaved by 1810.[4] The place was called "Negro Fort" in the press, and it was seen by some US citizens

used as racial descriptions. My sense is that the process of white people meaningfully reckoning with the history of whiteness remains nascent, and capitalizing the word in advance of white people learning our racial history is unlikely to be an effective means of carrying out that reckoning. One useful source with respect to the history of whiteness is Nell Irvin Painter, *The History of White People* (New York, NY: Norton, 2010).

[2] The first book-length work on this community is Nathaniel Millett, *The Maroons of Prospect Bluff and Their Quest for Freedom in the Atlantic World* (Gainesville: University Press of Florida, 2013). "The process of comparing Prospect Bluff with other maroon settlements provides a rare glimpse into how a community of successful North American slave rebels might choose to live, when entirely on their own terms. The comparative method demonstrates how full and remarkable a version of freedom had been achieved at Prospect Bluff" (Millett, *The Maroons of Prospect Bluff*, 98). See also, Matthew J. Clavin, *Aiming for Pensacola: Fugitive Slaves on the Atlantic and Southern Frontiers* (Cambridge, MA: Harvard University Press, 2015), 39–61. "It was the largest maroon colony of fugitive slaves in the history of the territory that would become the United States" (Clavin, *Aiming for Pensacola*, 40).

[3] Quoted in Clavin, *Aiming for Pensacola*, 52.

[4] The figure comes from census data reported in John Cummings, "Negro Population in the United States 1790–1915" (US Census Bureau, 1918), 57, www.census.gov/library/publications/1918/dec/negro-population-1790-1915.html (accessed August 20, 2020).

and politicians as a threat to the United States. Southern enslavers complained that the community served as a beacon for people escaping enslavement. Clavin writes that "according to one U.S. Army lieutenant, 'their numbers were increasing daily.'"[5] So one year after the British withdrawal, in July of 1816 when the inhabitations and gardens of the settlement stretched for 50 miles along the river, the US military surrounded the fort both on land and on the river and demanded the surrender of the 300–400 free people who were sheltered inside. The occupants refused to surrender, raised the English Jack, and defended the fort for days. Eventually, a shot from US gunboats on the river hit the gunpowder magazine and caused a massive explosion. That explosion killed many of the people inside the fort. The site of the fort and that deadly explosion is now located within what is seen as pristine national forest, the historic markers (which use the current name "Fort Gadsden") are rarely visited, and the story of the free Black people who grew gardens and fought to maintain their home is largely forgotten by the tourists who come to paddle the river. Kayaking is big.

At the beginning of my academic career, I thought my research would treat that place, whose ecology and history I loved. I planned an ethnographic project about the way people think about environmental ethics on a local level there. I went to work learning about ethnographic methods, and I spent time in Apalachicola doing fieldwork: attending local government meetings, learning about environmental activism, going out on the water with fishermen, and getting to know scientists who study the bay on which the town is located. That topic seemed to me rich and deep and ethically complicated. It also seemed that to do it well I would need to work on it for a long time. It occurred to me that a first book should be a project you can finish, not one that you can imagine working on for the rest of your life.

[5] Clavin, 52.

So I switched courses, and decided to write first about a book, *Walden*, and about a dead white man rather than a living, struggling community. Because I think Thoreau is endlessly compelling, this didn't feel like a loss, exactly, more like something I needed to do first. Needed to do now. A way of getting to know myself, and practice for everything else. But there have been days when it was hard to see how the work I was doing on these nineteenth-century Yankee texts was related to the place I started out caring about.

Then, one day, deep in the middle of this project, something amazing happened. It doesn't happen often, at least not to me, but I guess every now and then when we're lucky the fates can send us a sign that we're in the place we're supposed to be, doing what we're supposed to be doing. That day I was reading in Thoreau's *Journal* from the summer of 1845, the summer he went to live at Walden. And it was as if the parts of my life that sometimes seemed remote from one another were coming together in a way I could not yet explain. Just beginning to settle in to his life at the Pond, Thoreau wrote,

> And earlier today came 5 Lestrigones – Railroad men who take care of the road, some of them at least. They still represent the bodies of men – transmitting arms and legs – and bowels downward from those remote days to more remote. They have some got a rude wisdom withal – thanks to their dear experience. And one with them a handsome younger man – a sailor Greek like man – says "Sir I like your notions – I think I shall live so my self Only I should like a wilder country – where there is more game. I have been among the Indians near Apallachecola I have lived with them, I like your kind of life – Good-day I wish you success and happiness."[6]

[6] Henry David Thoreau, *Journal*, Volume 2: *1842–1848*, ed. Robert Sattelmeyer (Princeton, NJ: Princeton University Press, 1984), 160–61.

Thoreau recorded his encounter with the railroad men at work in Walden Woods in his usual, playful way, likening them to ancient Greek "Lestrigones" who had appeared in Homer's *Odyssey*, and praising the wisdom they had gained by experience. Then he quoted one of them, one who seems to have been a kindred spirit: "Sir I like your notions." It is fun to imagine what Thoreau said his notions were to elicit this response. Did he say, "I have come to the woods to live deliberately"? Did he say, "I want to see how little I can live on"? Did he say, "I love the wild, and I want to live among it"? But then, and this was what took me aback, the railroad man had been to Apalachicola! He had lived with the "Indians" there, in a "wilder country." He thought it would be an even better place to live than Walden Woods, and he told Thoreau so. I grew up with legends of old Indian tracks through the woods, grew up looking for arrowheads on the beach, grew up trekking out to see middens made of the shells of oysters and clams, just some of the "game" the Indigenous people lived on, evidence of the societies who loved the place before we settlers came. And here, in Thoreau's *Journal*, was a railroad man who had lived with them.

Because of Apalachicola's role as a port, it is not so surprising that railroad men in Concord would have been there. But to find that Thoreau wrote about the fact that they had, startled me. I jumped up, shouting. It gave me comfort, somehow, in the middle of a project I sometimes struggled to believe in, to find the Panhandle I loved in its earlier, wilder shape on those pages.

I think it made me feel that somehow, in some way I do not yet know, my life does hang together in all its half-formed pieces. The work I do is sometimes so interdisciplinary I have the feeling it will all fall apart, that the center cannot hold. This is a temptation. When I have it, I remember that Annie Dillard wrote:

> You take it on faith that the multiform and variously lighted latitudes and longitudes were part of one world, that you didn't drop chopped from house to house, coast to coast, life to life, but in some once comprehensible way moved there, a city block at a time, a highway mile at a time, a degree of latitude and longitude at a time ...[7]

When I am sitting elsewhere, writing, in Chicago or New Jersey or, now, in Australia, on Wurundjeri Country, and I remember how far from home, from the "wilder country" that I love, I am, I try to remember Dillard's faith. You take it on faith, she says, that the parts belong – somehow – together, in one world. And at the same time, I think, you have to remember that no matter how many parts there seem to be, there is only one you holding them together. You have to know who that is to tell us the story of your moving elsewhere "a city block at a time, a highway mile at a time, a degree of latitude and longitude at a time."

I want to write toward a wide, beautiful, complicated, suffering world. This work deals with issues related to race, religion, class, and environment. Writing about these things, I have discovered some complicated linguistic issues about how I identify myself with respect to that world, those races, religions, classes, places, beauty, and suffering. When I describe white people, or Black people, or poor people, or rich people, or Indigenous people, or people who live in places that suffer, or the pious ones, do I say "they"? "We"? I am only me. Thoreau wrote at the beginning of *Walden*, "I, on my own side, require of every writer, first or last, a simple and sincere account of his own life" (I, 2).[8] I try to remember that

[7] Annie Dillard, *An American Childhood* (New York: Harper & Row, 1987), 249.

[8] I give references to Thoreau's *Walden*, "Civil Disobedience," and "Slavery in Massachussetts" in the tradition of Stanley Cavell: "To make my references to *Walden* independent of any particular edition, I shall give citations by chapter and paragraph, roman numerals for the former, arabic for the latter. References to 'Civil Disobedience' are also according to paragraph, preceded by 'CD.'" Stanley

my own life shapes what I see to a large extent, especially when I write about people who are different from me, whose experience I only know distantly. I know I must often get it wrong. Myles Horton – educator for the US civil rights movement – wrote, about "Knowing Yourself,"

> You have to be careful not to think that you're somebody else. I've had to avoid thinking that I'm Nicaraguan or, when I was in India, Indian. I have a tendency to want to identify with people. I have to say to myself, "Look, Horton, get as close to people as you can, have as much interest as you can, but don't get things mixed up. You're white, and black people can't say they are color-blind. Whites and white-controlled institutions always remind them that they're black, so you've got to recognize color." That doesn't mean that you feel superior, it's just that you've got to realize that you can never fully walk in other people's shoes. You can only be a summer soldier, and when the excitement is over, you can go back home. That doesn't mean that you don't have solidarity with black people and aren't accepted; it just means that you have a different role to play.[9]

I'm a woman who grew up with all kinds of privileges, and whose early privileges have only accumulated since. Some of those privileges I am so grateful for; others have made me a smaller, more anxious, less feeling and caring person. In this work I aim to write about the issues I have come to care about, but being careful not to think that I'm somebody else. In this spirit, I identify myself as white in the text that follows, not to feel superior or inferior, but in an effort – an effort still incomplete, I think – to be clear with you and with myself about who I am and the role I mean to play.

Cavell, *The Senses of Walden* (New York: Viking Press, 1972), 4. All references to Thoreau's other writings in this work are given in footnotes to particular editions. In addition, I have retained original punctuation for all Thoreau quotations.

[9] Myles Horton, *The Long Haul: An Autobiography* (New York: Teachers College Press, 1997), 195.

Acknowledgments

This book began at Princeton University, where I was ably supported by a community of faculty, staff, and students whose joy in scholarship, commitment to transformative pedagogy, and natural collegiality inspired my own optimistic sense of what academic life might be. It was sustained through a visiting appointment at Brown University, where my students' grave suspicion of Thoreau's place in the history of settler colonialism deepened my appreciation for the difficulty of the task I had set myself: to help Thoreau speak to the present. I fear I have not met their challenge, but I trust they will carry the torch themselves. Since then, the book has been given the space, time, and resources it required by the Institute for Religion and Critical Inquiry at Australian Catholic University in Melbourne, Australia.

I have discussed material published here with many audiences, and I want to thank them all for their engagement. I should thank Richard Miller especially, for asking a key question about asceticism in 2014. His intervention helped to shape what this book has become. I also want to thank the people I have collaborated with on various conference panels about this material, including Hans-Christoph Askani, Maria Antonaccio, Fannie Bialek, Shira Billet, Steve Bush, David Brakke, Mark Cladis, Sarah Coakley, Daniel Delorme, C.J. Dickson, Emily Dumler, Daniel Fineman, Nicholas Friesner, Brian Hamilton, Carly Lane, Dana Lloyd, Vincent Lloyd, Elizabeth Mazzolini, Raymond Malewitz, Karline McLain,

Nicole Metildi, Deborah Mutnik, Willemien Otten, Scott Resnick, Dan Sherrell, Sarah Stewart-Kroeker, Kyle Sittig, Alex Torres, and Sarah Zager. I was touched to be welcomed so warmly to my first Thoreau Society event in 2019 by James Finley, John Kucich, and Alex Moskowitz. Conversation and correspondence with Willis Jenkins, Laura Dassow Walls, and Lance Newman have provided real encouragement.

Portions of the book have appeared elsewhere in print and I thank the publishers for permission to use the material, which has been significantly rearranged.

- "Thoreau's Woodchopper, Wordsworth's Leech-Gatherer, and the Representation of 'Humble and Rustic Life.'" In *Theology and Ecology across the Disciplines: On Care for Our Common Home*, edited by Celia Deane-Drummond and Rebecca Artinian-Kaiser. London: Bloomsbury, 2018.
- "Exemplarist Environmental Ethics: Thoreau's Political Asceticism against Solution Thinking." *The Journal of Religious Ethics* 47, 3 (September 2019): 525–50.
- "Active and Contemplative Lives in a Changing Climate: The Emersonian Roots of Thoreau's Political Asceticism." *Journal of the American Academy of Religion* 87, 2 (May 30, 2019): 311–32.

Many readers have responded to previous versions of this book. Jeffrey Stout read the first draft with tremendous care and helped me imagine it could become something good to read. Mark Cladis, Keri Day, Molly Farneth, Eric Gregory, Martin Kavka, Susannah Ticciati, Cornel West, and the anonymous readers from Cambridge University Press all provided generous written comments. Other readers have included Leora Batnitzky, Anat Benzvi, Shira Billet, Wallace Best, Liane Carlson, Rachel Davies, Jessica Delgado, Emily Dumler-Winckler, Lexi Eikelbloom, Rick Elgendy, Eddie Glaude, Jonathan Gold, Clifton Granby, Joshua Nunziato, Seth Perry, Al Raboteau, Susan Stewart, Sarah Stewart-Kroeker, Judith

Weisenfeld, and the members of both the Religion and Critical Thought workshop and the Religion in the Americas workshop at Princeton University. Fannie Bialek, Steve Bush, Molly Farneth, Daniel May, and Joshua Dubler read the whole manuscript and provided a wonderful conversation about revision. I hope a small piece of the potential they saw in this work exists now in the world.

Alex Wright at Cambridge University Press and all the Press staff have been a tremendous support. I thank them for their good work. William Lamson shared his photograph for the cover image, and Adriane Colburn taught me about his beautiful camera obscura installation and the video he made with it: *Untitled (Walden)*, 2014.

I was formed as a writer and a thinker before this project ever began by the wise teaching of Elizabeth Bernhardt, Adriane Colburn, Renee Courey, Kris Culp, Arnold Eisen, Linda Eyster, Franklin Gamwell, Van Harvey, Kevin Hector, Cynthia Lindner, Barbara Pitkin, Eric Slauter, Brent Sockness, and Lee Yearley. I am grateful for the lessons they taught me.

For their encouragement and patience and care, I want to thank Rebecca Anderson, Owen Billington and Rebekah Kerr and Michaela Psihogios-Billington, Lindsey Braun, Sylvia Clark, Josh Daniel and Megg Hoover, Rick Elgendy, Natalie and Josh Erdossy, Carolina Glauster, Steve Morrison, Annette Thornburg Owen, Sylvia Spicer, the Jacobs-Vandegeers, and the High Rise baking collective at Fitzroy Community Food Centre. Then, in the final crunch, there were the pinch hitters: the revolutionaries from Redgum Cleaning Cooperative, the grocery fairies at Ceres Fair Food, Dan Frankel, and the monks of Tarrawarra Abbey in the Yarra Valley.

Though I admire people who stay put, as Thoreau did, and I often wish I could do it myself, I belong to a generation and a class whose life consists mostly of coming and going. I have been coming and going from some amazing communities over the last many years: in Tallahassee and Franklin County, Florida; in Boston; in London; in California; in Italy and environs; in St. Paul, Minnesota; in Chicago; in New Jersey and New York; in Austin, Texas; and in Melbourne, Australia. In those places – and in airports, train stations, and bus depots on the way – I have often received the kindness of strangers, who listened to me talk about this work with interest, and encouraged me by suggesting they might want to read it themselves. To those communities and to those strangers I just want to say: thank you. Many of the virtues of this work were born in my relationships to you.

Family of all kinds have given their good will and hospitality, especially Amara, Al, Sadie, Tate, Sam, and Lucy Hastings. My parents, Mary Balthrop and Van Lewis, encouraged me to read when I was a child. They left me time and space to climb trees and keep notebooks. They taught me that none of us is free until all of us are, and they showed me how to gather your people around you and love them like crazy. Their parents, Ellen and Ed Balthrop and Clifton and George Lewis, taught us all that the heart of the gospel is the call for justice.

Anat Benzvi became my writing partner before I realized it, helped me (every week, sometimes more) through the whole of this project, and continues to remind me that whatever it takes to keep writing is what you have to do. “If in order to write you need … a certain light yellow paper, a certain special pen, a dim light shining from the left, it is useless to tell yourself that just any pen will do, that any paper and any light will suffice.”[1] I have dedicated the book to her because it probably would not exist without her, and in any case it would have been a lot less fun.

[1] Giorgio Agamben, *Profanations*, trans. Jeff Fort (New York: Zone Books, 2007), 10.

I completed this work halfway around the world from where it began. From the window where I wrote the bulk of it, in Melbourne, Australia, I could see the weather and the children come and go. My thanks to David Newheiser for taking me there. We have cared together (through much contestation!) about many of the ideas presented here, and his presence in my life has shaped every page.

Introduction: Why Thoreau Would Love Environmental Justice

The Book's Aims

Henry David Thoreau's *Walden*, published in 1854, is still so regularly taught in US high schools that US Americans usually know it by instinct. Whether or not they actually read *Walden*, they understand its basic plot: Thoreau went to the woods near Concord, Massachusetts "to live deliberately," as he famously wrote. He built a tiny house by the shores of Walden Pond, in a friend's forest. He grew beans and read books and went on walks. He laid on his belly to peer through the ice of the pond when it was frozen over during the winter. And he recorded his experiences in journals that he developed over nearly ten years into *Walden*. This has made Thoreau into a saint of the environmental movement, sometimes.[1]

[1] Lawrence Buell made the comparison to sainthood explicit and analyzed it in his important work on Thoreau and nature writing. There, he also analyzes Walden Pond as a site of pilgrimage. Lawrence Buell, *The Environmental Imagination: Thoreau, Nature Writing, and the Formation of American Culture* (Cambridge, MA: Belknap Press, 1996), 328–32. Rod Giblett has written on Thoreau as "the patron saint of swamps." Rodney James Giblett, *Postmodern Wetlands: Culture, History, Ecology* (Edinburgh: Edinburgh University Press, 1996). April Anson calls Thoreau the "patron saint of tiny houses." April Anson, "The Patron Saint of Tiny Houses," in *Henry David Thoreau in Context*, ed. James Finley (Cambridge: Cambridge University Press, 2017). Contemporary interpreters regularly use the phrase "environmental saint" as though its meaning were obvious. See, for example, Kent Curtis, "The Virtue of Thoreau: Biography, Geography, and History in Walden Woods," *Environmental History* 15, 1 (2010): 32. Of course, environmentalists are not agreed Thoreau should have this status, and there is a

But, as I will describe, he is a complicated figure to hold up as a hero, perhaps especially for environmentalism. And his image as 'saint of the woods' has sometimes obscured his commitment to justice in human communities.

Bring to mind two different figures of Thoreau. On the one hand, there is the Thoreau we have from *Walden*, the one whose nature piety inspired him to live in the woods, to spend time among the birds and the trees and the woodchucks. This is the Thoreau whose writings grew more and more focused on the observation of nature as he aged, who came to believe that the observation of the world around him was his most important activity. This Thoreau was a great naturalist. Then, on the other hand, there is the figure of Thoreau we have from the essay that has come to be called "Civil Disobedience," the Thoreau whose night in jail for not paying tax inspired Gandhi – and then Martin Luther King, Jr. – to nonviolence in the pursuit of social justice. This Thoreau was an active abolitionist who admired John Brown and even made him into a Christ figure.

I want to tell a story that can unite these two figures of Thoreau – his nature piety and his political commitment to justice – into one man, one life.[2] We know Thoreau opposed

persuasive argument that Thoreau's influence on the environmental movement has in fact been negative. See William Chaloupka, "Thoreau's Apolitical Legacy for American Environmentalism," in *A Political Companion to Henry David Thoreau*, ed. Jack Turner (Lexington: The University Press of Kentucky, 2009).

[2] The "two Thoreaus" observation is not new, and the tension we sometimes see between them is not simply (as I suggest below) a result of a segregated (and racist and misogynist) reception history. An early biographer wrote about his motivation for writing Thoreau's biography: "As Thoreau could do what he did, and never feel as though there was any inconsistency between Walden life and anti-slavery action, I was desirous to satisfy myself, by closer scrutiny, of his real aims and objects." Alexander H. Japp, *Thoreau: His Life and Aims* (Boston: Osgood, 1877), viii. In the twentieth century the theme remained in circulation: Leo Marx, "The Two Thoreaus," October 26, 1978, www.nybooks.com/articles/1978/10/26/the-two-thoreaus/ (accessed August 20, 2020). A late twentieth-century interpreter in

slavery, but many readers of Thoreau read his opposition to slavery apart from his interest in nature. This book argues that these two sides of Thoreau should be read together. Thoreau didn't just happen to love nature and also be committed to economic and political justice, including the abolition of slavery, as though those were separate interests. Those two features of his work were part of one thing: a form of piety that entailed pursuing spiritual flourishing for all.[3]

Walden is the book in which these two figures come together most vividly, so I make this argument by way of an interpretation of *Walden*, one that draws out the justice concerns that were driving much of it and that are often, surprisingly, neglected. I reinterpret the nature piety in *Walden* as the ground for Thoreau's radical political commitments.

political science, Jane Bennett, focuses on one Thoreau (the naturalist Thoreau) so as to situate the other (the political Thoreau) within it. "The Thoreau most vocal in these debates is not the Thoreau of 'Resistance to Civil Government' or the antislavery lectures, but the Thoreau of *Walden*, the journals, *The Maine Woods, A Week on the Concord and Merrimack Rivers,* and the natural history essays. I find these naturalist writings more engaging than the political writings because they map out a larger project within which, among other things, Thoreau's arts of civil disobedience and political dissent are set." Jane Bennett, *Thoreau's Nature: Ethics, Politics, and the Wild* (Thousand Oaks, CA: Sage Publications, 1994), xx. At the time Bennet wrote, looking for the political Thoreau in the naturalist Thoreau was innovative. I join a new edge of Thoreau scholarship that tries to speak to current tensions between nature piety and social justice by arguing that the "two Thoreaus" are one. As Thoreau's most recent biographer wrote: "Today, two hundred years after his birth, we have invented two Thoreaus, both of them hermits, yet radically at odds with each other. One speaks for nature; the other for social justice. Yet the historical Thoreau was no hermit, and as Thoreau's own record shows, his social activism and his defense of nature sprang from the same roots." Laura Dassow Walls, *Henry David Thoreau: A Life* (Chicago: University of Chicago Press, 2017), xviii.

[3] Jeffrey Myers has argued that Thoreau represented a new resistance to racial and ecological hegemony. Jeffrey Myers, *Converging Stories: Race, Ecology, and Environmental Justice in American Literature* (Athens, GA: University of Georgia Press, 2005).

This unified figure offers an image in which environmentalism and efforts for a just political community (including economic and racial justice) do not just happen to coincide but belong to one another, are integral, require one another.[4] Thoreau's love of nature led him to love justice. Even if interpreters (especially white interpreters) have often evacuated *Walden* of its radical political significance and basic call for justice, the reading of *Walden* I offer in this book can reconfigure Thoreau's significance for contemporary environmental politics.

I think there are reasons readers have often leaned toward one or the other of the two Thoreaus in their interpretation of *Walden*. The main reason is that readers of Thoreau have generally been more invested in one of the two figures I described or the other – because they lived in a context in which one or the other of these radical visions was most pressing.[5] For Gandhi, in colonial India, Thoreau's resistance to civil government offered an example of what resistance to political injustice could look like. But for Rachel Carson,

[4] In this I hope to persuade those who share the growing agreement on this point among many with environmental concerns that Thoreau is an ally rather than a foe. The articulation of this point as "integral ecology" was one of the reasons Pope Francis's encyclical was welcomed warmly by environmentalists: Francis, *Laudato Si'* [Encyclical Letter on Care for Our Common Home], http://w2.vatican.va/content/francesco/en/encyclicals/documents/papa-francesco_20150524_enciclica-laudato-si.html (accessed August 5, 2020). See also Jedediah Purdy, *After Nature: A Politics for the Anthropocene* (Cambridge, MA: Harvard University Press, 2015). Purdy has argued that the challenges of this age call for an environmental politics that commits to a deepened democracy, since "taking responsibility for nature and taking responsibility for democracy come together" in a world determined by human powers (286).

[5] This is just to say that Bob Pepperman Taylor's confession is a common (and often laudable) reading practice. "I had always read him with my own agenda as the overwhelming concern." Bob Pepperman Taylor, *America's Bachelor Uncle: Henry Thoreau and the American Polity*, American Political Thought (Lawrence, KS: University Press of Kansas, 1996), x.

facing the evidence of the harms of the widely used insecticide DDT in the United States, Thoreau's nature piety was most compelling. In both cases, readers of Thoreau faced real, pressing problems that shaped their reception of his writing. Of course, it is not the case that Carson ignored the claims of economic and racial justice, or that Gandhi was unconcerned with the health of the land. But different communal contexts (often shaped in the United States by ongoing effects of white supremacy, especially Jim Crow, intense segregation, and resegregation) led to one emphasis or another in the way readers have told the story of who Thoreau is. One premise of this book is that white supremacy perverted Thoreau's twentieth-century reception.

Since the environmental justice movements of the 1980s and 1990s, the presumed whiteness of US environmentalism is thankfully passing away, though of course its actual whiteness in the large national organizations, like whiteness of all kinds, persists.[6] For too long, and still, white racial cultures of environmentalism have had tense relationships with communities of color, have failed to describe and fight environmental racism that harms such communities. The US history of land access (that it was stolen from Indigenous peoples) and labor

[6] On environmental racism and environmental justice movements, the most prominent scholar may be Robert Bullard. His classic work, *Dumping in Dixie*, was among the first academic studies to document the fact of race- and class-based environmental inequality. Robert D. Bullard, *Dumping in Dixie: Race, Class, and Environmental Quality* (Boulder, CO: Westview Press, 1990). Dorceta Taylor has been at the forefront of documenting the power of privilege in shaping American environmentalism. See especially Dorceta E. Taylor, "American Environmentalism: The Role of Race, Class and Gender in Shaping Activism, 1820–1995," *Race, Gender & Class* 5, 1 (1997): 16–62; Dorceta E. Taylor, "The State of Diversity in Environmental Organizations: Mainstream NGOs, Foundations & Government Agencies" Green 2.0. www.diversegreen.org/wp-content/uploads/2015/10/FullReport_Green2.0_FINAL.pdf (accessed August 5, 2020); Dorceta E. Taylor, *The Rise of the American Conservation Movement: Power, Privilege, and Environmental Protection* (Durham, NC: Duke University Press Books, 2015).

(that it was so often stolen from kidnapped Africans enslaved in the United States and their enslaved, US-born children) has meant that white people have had particularly privileged relationships to the places we lived and recreated and sought to preserve. White supremacy has made it so that white citizens often have greater social, economic, and political powers to protect the places we love than communities of color; white environmentalism too often kept our places clean, and sent our environmental harms to be endured by communities of color.[7] But the movements for environmental justice that began in the 1980s and 1990s and have only grown in the years since are teaching white environmentalists that our privileges were never *ours*. The care and connection we experience to the places that we live is real, but as Thoreau believed, ownership can fool us. When we think we own the land alone, we can forget the alternative view: that it was given to all in common.[8] Thoreau complained of those landowners who put up fences – they interrupted his walking routes. But the insight was deeper: proprietary relationships can disfigure the ones who think of themselves as owners.

[7] David Pellow's work on environmental injustice describes it as a form of social violence and associates it with police violence and hyperincarceration. David Naguib Pellow, *What Is Critical Environmental Justice?* (Cambridge, UK: Polity, 2017).

[8] I return briefly to Thoreau's worries about ownership in Chapter 4. Readers interested in the philosophical debate Thoreau was entering might take interest in a contemporary philosophical treatment of the topic in Jeremy Waldron, *The Right to Private Property* (Oxford: Clarendon, 1988). Waldron critically examines the idea that private property is a fundamental human right. In Thoreau's time and place, the suspicion of private property was common. Bronson Alcott's suspicion of private property contributed to the community he helped form at Fruitlands. Orestes Brownson admitted an individual right to property, but advocated the abolition of inherited property. "As we have abolished hereditary monarchy and hereditary nobility, we must complete the work by abolishing hereditary property." Orestes Augustus Brownson, *The Laboring Classes: An Article from the Boston Quarterly Review* (Boston, MA: B. H. Greene, 1840), 24.

Much of the aim of telling the story the way I do is a desire to inspire those communities of white environmentalists I often find myself among to cease our own segregation of Thoreau. To let him be the whole person that he was. To see his radical commitment to justice as the outgrowth of the nature piety for which we have admired him. And to let him teach us to be the more wholesome people we might become, persons who can acknowledge our interdependence and work for the benefit of the goods we can only share in common if we want to avoid the moral and spiritual corruption that comes with deformed, unjust relationships with other people, other creatures, natural objects, ecosystems, and the land.

I see a problem with the way I have set this up, however. This story could be read as one that tries to make Thoreau into a predecessor of environmental justice movements, those twentieth-century political movements that showed the ways in which environmental harm is so unevenly distributed to communities of color and the poor. I like that about the story I am telling, in that it aims to make Thoreau an ally of frontline communities that are fighting for their wellbeing. But I am also attentive to the fact that Thoreau was no saint with respect to racial and class politics from the perspective of our times. And, more to the point, he was not the one who did the organizing – the work – required to bring environmental justice and movements against environmental racism into being and into the public view. The people who did that were citizens, patriots, who deserve our admiration and support.[9] So part of me worries

[9] One window into this activism through a particularly important case is Elizabeth D. Blum, *Love Canal Revisited: Race, Class, and Gender in Environmental Activism* (Lawrence: University Press of Kansas, 2008). Another important history that helped scholars see the ways in which mainstream white environmentalism failed to account for the difference race and class make to environmental problems is Laura Pulido, *Environmentalism and Economic Justice: Two Chicano Struggles*

that this story will read as an aggrandizement of an imperfect man, at the expense of the vast coalitions of democrats who actually do the consistent, grinding work required to make environmental justice a reality.

When you're a person who likes Thoreau, as I do, writing about him carries with it one great danger: that the infatuation will blind you, that your admiration will lead you to make larger claims than the evidence demonstrates, and especially that you will take him to be exemplary, a moral model on a grand scale, when he also of course represents his time and its foibles. I feel the danger pressing in.[10] I am inspired by the life Thoreau lived, especially by the ways in which he articulated the concerns that we share. He resisted the emaciated vision of the human promoted by industrial economy, and I find this feature of his writing deeply heartening. He was funny, and he struggled to find his way, and he loved and was loved deeply. In this way, I am drawn to how he articulated his humanity, and, by doing that, sometimes enables the rest of us to be a little more human.

in the Southwest (Tucson, AZ: University of Arizona Press, 1996). See also Shannon Elizabeth Bell, *Our Roots Run Deep as Ironweed: Appalachian Women and the Fight for Environmental Justice* (Urbana, IL: University of Illinois Press, 2013). Broader histories of the US environmental movement can be found in Robert Gottlieb, *Forcing the Spring: The Transformation of the American Environmental Movement* (Washington, DC: Island Press, 2005); Chad Montrie, *A People's History of Environmentalism in the United States* (London: Continuum, 2011). There is a particularly helpful bibliographical essay on the historiography of environmentalism in Montrie, *A People's History of Environmentalism*.

[10] I have even written myself on how Thoreau might serve as an example for contemporary environmental ethics, though I claim he ought to be an example of something rather different than simply "living lighter on the earth." Alda Balthrop-Lewis, "Exemplarist Environmental Ethics: Thoreau's Political Asceticism against Solution Thinking," *The Journal of Religious Ethics* 47, 3 (September 2019): 525–50.

But I also know that my attachment to him sometimes leans in the direction of adulation. And I know that a lot of the Thoreau literature leans this way. Such a tendency can be distasteful. He was not a perfect man.

In this context, my attempt to cast Thoreau as a proto-environmental justice figure could be read as undermining the importance of the citizens who created environmental justice movements in the first place. I do not attribute the development of those movements to Thoreau. What I mean to do is offer an interpretation of *Walden* that will unify the two strands I described before, the nature piety and the social justice, to show those who have been inspired by his nature piety that their piety entails a social justice politics, and those who have been inspired by Thoreau's vision of individualist politics that such a politics rests on a relation to nature that ought to be characterized by piety, which is to say reverent acknowledgment of dependence.

Thoreau's Religion is thus a new reading of *Walden*. My sense is that people do not usually read *Walden* this way because of white supremacy. It is telling that Gandhi and Martin Luther King, Jr. – leaders of movements against forces of white supremacy – are the most famous figures to put Thoreau to use for social justice causes. They read him with the struggles of their own communities in mind. For such communities, in contrast to many white communities with access to wealth and land, nature was not always a place of peace, and a naïve view of Thoreau's romanticism was perhaps less tempting. And it is telling that the predominantly white, wealthy environmentalist movement of the twentieth century focused so closely on the nature piety of *Walden*.[11]

[11] Here, I may accept too quickly the standard narrative of the environmental justice movement that Jedidiah Purdy complicates. Jedediah Purdy, "The Long Environmental Justice Movement," *Ecology Law Quarterly* 44, 4 (2017): 809–64.

Those readers came from communities in which forced land labor was past, coerced labor largely hidden, and the wildness of the woods indicated peace.[12]

For Thoreau, the woods were not only a place of peace. They were also where people of color and poor people we now consider white (largely Irish) lived and worked. In going to the woods, he opened himself to encounter with people outside his social, racial, and class position. During his time in Walden Woods, Thoreau made his world a little less segregated. He went to live in a neighborhood that had, in the generation before, been the home of formerly enslaved people and others outside of more elite Concord society. It was then the working place of Irish laborers. He traveled

[12] There is an important strand of literary interpretation that has argued that the view of wilderness and nature as a homeland and place of peace (over and against other images of nature, for instance, as a place of exile and fear) is inflected by white experience and fails to account for experiences of other groups, especially Black and African American communities. For examples see Melvin Dixon, *Ride Out the Wilderness: Geography and Identity in Afro-American Literature* (Urbana, IL: University of Illinois Press, 1987); Paul Outka, *Race and Nature from Transcendentalism to the Harlem Renaissance* (New York: Palgrave Macmillan, 2008). Outka is refreshingly unmotivated to redeem Transcendentalist authors from the racism of their milieu, and has argued that environmental practices contributed historically to the construction of whiteness and blackness in America. Outka is much less attentive to the historical location of his studies in nineteenth-century European, British, and American humanism, which sometimes makes him inattentive to the settler colonial narrative in which the story of race he tells plays out. He is also, perhaps therefore, inattentive to the ways in which relationships to land among the First Nations of the Americas might complicate his story. Other work on the role of literature in shaping American views of nature and race includes Myers, *Converging Stories*. Recent important scholarship collects and analyzes Black writing about nature and agriculture. Kimberly N. Ruffin, *Black on Earth: African American Ecoliterary Traditions* (Athens, GA: University of Georgia Press, 2010); Sonya Posmeniter, *Cultivation and Catastrophe: The Lyric Ecology of Modern Black Literature* (Baltimore, MD: John Hopkins University Press, 2020).

with and befriended an Indigenous guide. He got to know the poor white people who also lived in the woods. In everyday ways, he tried to get to know what life was like for others.

Eventually, he returned to what he called – with pointed irony – "civilized life." He took up residence as a rent-paying boarder in the Thoreau family home, which functioned as a boarding house. In this way, he benefitted from inherited wealth that has made much of the history of philosophy possible. Transcendentalism, like the first-generation theorists of US democracy, and for that matter like all intellectual life basically since Aristotle, famously relied on inherited wealth. As Bruce Kuklick has written about Transcendentalism, "Cambridge and Boston became the home to America's first 'intellectuals' and, assisted by inherited wealth, an associated genteel literary society."[13] Kuklick's aside about inherited wealth hides a major tension at the heart of intellectual life in an allegedly democratic culture. The tension is between the elite life of the universities and the movements for democratic equality that have unfolded over the last 300 years.

Thoreau's place in this history is as a member of the philosophical elite who had received the advantage of university education and wanted to do something with it that would enrich his life and make the world a little better. Most readers of *Thoreau's Religion* will recognize some form of a similar advantage in their own lives; in whatever form it came to you, with whatever coordinated struggles, some set of fortunate circumstances has given you the education, desire, and time to read this book. You share that, at least, with Thoreau.

[13] Bruce Kuklick, *A History of Philosophy in America, 1720–2000* (New York: Oxford University Press, 2001), 77.

Asceticism

A major feature of my interpretation of *Walden* is that it represents Thoreau as an ascetic. "Asceticism" names forms of disciplined, religious life often characterized by renunciation. In one of asceticism's characteristic forms, in the lives of Christian monks and nuns, the asceticism is given shape by three vows: of poverty, chastity, and obedience. The vow of poverty entails a renunciation of material wealth. The vow of chastity entails a renunciation most obviously of sexual activity, but also of the often-associated bonds of family. The vow of obedience entails a renunciation of individual autonomy. Even Christians who do not take such vows can practice asceticism – by fasting, for instance, or practicing silent prayer. Different forms of practices like these are prevalent across different religious traditions.

Those who do not practice such asceticism tend to think of it as rather foreign these days. Why would you deny yourself the goods of the world, when they are there for the taking?[14] Perhaps especially in the modern period, and even more certainly in the late twentieth- and early twenty-first centuries, such religious renunciation has been seen by many in Western, secular societies with deep suspicion, and the associated religious traditions have witnessed major decline.[15]

[14] Interesting answers to this question are to be found in Ross Posnock, *Renunciation: Acts of Abandonment by Writers, Philosophers, and Artists* (Cambridge, MA: Harvard University Press, 2016).

[15] I am thinking here of examples from the Christian tradition, that I know best. See, for example, Patricia Wittberg, *The Rise and Fall of Catholic Religious Orders: A Social Movement Perspective* (Albany, NY: SUNY Press, 1994). Of course, the coming to light – especially since the early 2000s – of the abuses of Christian churches against their members has not helped the reputation of Christian ascetic practices. I am thinking here especially of the report in 2002 by *The Boston Globe* about sexual abuse in the Catholic Archdiocese of Boston, and the 2013–2017 Australian Royal Commission into Institutional Responses to Child Sexual Abuse, because those were contexts to which I had attachments in those years.

Modern worries about asceticism are diverse. One is that asceticism is bad for the person who practices it, that the self-denial entailed is unhealthy or damaging in some way. Perhaps, for example, fasting is a religious good, but it expresses a denial of the body that is subjugating.

Another worry, though, is that asceticism is bad for the world. According to this view, all ascetic practice does is offer the practitioner reassurance that she is good, without actually doing good. After all, how on earth would *my* self-denial do *you*, or the community I am a part of, any good? Perhaps those things aren't associated with one another. And to the extent that I convince myself my ascetic practice is good, I excuse myself from the actually good work I could do for my community, and in this way asceticism is a form of quietism. Under this view, asceticism acknowledges that there are problems that need to be addressed, it aims to address them, but it is so ineffective that its ultimate result is support of the status quo. By refusing to engage with the world, ascetics give the world up to the suffering it currently holds.[16]

My view is that asceticism can be both of these things, and neither, depending on the practice and the context. In Thoreau, I think, we have an example of a *political* ascetic;

[16] Contemporary critiques of Christian theologies of sacrifice go one step further from the accusation that asceticism is a form of quietism to suggest that, in many of their formulations, such theologies reinscribe hierarchies of dominant power, especially with respect to gender. See especially Linn Marie Tonstad, *God and Difference: The Trinity, Sexuality, and the Transformation of Finitude* (New York: Routledge, 2016), chapter 3. Tonstad's target in that chapter is Sarah Coakley, who is a prominent Christian interpreter of ascetic practice. But since, in Coakley's account of asceticism, its central practice is kenosis via contemplative prayer – even to the extent that asceticism and contemplation sometimes seem interchangeable in her account – she does not write much about the economic, labor concerns that I am focused on in this work. Kathryn Tanner's 2016 Gifford Lectures were concerned with the ways in which Christian teaching and practices might resist contemporary exploitative economies. Kathryn Tanner, *Christianity and the New Spirit of Capitalism* (New Haven, CT: Yale University Press, 2019).

that is, one who was motivated to his renunciations by the instinct that our everyday choices make up our politics. On his rendering of asceticism, it entails renunciation. The first, most obvious renunciation he enacts is moving away from town, to a small house. But his asceticism is not primarily about renunciation. This book aims to show what else it is about. And the book opens new perspectives on ascetic practice as a whole.

In fact, much religious asceticism is – like his – about more than what its practitioners reject. It is also about the positive practices they pursue (such as, typically, labor and prayer), which are often an expression of the piety they mean to enact.[17] And their positive practices are more about what they gain through these practices than they are about the renunciations such practices require, real as those renunciations are. Further, the gains of the individual practitioners should not be the end of our understanding of what asceticism is for and does. Attention to the context out of which ascetic practice is born often uncovers that the practices are not only formative for the practitioner but also for the society from which the practitioner withdraws. The ascetic practitioner participates in the society from which he withdraws by withdrawing from it, and he sometimes establishes or contributes to a new society through his ascetic practice. Further, these two societies are often mutually constituting. There is not just one social and political world; there are many. And withdrawing from any means reinvesting in another. Such an act is its own sort of politics. It is in this sense that I describe political

[17] I tend to use "piety" in the sense explicated by Jeffrey Stout as "virtuous acknowledgement of dependence on the sources of one's existence and progress through life," though I think when I use it it may have a somewhat more practical emphasis. Jeffrey Stout, *Democracy and Tradition* (Princeton, NJ: Princeton University Press, 2004), 30.

asceticism as a form of religious practice that intervenes in the political discourse and action of its world.

On Emerson and Asceticism

Thoreau's interest in ascetic practice may have been inspired by Emerson – as so much was in the period in which he wrote *Walden*.[18] But where Emerson alluded to ascetic life as a symbol, Thoreau literalized the symbol in his experiment at Walden.

Let me explain one instance in which Emerson alluded positively to asceticism, one that suggests he had the image of the monastery on his mind in the period in which Thoreau first met and befriended him. Emerson delivered an oration before the Literary Societies of Dartmouth College on July 24, 1838, a mere nine days after delivering the famous "Divinity School Address." It was entitled "Literary Ethics," and in it, Emerson described the "resources, the subject and the discipline of the scholar."[19] Especially the section on "discipline"

[18] Readers interested in the friendship between Thoreau and Emerson can turn to Harmon Smith, *My Friend, My Friend: The Story of Thoreau's Relationship with Emerson* (Amherst, MA: University of Massachusetts Press, 1999); John T. Lysaker and William Rossi, eds., *Emerson and Thoreau: Figures of Friendship* (Bloomington, IN: Indiana University Press, 2010); David O. Dowling, *Emerson's Protégés: Mentoring and Marketing Transcendentalism's Future* (New Haven, CT Yale University Press, 2014), 66–100; Jeffrey S. Cramer, *Solid Seasons: The Friendship of Henry David Thoreau and Ralph Waldo Emerson* (Berkeley, CA: Counterpoint, 2019). I extend some of the material in this section to a broader interpretation of Emerson and Thoreau's relationship and its contemporary significance in Alda Balthrop-Lewis, "Active and Contemplative Lives in a Changing Climate: The Emersonian Roots of Thoreau's Political Asceticism," *Journal of the American Academy of Religion* 87, 2 (May 30, 2019): 311–32.

[19] Ralph Waldo Emerson, *Ralph Waldo Emerson: Essays & Poems*, ed. Joel Porte, Harold Bloom, and Paul Kane (New York: Library of America, 1996), 96.

offered a gentle but urgent call for those gathered to take up a more rigorous form of scholarly life.

In the "Divinity School Address," Emerson had addressed graduating divinity students who wanted to respond to "the evils of the church that now is." He had suggested that what was required of them was to breathe the breath of new life through the forms already existing. "Let the breath of new life be breathed by you through the forms already existing."[20] In "Literary Ethics," Emerson took up one of those forms. There, Emerson said that in order to create an American intellectual culture, the scholar would need to adopt a "rule of his ambition and life." The language of a "rule" related Emerson's understanding of the scholarly life to traditions of Christian monasticism, in which monastic communities were governed by a rule, usually written by their founder. The earliest examples of these rules – for example in the Rules of Basil, Benedict, and Augustine – remain important in contemporary Christian life.[21] The rule organized everything about communal life – when to pray, when to work, when to be alone, when to gather together, how to settle conflicts. Emerson's use of "rule" alluded to these monastic communities and introduced a series of paragraphs in which intellectual life was implicitly likened to monastic life. Those paragraphs took an old form and tried to breathe new life into it.

In those paragraphs, Emerson again evoked life in the monastery by his appeal to the benefits of solitude, which he described in glowing terms. "But go cherish your soul; expel

[20] Emerson, *Ralph Waldo Emerson*, 91.

[21] They are also figures of appeal for a wide variety of contemporary thinkers. One interesting example is in journalist Andrew Nikiforuk's analogy between slavery and the use of fossil fuels, which ends with an appeal to medieval monasticism. Andrew Nikiforuk, *The Energy of Slaves* (Vancouver, BC: Greystone Books, 2012). "The rise and fall of the Benedictines reads like an energy fable" (248).

companions; set your habits to a life of solitude; then will the faculties rise fair and full within, like forest trees and field flowers; you will have results, which, when you meet your fellow-men, you can communicate, and they will gladly receive."[22] Solitude, such as that in the monastery, was not utterly desolate. It could even be achieved around other people. "Think alone, and all places are friendly and sacred. The poets who have lived in cities have been hermits still." The solitude of the "hermit" (another invocation of ancient forms of asceticism) was for thinking. It was not for itself. Emerson wanted to make this clear. He said, "Of course, I would not have any superstition about solitude. Let the youth study the uses of solitude and society. Let him use both, not serve either." Indeed, solitude had society as its end. "The reason why an ingenious soul shuns society, is to the end of finding society. It repudiates the false, out of love for the true." In this sense, Emerson echoed the ancient Christian practice in which the monk's retreat to the desert hermitage was not primarily a rejection of society, though there was a sense in which it required that. The eremitic life was undertaken in an effort to grow closer to God – it repudiated the false, not for the sake of that repudiation, but because love for the true required it.

The desert monks left the cities of Egypt to pray in the desert. Emerson said, "You can very soon learn all that society can teach you for one while. Its foolish routine, and indefinite multiplication of balls, concerts, rides, theatres, can teach you no more than a few can." It was not that balls, concerts, rides, and theaters were worthless. The point was that to learn from them you need not indefinitely multiply your attendance at them. Instead, Emerson said, you have

[22] Emerson, 105.

another option. "Then accept the hint of shame, of spiritual emptiness and waste, which true nature gives you, and retire, and hide; lock the door; shut the shutters; then welcome the imprisoning rain, – dear hermitage of nature."[23] In this image, the scholar need not retire to the desert to find a hermitage, but can welcome the weather, in this case "the imprisoning rain," as his hermitage.

And then he said, continuing the extended allusion to monastic life and finally making it explicit, "You will pardon me, Gentlemen, if I say, I think that we have need of a more rigorous scholastic rule; such an asceticism, I mean, as only the hardihood and devotion of the scholar himself can enforce."[24] In this sentence, Emerson's allusion to monastic life came out full force. "Scholastic" has at least two significances. First, it referred to the scholar to whom he spoke and his scholastic life of study. But second, it referred to the traditions of Christian learning that flourished in medieval monastic communities, which were centers of intellectual life in Europe in the early medieval period.[25] Emerson's asceticism was thus partaking in what had been the practices of medieval Christians. It would breathe the breath of new life into the forms already existing.

But, of course, Christian asceticism had its own roots in the ancient Greek and Roman philosophies with which it was in conversation as it developed. Emerson also alluded to those ascetics, when he wrote, "Let us sit with our hands on our mouths, a long, austere, Pythagorean lustrum." The "lustrum"

[23] Emerson, 105. [24] Emerson, 106.

[25] Benedictine monks in particular adapted the motto "pray and work" from the Rule of Benedict to include scholarship as part of the command to work. Diarmaid MacCulloch, *Christianity: The First Three Thousand Years* (New York: Penguin Books, 2009), 318. On Christian scholasticism more broadly see Josef Pieper, *Scholasticism: Personalities and Problems of Medieval Philosophy*, trans. Richard and Clara Winston (New York: McGraw-Hill, 1964).

referred to a ritual from the Roman republic, in which censors made a purificatory sacrifice on behalf of the people once every five years. The word therefore also meant a five-year period. Pythagoras was famous for valuing silence, and those he taught were required to spend a five-year period in silence. This was in marked contrast to the schools of traditional Greek education, which emphasized public speaking.[26] Emerson thus compares his asceticism to that of an ancient philosophy purposefully marked by silence. "Let us live in corners, and do chores, and suffer, and weep, and drudge, with eyes and hearts that love the Lord. Silence, seclusion, austerity, may pierce deep into the grandeur and secret of our being, and so diving, bring up out of secular darkness, the sublimities of the moral constitution."[27] The aim of such labor was not self-abnegation, though the weeping and drudging could make a reader think that. But beyond the suffering and chores, there was a clear positive aim. It was the renewal of "the moral constitution."

This constitution was at risk, in Emerson's view, threatened by a "secular darkness." His own religious upbringing and training had been thoroughly Unitarian, and Unitarianism was in turn a reform of Puritanism, which had been a reform of Calvinism. In this context, Emerson's use of the images of the monastery – the rule, the hermitage, the asceticism – appealed to a more ancient Christianity. It may have been because of this that he had to say, "You will pardon me, Gentlemen." He was likely apologizing because of Proestant suspicion of monasticism. His appeal to a more ancient Christianity aimed to breathe the breath of new life into a form that had been thoroughly criticized.

[26] Carl Huffman, "Pythagoras," *The Stanford Encyclopedia of Philosophy* (Summer 2014 Edition), ed. Edward N. Zalta, https://plato.stanford.edu/archives/sum2014/entries/pythagoras/ (accessed August 14, 2020).

[27] Emerson, *Ralph Waldo Emerson*, 106.

My reading of Thoreau is marked by attention to the sense in which he was working within the traditions to which he appealed, perhaps especially within Christianity. This is uncommon in literature on Thoreau, where many scholars accept the common view that he rejected religious tradition in general.[28] One reason people have sometimes considered Thoreau areligious is that the traditions to which he appealed in his defense of the way of life he promoted in *Walden* were extremely diverse. Thoreau invokes a wide variety of spiritual authorities, people he takes to have had insight into the making of a good day and the relationship of that daily structure to the good life as a whole. These are people he hopes to emulate and to encourage his readers to emulate.

The quintessential examples of the benefits of asceticism and what he called "voluntary poverty" for Thoreau were in the practices of "the ancient philosophers, Chinese, Hindoo, Persian, and Greek" (I, 19).[29] But he found more recent – and

[28] Contemporary readers of Thoreau sometimes seem to resist the resonances of Transcendentalist asceticism with that of Christian monks and nuns. For example, literary scholar Robert Harrison contrasts Thoreau's retreat at Walden with that of Christian monks and nuns: "Thoreau goes into the forest not like medieval Christian saints who sought out an extreme condition where a preestablished truth could impose itself more rigorously upon them, but as one who would put to the test the meaning of being on the earth." Robert Pogue Harrison, *Forests: The Shadow of Civilization* (Chicago, IL: University of Chicago Press, 1992), 221. It is a mischaracterization of "medieval Christian saints" to assert that they all agreed that their retreats, when they undertook them, were aimed at the imposition of "a preestablished truth."

[29] I am convinced that the diversity of global influences on previous generations of American thinkers has been obscured by structures of white supremacy in the American academy. For an account of American literature in its global context, including Thoreau, see Wai Chee Dimock, *Through Other Continents: American Literature across Deep Time* (Princeton, NJ: Princeton University Press, 2008). She writes, "I have in mind a form of indebtedness: what we called 'American' literature is quite often a shorthand, a simplified name for a much more complex tangle of relations. Rather than being a discrete entity, it is better seen as a crisscrossing set of pathways, open-ended and ever multiplying, weaving in and

perhaps therefore makes more frequent appeal to – examples of simple living in the practices of American Indians, the Indigenous peoples of the Americas. Thoreau thought American Indian practices of simplicity were worthy of imitation. In addition to his continual appeal to the wisdom of ancient philosophers and Indians, Thoreau also had traditional Christian practice in mind as a model, both one to imitate and one to be overcome. He seems to have had in mind not only the Protestant movements for simplicity in North America ongoing in his time among Quakers and Shakers, but also ancient and medieval Christians, as had Emerson.[30] Three examples: Thoreau pines for an Abelard for his own period in a passage in which he suggests that the village should spend its money on education: "Can we not hire some Abelard to lecture to us?" (III, 12). Abelard had started a school of philosophy sometime soon after 1100, in Paris, when he was just past twenty.[31] Thoreau thought his sort of teaching would be good for Concord. Second, Thoreau writes of a neighbor, "he belonged to the ancient sect of Coenobites" (IX, 2).[32]

out of other geographies, other languages and cultures" (3). Thoreau read in seven languages: English, French, Latin, Greek, German, Italian, and Spanish.

[30] One of the many ways that Thoreau would have known about Shaker spirituality, Charles Lane published an essay on a visit to a Shaker community in the same issue of *The Dial* as Thoreau's essay "A Winter Walk." Charles Lane, "A Day with the Shakers," *The Dial*, October 1843. Lane wrote about arrival at the village, "No formal introduction is required; on the contrary, there is a general disposition on the part of both the more intelligent men and women to enter into free conversation at once upon their distinguishing practice of self-sacrifice" (166). Medieval examples were also very present for Thoreau. "The Middle Ages as an idea, however, held great appeal for Thoreau." Kathleen Coyne Kelly, "Medievalism," in *Henry David Thoreau in Context*, ed. James S. Finley (New York: Cambridge University Press, 2017), 71.

[31] Josef Pieper, *Scholasticism*, 79. Abelard was also first to use the term "theology." MacCulloch, *Christianity*, 398.

[32] This is also a pun. The man he describes turns out not to be a very good fisherman, thus see-no-bite.

Coenobitic monasticism refers to communal forms of Christian ascetic practice, as opposed to those that emphasize eremitic practice. Where eremitic monks live alone in hermitages, praying with others only intermittently, coenobitic monks live together in cooperative communities. And finally, when describing the fish in Walden Pond, Thoreau makes a pun on the name of a twelfth-century Christian poverty movement by calling the fish Waldenses (XVI, 5).[33]

Some interpreters assume the diversity of sources Thoreau was drawing upon demonstrate that he was areligious, and especially that he had rejected Christianity. On this understanding, true identification with one tradition requires the disavowal of others, and people who are influenced by many traditions have renounced religion entirely. Yet, diversity of influence does not areligiosity make.[34] An insistence on purity of influence would leave out most of the people we take as examples of their religions. Take Thomas Aquinas as an example. He was a medieval Christian theologian whose

[33] For more on the political significance of the movement that Waldo of Lyons was part of, and that Thoreau was thus appealing to, see Brian David Hamilton, "The Politics of Poverty: A Contribution to a Franciscan Political Theology," *Journal of the Society of Christian Ethics* 35, 1 (2015): 29–44. Unlike in Thoreau's treatment of ancient philosophy and American Indian economic practice, none of these references to Christian practices of simplicity is a thoroughgoing commendation of a particular practice. Yet they do show that Thoreau was aware of Christian ascetic traditions and to some extent identified with them. The Abelard reference in particular seems to indicate that he took them to be in some sense authoritative, though it is also, as in each of these cases, a sort of joke. I discuss the significance of Thoreau's humor further in Chapter 5.

[34] Contemporary scholarship in American religious history on the practices of those who are "spiritual but not religious" makes this abundantly clear. For example, Courtney Bender, *The New Metaphysicals: Spirituality and the American Religious Imagination* (Chicago, IL: University of Chicago Press, 2010). I do not investigate the relationship of those contemporary practices to Thoreau and the other Transcendentalists, but readers who are interested in that might look to Leigh Schmidt, *Restless Souls: The Making of American Spirituality* (San Francisco, CA: HarperOne, 2005).

Summa Theologica is a classic work of Christian theology and is taken by many theological traditions as a normative standard for orthodox teaching.[35] But in Thomas's time, his independence of mind and attention to a wide diversity of sources – especially his willingness to take Islamic theology seriously – often got him in trouble with bishops and professorial colleagues in Paris.[36] This eagerness to attend to diverse sources in pursuit of the truth is a hallmark of traditional theology, not contrary to it.

In taking them as authoritative, Thoreau cast himself as carrying on these traditions in some sense.[37] By appealing to them as authorities, he also affirmed a view of knowledge as socially – rather than independently – achieved.

On Truth as Thinking in Place

In "Literary Ethics," Emerson anticipated that his audience might worry the form of asceticism he enjoined was pointless, in that it hid from the world the fruits of its efforts. He knew about the quietist objection to asceticism, that it retreats from the world. Such a worry, he insisted, was unnecessary, given the nature of thought.

> You will not fear, that I am enjoining too stern an asceticism. Ask not, Of what use is a scholarship that systematically retreats? or, Who is the better for the philosopher who conceals his accomplishments, and hides his thoughts from the waiting world? Hides his thoughts! Hide the sun and the moon.

[35] Thomas was also a member of the Dominican order, an order that arose out of the Waldensian movement for poverty to which Thoreau had jokingly appealed. "Dominic's reform movement arose out of Waldensianism." Josef Pieper, *Guide to Thomas Aquinas* (San Francisco, CA: Ignatius Press, 1991), 26.

[36] I thank Denys Turner for conversation and instruction on this point.

[37] "To find oneself in a cultural tradition is the beginning, not the end, of critical thought." Jeffrey Stout, *Ethics after Babel* (Boston, MA: Beacon Press, 1988), 73.

Thought could be hidden no more than the sun and the moon could be hidden. This was because, "Thought is all light, and publishes itself to the universe. It will speak, though you were dumb, by its own miraculous organ. It will flow out of your actions, your manners, and your face. It will bring you friendships."[38] Thought cannot help but "publish itself to the universe." Thought takes place in a person, one who is necessarily situated in the world, who could no more retreat from the world than he could hide the sun or the moon. And a person's thought has "its own miraculous organ." It "flows out of" the very living of the person who thinks. And crucially it brings him friendships, through which he lives in society, and a society that will welcome his thoughts. Because of this, the ascetic scholar must retire to his hermitage to welcome thought, and trust that thought will, in the end, publish itself to the world.

This was part of a theory of truth Emerson articulated in "Literary Ethics," one that must have appealed to Thoreau. Emerson said,

> Truth is such a flyaway, such a slyboots, so untransportable and unbarrelable a commodity, that it is as bad to catch as light. Shut the shutters never so quick, to keep all the light in, it is all in vain; it is gone before you can cry, Hold. And so it happens with our philosophy. Translate, collate, distill all the systems, it steads you nothing; for truth will not be compelled, in any mechanical manner.[39]

Truth's refusal to succumb to systems was part of what made his *Journal* and other ephemeral forms so important to Thoreau. Sharon Cameron and William Howarth argue that the *Journal* is Thoreau's great work, and it seems like it would

[38] Emerson, *Ralph Waldo Emerson*, 112. [39] Emerson, 103.

have made sense for someone with this theory of truth to develop loyalty to such a form.[40]

What is appealing about the *Journal*, given this theory of truth, is that it does not attempt to compel truth into a mechanical manner. It relates to ideas through time, as thought can only run through time. Thought is a primary way of relating to truth, but without time, there is no thought. What it means that truth will not be compelled in a mechanical manner is that truth must develop over time. This gives Thoreau's cyclical reflections on the seasons over the years of the *Journal* a significance that may be difficult to see at first. Every thought comes in a context, and develops through time. That old "slyboots" truth must be seduced, with gentle reverence and patience, through daily practice, into an organic form rather than a mechanical form.

This means that philosophy is not a system, as a machine is a system, one that can be ordered with ease into parts. The asceticism is the ordering, which is to say it is the rule of living, in which thought and thus truth can thrive.

Emerson had said thought will "publish itself" when ordered in an ascetic life. That phrase appeared also in Thoreau's *Journal* soon after Emerson delivered "Literary Ethics." On August 10, 1838, Thoreau wrote – under the heading, "Truth" – "whatever of past or present wisdom has published itself to the world, is palpable falsehood till it come and utter itself by my side."[41] Emerson and Thoreau

[40] Sharon Cameron, *Writing Nature: Henry Thoreau's Journal* (New York: Oxford University Press, 1985); William L. Howarth, *The Book of Concord: Thoreau's Life As a Writer* (New York: Viking Press, 1982). Ian Hasketh has also argued that the journal form played an important role in the nineteenth-century development of "the scientific self." Ian Kasketh, "Technologies of the Scientific Self: John Tyndall and His Journal." *Isis* 110, 3 (September 1, 2019): 460–82.

[41] Henry David *Thoreau, Journal, Volume 1: 1837–1844*, ed. Elizabeth Hall Witherell et al. (Princeton, NJ: Princeton University Press, 1981), 49.

shared a commitment to the idea that truth "publishes itself," that the scholar's duty is to establish the discipline that will allow her to hear it uttered by her own side, and that this is part of what it means to live a good life. But *Walden*, Thoreau's own experiment with ascetic life, suggests Thoreau thought that Emerson's use of the image of the monastery did not go far enough. It did not actually *breathe* into the old ascetic forms.

Thoreau responded to Emerson's use of monastic allusion both by literalizing it, and by playing with it in *Walden*. In perhaps the most playful reference of all to Emerson's call for a more ascetic scholarship, Thoreau describes the fish in Walden Pond as ascetic (IX, 6).

My methodological orientation in this book assumes that for Thoreau, truth requires thinking in place; that is, it requires thinking in relation to all of the members of one's imagined society and one's imagined ethical inheritance. This commitment drives my argument in Chapter 1 about the importance of Walden Woods as a neighborhood, my argument in Chapter 2 about the rhetorical posture of *Walden* as a piece of public reasoning with the townsmen, my suggestions in Chapter 4 about the sociality of reason, and my argument in the Conclusion against what I call there "solution thinking." In each case, the point is to say that thinking well is impossible without attention to the social and political context of thought.

On History and Nature as Lively

Thoreau thought truth could only be uncovered by thinking in place. He also thought history was significant for the present. He came to this view in part through his response to the failures of his own formal education, especially a curriculum at Harvard that he viewed as pointless. American nature writing has had a central role in reflection on religion and ecology across the university for some time now. Let's say you take Thoreau as the progenitor of a nature writing tradition that runs down from him through John Muir, Aldo Leopold, and Edward Abbey to Wendell Berry, Annie Dillard, Barry Lopez, Lauret Savoy, and so many others. You needn't think of Thoreau as the beginning, since he had his own sense of progenitors, but you might.[42] Many do. In such a case, you might say that the nature writing tradition began as a response to what Thoreau saw as the failure of the university – his example was Harvard – to take reflection on religion and ecology seriously.

Teaching and learning at Harvard in Thoreau's generation focused on recitation and the collection of points to what was considered an absurd extent by students. Teachers were expected to deliver content and to score student performances in every aspect of college life. But teachers were not expected to cultivate the intellectual lives of young students. Robert Richardson writes that "the curriculum was largely fixed and generally detested."[43] Josiah Quincy III had been made the president of Harvard after losing his seventh election to remain mayor of Boston. He was appointed at a moment when Harvard seemed particularly vulnerable. "He had been chosen by the Corporation neither for his scholarly attainments which were considerable, nor his teaching experience which was non-existent, but for his demonstrated capacity to

[42] Michael Branch tells the story of American nature writing before Thoreau and proposes "a corrective thought experiment" that tries "to imagine the American nature writing traditions slowly building toward Thoreau, rather than spontaneously issuing from him." Michael P. Branch, *Reading the Roots: American Nature Writing before Walden* (Athens, GA: University of Georgia Press, 2004), xvi.

[43] Robert D. Richardson, *Henry Thoreau: A Life of the Mind* (Berkeley, CA: University of California Press, 1988), 10.

govern the recalcitrant."[44] He designed and kept the books on the elaborate, standardized marking system, meant to forestall both the grading that had up to then been left to the discretion of teachers and the complaints of favoritism that such a system risked. In the course of a four-year career, a student could accumulate as many as 29,920 points.[45]

Students despised Quincy's firm hand. This was true to the extent that in the spring of Thoreau's freshman year, 1834, the most violent student rebellion in Harvard's history broke out. The conflict went on for weeks. Quincy's effigy was burned by the Junior class. In this context, curricular activity at Harvard may have been attached in Thoreau's mind to the conflict that had raged on campus at Harvard. His extracurricular reading seems to have been more indicative of his interests than any of his schooling. Withdrawal from the melee could have seemed the most important way to get an education.

A big part of what Thoreau found inspiring about his relationship with Emerson was that Emerson had a more capacious understanding of what learning was for, and from whence it came, than the marking system at Harvard would have implied. This included Emerson's philosophy of history, which was based largely on what he knew of German philosophy. Whereas the Harvard curriculum emphasized rote memorization, which set the history it covered at a distance from the students who were obliged to do that memorizing, Emerson believed that history was vivid and lively in a way Thoreau found freeing.

[44] Robert A. McCaughey, "The Usable Past: A Study of the Harvard College Rebellion of 1834," *William and Mary Law Review* 11, 3 (April 1, 1970): 596.

[45] McCaughey, 597.

Indeed on Emerson's account, one of the things that nature provided was help understanding what history is and means. I think you can see this in his lecture "Literary Ethics." In the first part, on the resources of the scholar, he describes a young person who is so "intoxicated with his admiration of a hero" from history that he doesn't see the things he has in common with that hero. This is the danger Emerson saw in the form of education being practiced at Harvard; it stressed in history "the distinctions of the individual" rather than "the universal attributes of man."[46] The youth in Emerson's illustration has read about the Emperor Charles the Fifth, and in imagining who the Emperor was, "He is curious concerning that man's day. What filled it?" Emerson suggests that if the youth can understand that what he admires in the Emperor he can also find in his own soul, he'll see things – especially the promise of his own life – differently. In response to the youth's question about the Emperor's day, "The soul answers – Behold his day here!" The youth has in common with the Emperor, on Emerson's description, the sighing of the woods, the quiet of gray fields, the cool breeze that sings out of the northern mountains, the hopes of morning, ennui of noon, regrets at want of vigor – all aspects of nature in some sense, those things that exist in the world. Emerson describes features of the world that he thinks will have persisted from the period in which the Emperor lived to the period in which the youth lived. Nature persists. This means that the world we belong to is like that world in which our heroes lived. Which in turn means that the things we admire in them are also accessible to us. What was a day of his? "Day of all that are born of women."[47]

[46] Emerson, *Ralph Waldo Emerson*, 99. [47] Emerson, 99.

This, in turn and perhaps counterintuitively, means that a person ought not think of themselves as living at the climax of history. To do so would be to misunderstand history itself.

> The whole value of history, of biography, is to increase my self-trust, by demonstrating what man can be and do. This is the moral of the Plutarchs, the Cudworths, the Tennemanns, who give us the story of men or of opinions. Any history of philosophy fortifies my faith, by showing me, that what high dogmas I had supposed were the rare and late fruit of a cumulative culture, and only now possible to some recent Kant or Fichte, – were the prompt improvisations of the earliest inquirers; of Parmenides, Heraclitus, and Xenophanes.[48]

History teaches that we have access to the same possibilities now that we read about in history. The sentiment is at the same time optimistic about human possibility and, perhaps more subtly, demonstrates Emerson's exacting doctrine of human responsibility. Emerson is famously a perfectionist – in that he thought that humans could always attain a better self. His perfectionism has become one of the intellectual tropes for which he is most famous.[49] And this has led some of his readers (and those who do not read, but think they know) to imagine that Emerson expected human progress would come about necessarily through history also. But Emerson's philosophy of history – even as it expressed perfectionist hopes for individual humans – also shows that he did not think perfectionism was inevitable in history or in any

[48] Emerson, 98.
[49] Perhaps especially because of Stanley Cavell's "Emersonian perfectionism." Stanley Cavell, *Conditions Handsome and Unhandsome: The Constitution of Emersonian Perfectionism: The Carus Lectures, 1988* (Chicago, IL: University of Chicago Press, 1991); Stanley Cavell, *Cities of Words: Pedagogical Letters on a Register of the Moral Life* (Cambridge, MA: Belknap Press, 2005).

human life.[50] Moral progress was uncertain and required moral effort by individuals in every age. This contributed to the central argument of the conclusion of *Walden*, that there is no moral progress without moral effort.

According to Emerson's view of history, every telling of history uncovers both something about the teller and an important feature of the past itself, a feature only discoverable by that telling of history.

> Is it not the lesson of our experience that every man, were life long enough, would write history for himself? What else do these volumes of extracts and manuscript commentaries, that every scholar writes, indicate? Greek history is one thing to me; another to you.[51]

This is not to say that all is relative, because there is of course the material record to which each of us is obligated. But in this understanding of the nature of historical practice, it is our uncovering of the past, as it speaks now. One of the things that education can give is the capacity to see the history we have been taught anew through our own eyes.

This doctrine of history was what enabled Thoreau to connect, as he did, his daily life in the woods – for example, the wars of the ants – to the heroic periods he knew from classical history. History was always encroaching, sneaking through the cracks of the present. And this, in turn, enabled Thoreau to believe that he might himself, though living far

[50] Christopher Lasch argues that Emerson (relying on his Calvinism) was among those who resisted doctrines of progress, insisting on human limitations. "The 'terror of life' cannot be 'talked or voted away,' and freedom is not something that can be guaranteed by a constitution, a 'paper preamble.'" Christopher Lasch, *The True and Only Heaven: Progress and Its Critics* (New York: W. W. Norton & Company, 1991), 262.

[51] Emerson, *Ralph Waldo Emerson*, 103.

from heroes, write a heroic book. The same spirit that had inspired Virgil's *Georgics* lived on, even in Concord.

It also means that the profusion of interpretations of Thoreau reflect how Emerson and Thoreau themselves thought of history. Controversy over what to make of Thoreau began even before he died, and has continued unabated ever since. Interpretations can be more and less justified by the evidence, but the understanding of history that Emerson gave Thoreau would have indicated not that one account of Thoreau will be vindicated in some far future, but instead that we learn more than we knew before from each person's telling – both about the teller and about the people and places in his story. Were life long enough, each of us would have their own Thoreau. This requires that we embrace readings of him across what we now call disciplines, though of course even to separate them is somewhat of an anachronism, since in Thoreau's period they were not what they are now.[52]

Social History

Where the mainstream view among interpreters is that Thoreau was a Transcendentalist, my interpretation seeks to draw him to a certain extent away from the historiography of Transcendentalism – which has so often focused on famous men – and back into the diverse world in which Thoreau actually lived.[53] In this, I have been inspired by historians

[52] Laura Dassow Walls, *Seeing New Worlds: Henry David Thoreau and Nineteenth-Century Natural Science* (Madison, WI: University of Wisconsin Press, 1995).

[53] The historiography of Transcendentalism is changing, however. Sandra Petrulionis has been especially important for the recovery of Concord's women in the history of Transcendentalism. Sandra Harbert Petrulionis, *To Set This World Right: The Antislavery Movement in Thoreau's Concord* (Ithaca, NY: Cornell University Press, 2006).

who have challenged our assumptions about what sorts of histories the sources enable us to tell, especially women's historians and historians of African American communities. From these historians I have learned that to claim we lack sources is often a sophisticated way of perpetuating a silence that was always unjust. As Albert Raboteau wrote in his groundbreaking *Slave Religion: The "Invisible Institution,"* "it is the neglect of slave sources by historians which has been the main cause of this invisibility."[54] In women's history, too, historians have often assumed that sources did not exist. But those historians who have uncovered histories of everyday people, people who left less of a written record than the elite who have generally made history, have inspired my interpretation of Thoreau.

In the interpretation of *Walden* I offer in this book, I make use of the broadening of history accomplished by the social historians of the past fifty years. Most readings of Thoreau situate him in the history of ideas, whether as a Transcendentalist, an inheritor of classical sources, or the progenitor of the nature writing tradition that so deeply influenced – for good or for ill – the environmental movement. My starting point is, rather, to situate Thoreau in US labor and social history, including especially the history of working women, free Black people, and those who defied enslavement. In this I join a growing edge of Thoreau scholarship, advanced especially by Lance Newman's *Our Common Dwelling*, which insists that the material and economic context of Thoreau's writing has been largely neglected and ought to be recovered.[55]

[54] Albert J. Raboteau, *Slave Religion: The "Invisible Institution" in the Antebellum South* (New York: Oxford University Press, 1978), x.

[55] Lance Newman, *Our Common Dwelling: Henry Thoreau, Transcendentalism, and the Class Politics of Nature* (New York: Palgrave Macmillan, 2005).

While Thoreau is famous for his opposition to slavery, that opposition is most often read apart from Thoreau's interest in nature. I read these two strands together. Thoreau's focus in *Walden* was, after all, not only on the contemplation of nature, but also on doing his own work. This was, I think, his way of finding out the material needs of citizens and resisting forms of unjust labor. His experiment at Walden was contemplative, and it was also an experiment driven by his political and moral disappointment toward a politics that could sustain social justice for all.

Local history was of great interest to Thoreau. Take, for example, a passage in *Walden* that describes the former inhabitants of the woods. Later in his life, Thoreau was especially interested in the history of the Indigenous peoples of the Americas, and he planned to write a book on the subject. But even early, in the period he spent living in Walden Woods, Thoreau was invested in knowing the history of the place. As with much else in his life, he thought he could learn this history from nature, by which he meant the world he could observe. And so he went on a walk in the woods. Not only a natural historian, but an oral historian as well, as interpreters often forget, Thoreau took his knowledge of the past from the world around him, and from the people he knew. This was a walk through woods that "within the memory of many of my townsmen . . . resounded with the laugh and gossip of inhabitants." He remembered when the road was heavily covered by pines, so close that they "would scrape both sides of the chaise at once" (XIV, 1). Thoreau goes on to write a paragraph on each of four formerly enslaved Black people who had occupied the woods before him.

History, like that of Walden Woods, was alive for Thoreau in ways we might sometimes find quite foreign. Same too with what he called nature. Indeed, as I have described, one of the reasons that nature is as important for Thoreau as it is, is that it allows access to what the heroes had. The meaning of histories stayed in places, and the meaning of the leaf could be found in the tree.

As Sandra Petrulionis and Laura Dassow Walls wrote in 2007, with reference to Lance Newman's "Thoreau's Materialism," attention to the concrete historical situation in which Thoreau wrote *Walden* offers new views on how its contents reveal Thoreau's own political aims, even when his writing seems most politically sedate.[56]

Social Justice

The title of this book is *Thoreau's Religion: Walden Woods, Social Justice, and the Politics of Asceticism*. The three terms of the subtitle are intended to summarize my interpretation of what Thoreau's religion is: an ascetic practice that aims to set right his social and political relationships as he came to understand them through the course of his life in Walden Woods. His life in the woods revealed to him an alternative social world to the one he knew in Concord. It suggested to him that setting right all of his relationships – including those with the more-than-human, those with outsiders to Concord society, and his own relationship to himself – could contribute to a more just social and political world. And it taught him a form of ascetic practice that would give due reverence to God, enable delight in the practitioner, and contribute to the just reformation of relationships.

Thoreau's religion, perhaps surprisingly, was oriented by both reverence for the woods and a form of social justice. This

[56] Sandra Harbert Petrulionis and Laura Dassow Walls, eds., *More Day to Dawn: Thoreau's* Walden *for the Twenty-First Century* (Amherst, MA: University of Massachusetts Press, 2007), 244.

reading of Thoreau finds in him a contrasting understanding of justice from one that has been taken for granted by many political philosophers, especially twentieth-century liberal political philosophers who are often interested in Thoreau and read him as invested in their conception of justice. Liberal political philosophy considers liberty the primary political value (as opposed to, for example, equality or belonging), and often seeks principles to guide the governance of the modern liberal state. On one influential liberal view, justice obtains when fairness is enacted.[57] In much liberal political theory, what justice requires is knowing the right principles and then applying them. In my reading, Thoreau thinks something else. He thinks that justice obtains not when a principle from outside is applied to our situation (whether fairness or something else), but rather when we set the relationship between us right.[58] This kind of justice, when we get our relationship to each other right, is a kind of relational justice, which is to say that it ought to be worked out between us not outside of us. Thoreau thought social justice (which is to say, a society in which all enjoy justice) required this kind of relational justice.

This is important because imagining justice as a principle applied from outside often fails to offer requisite attention to the particularities of the relevant relational situation. In fact, when people try to enforce an external principle, it can further

[57] The early articulation of this view in the twentieth century, often summarized "justice as fairness," is found in John Rawls, *A Theory of Justice* (Cambridge, MA: Belknap Press, 1971). Rawls was deeply concerned that society should be just. I take it he had a different understanding of what justice is than Thoreau.

[58] Carol Gilligan argued in the early 1980s that moral philosophy had been dominated by a masculinist vision of justice that focused on abstract principles. She studied women who conceptualized morality in more relational terms, asking not, "what principle applies?" but instead, "how should I respond?" Carol Gilligan, *In a Different Voice: Psychological Theory and Women's Development* (Cambridge, MA: Harvard University Press, 1982).

contribute to injustice. I discuss this further in Chapter 3, where I interpret Thoreau's critique of philanthropy as resting on the grounds that it fails to render this kind of justice.

Justice as fairness has often assumed, like much Western philosophy, that humans are the morally salient members of society. Thoreau's vision of justice, in which relational setting right *just is* what justice is, included from the beginning human relationships to the natural world. As I argue in Chapter 1, Thoreau considered every thing in Walden Woods a member of society there, and thus a member of a community in which he sought to cultivate social justice. As I argue in Chapters 2 and 3, he opposed contemporary economic practices, on the grounds that they failed to render this kind of justice. As I argue in Chapters 4 and 5, his asceticism aimed to sustain deeper relationships to all the world's delightful goods. This is an explosively expansive account of social justice.

Chapter Plan

The book is divided into five chapters. The first chapters are focused on responding to common interpretations of Thoreau as, first, fiercely independent, second, inconsequential with respect to politics, and, third, spiritually eccentric to the point of being irreligious.[59] Too often, the Thoreau of *Walden* is

[59] There has been a relatively recent turn to studying religion in the wider historical study of the Transcendentalists. K. P. Van Anglen, "Transcendentalism and Religion: The State of Play," *Literature Compass* 5, 6 (November 1, 2008): 1010–24. That trend is still growing among scholars of Thoreau. The best available book-length work on Thoreau and religion is Alan D. Hodder, *Thoreau's Ecstatic Witness* (New Haven: Yale University Press, 2001). An early foray into the study of Thoreau's religion is William J. Wolf, *Thoreau: Mystic, Prophet, Ecologist* (Philadelphia, PA: United Church Press, 1974). Catherine Albanese wrote that Wolf's book tended "to make the results of present-day biblical scholarship and theological inquiry normative," but that it might be a

imagined as asocial, apolitical, and areligious. By way of addressing these caricatures, the first three chapters respond to each in turn. Chapter 1, "Thoreau's Social World," presents a view of his time in the woods as taking up membership in an alternative society – not the one people expected him to belong to, admittedly, but a society nonetheless. Chapter 2, "The Politics of Getting a Living," describes how Thoreau's time in the woods instantiated his political views in ways the literature on Thoreau does not usually highlight. Chapter 3, "Thoreau's Theological Critique of Philanthropy," begins to explicate some of Thoreau's theological commitments. It offers a close reading of Thoreau's critique of philanthropy at the end of "Economy." This critique was motivated by Christian theological commitments and a theological ethics oriented by relational justice. Chapter 4, "Political Asceticism," describes Thoreau's interest in ascetic practice and voluntary poverty, which I interpret as his own positive social, political, and religious response to his strong critique of philanthropy. Chapter 5, "Delight in True Goods," responds to worries that asceticism is dour. The chapter is motivated by a concern that contemporary environmentalism is often tempted to despair, confronted as it is by an apocalyptic

"harbinger of future work on the religious meaning of Henry David Thoreau." Catherine Albanese, review of *Thoreau: Mystic, Prophet, Ecologist*, by William J. Wolf, *Church History* 44, 1 (1975): 133–34. For a helpful footnote that collects some of the scholarship on Thoreau and religion before Hodder, see John Gatta, "'Rare and Delectable Places': Thoreau's Imagination of Sacred Space at Walden," in *There Before Us: Religion, Literature & Culture from Emerson to Wendell Berry*, ed. Roger Lundin (Wm. B. Eerdmans Publishing Co., 2007), 25. Laura Dassow Walls is quite sensitive to religion in her excellent new biography, Walls, *Henry David Thoreau*. Stanley Cavell is the interpreter of *Walden* most attentive to the influence of Christianity on Thoreau. Cavell, *The Senses of Walden*. Other recent book-length works that attend to the influence of religion on Thoreau include Malcolm Clemens Young, *The Spiritual Journal of Henry David Thoreau* (Macon, GA: Mercer University Press, 2009); Kevin Dann, *Expect Great Things: The Life and Search of Henry David Thoreau* (New York: TarcherPerigee, 2017).

future. The chapter focuses on the puzzling coincidence of Thoreau's earnestness with his humor. I argue that there are some things – political asceticism may be one of them – that are best articulated while laughing. Dark jokes about the end of the world sometimes help us through, but true engagement with the goods that remain will sustain whatever future we have.

In the conclusion, "The Promise of a Delighted Environmental Ethics," I look at what significance my interpretation of *Walden* might have to work ongoing among those who study religious environmental ethics. Finally, the epilogue "On Mourning" returns to the Florida Panhandle I discussed in the preface, where Hurricane Michael hit in the summer of 2018. There, I discuss the importance of mourning goods as they pass away. Such mourning is an important way of valuing good things and thus relating justly to them.

1

Thoreau's Social World

> Confucius says truly, "Virtue does not remain as an abandoned orphan; it must of necessity have neighbors."
>
> *Walden*, (V, 10)

One of the most popularly salient images of Thoreau taken from *Walden* is Thoreau as an asocial hermit, whether an honest one or a hypocrite. The Honest Hermit view sees his time in the woods as a praiseworthy retreat from other people in pursuit of higher values among nature. The Hypocrite Hermit view takes his forays into town – and the assumption that his mother did his laundry especially – as a sign that while he aimed to look holy out there in his hermitage, and would have been holy if he had achieved what he claimed, he did not live up to his own standard.[1] Both of these views respond to

[1] Rebecca Solnit has written about how strange it is that Thoreau's washing has become such a focus of attention. "There is one writer in all literature whose laundry arrangements have been excoriated again and again, and it is not Virginia Woolf, who almost certainly never did her own washing, or James Baldwin, or the rest of the global pantheon. The laundry of the poets remains a closed topic, from the tubercular John Keats (blood-spotted handkerchiefs) to Pablo Neruda (lots of rumpled sheets). Only Henry David Thoreau has been tried in the popular imagination and found wanting for his cleaning arrangements, though the true nature of those arrangements are not so clear." Rebecca Solnit, "Mysteries of Thoreau, Unsolved," *Orion*, June 2013, 18. Laura Dassow Walls points out that at the Thoreau boarding house, where Thoreau paid rent for the rest of his adult life after the Walden experiment, laundry was done by live-in servants. So presumably the charge against Henry was never quite accurate to begin with; everyone's laundry was done by servants. The charge reflected the accusers' own presumptions. Thoreau's mother did not do her own washing either. Walls's

passages where Thoreau describes his avoidance of society and his appreciation of solitude. And they take him quite literally at his word when he writes, "I find it wholesome to be alone the greater part of the time. To be in company, even with the best, is soon wearisome and dissipating" (V, 12). Those two views also leave open two other possibilities: first, that even if he was not a hypocrite, his aim was not praiseworthy – that is, being a hermit does not let you pursue higher values anyway; and second, the view I will defend, that the aim of living without society was never really his anyway, because the higher values he pursued were intimately related to society, or to relationships with others.[2]

Against an asocial reading of *Walden*, I argue that Thoreau's longing for solitude was tied to his deep interest and investment in (if also discomfort with) the dynamics of social life. There are a few main reasons to take this view.

comment: "No other male American writer has been so discredited for enjoying a meal with loved ones or for not doing his own laundry." Walls, *Henry David Thoreau*, 195.

[2] I am not, of course, the first interpreter of Thoreau to make this claim. A collection of essays on Thoreau, helpfully focused on his reception on both sides of the Atlantic, noted that almost all of the essays it contained emphasized "*relationality* as a central feature of Thoreau's writings." François Specq, Laura Dassow Walls, and Michel Granger, eds., *Thoreauvian Modernities: Transatlantic Conversations on an American Icon* (Athens, GA: University of Georgia Press, 2013), 3. Even where they are inclined to emphasize Thoreau's solitude over his sociability, many of his finest readers have seen that the dynamics of sociability and solitude are deeply intertwined in his life and writing. For example, Jane Bennett insists that Thoreau rejected standard politics for practices of self-craft, thus focusing on the individual over against the social, but she acknowledges the centrality of friendship in Thoreau's practices of self-fashioning. Bennett, *Thoreau's Nature*, 20. Still, she emphasizes Thoreau's resistance to social life as a necessary condition for cultivating the nonconformist self. Thoreau's own writing has been partially responsible for the asocial reading of *Walden*. My interpretation in this chapter aims to acknowledge the evidence in *Walden* that might tempt readers to the asocial view of his project there, while joining those who see Thoreau relationally by opening a new view on the social world Thoreau joined in the woods.

The first and most obvious is that Thoreau describes the social relationships he had in the woods in *Walden*, and the terms in which he describes them make clear that he also valued them. Even in his first few days at the pond, when – if he was bent on enforcing a rigorous solitude – we would expect him to avoid human contact, he records in his journal conversations with a man he met there, Alek Therien, who becomes his friend *while* he is living in the woods. Not only did Thoreau go to Walden Woods with friendships and familial relationships that he maintained; he also cultivated new relationships there, both intimate and remote.

Second, Thoreau was invested in a vision of social life that included more-than-human and more-than-living beings, or, as he usually called the social actors of the woods: "inhabitants."[3] It is easier to understand him as asocial (though still, I think, incorrect) when the only social actors you acknowledge are living human beings; but it is nearly impossible to maintain the asocial view when you take natural objects, animals, plants, and the human dead as involved in social life and relationships. Thoreau thought such beings were part of the social world and describes cultivating relationships with them, whether by keeping appointments with trees, weeding beans, or by "conjuring" the now-dead "former inhabitants" of Walden Woods.[4] This interpretation of Thoreau's sociality as including objects, plants, animals, and the human dead

[3] The phrase "more-than-human" was coined (perhaps first by David Abram in 1996) to replace "non-human," in the conviction that "non-human" placed moral priority on humans in a way that abetted human domination of other forms of life. David Abram, *The Spell of the Sensuous: Perception and Language in a More-than-Human World* (New York: Pantheon, 1996). "More-than-living" is not common in current usage.

[4] In his insistence on the social membership of a wide variety of creatures, Thoreau has what may be a surprising resonance with some forms of "ecological feminism" that developed in the 1990s. Val Plumwood, *Feminism and the Mastery of Nature* (London: Routledge, 1993).

relates to a growing field of scholarship being conducted across the humanities and social sciences – often under the rubric "multispecies" and indebted to the work of critical theory – which shows just how diverse social networks are and how much we miss of social life when we limit our understanding of "the social" to "the living human."[5]

With all this in mind, this chapter argues against a view that sees the Thoreau of *Walden* having departed from society in general, that sees him as asocial. Rather, I show a dynamic within Thoreau's writing between his desire for solitude and his investment in community.[6] I demonstrate Thoreau keeping company with a community of spirit that is peopled by exemplary individuals – both dead and alive, both flora and fauna. Among the individuals whom Thoreau took as neighbors in Walden Woods, some are easily legible as social actors. Alek Therien was a woodchopper who lived in the woods, and with whom Thoreau developed a relationship from his first days living by the pond. Others are less obvious, but no less important. Thoreau's writing describes an

[5] Bruno Latour and actor-network theory are influential in this line of thinking. A key text for the field is Bruno Latour, *Reassembling the Social: An Introduction to Actor-Network-Theory* (New York: Oxford University Press, 2005). Donna Harraway and Anna Tsing have been especially influential lately, in a purposefully feminist direction. For a helpful introduction (focused on plant sociality, but not on non-living social worlds), see Anna Tsing, "More-than-Human Sociality: A Call for Critical Description," in *Anthropology and Nature*, ed. Kristen Hastrup (New York: Routledge, 2013). For examples of recent work in this line of scholarship, see the May 2016 issue of *Environmental Humanities*, especially Vinciane Despret and Michel Meuret, "Cosmoecological Sheep and the Arts of Living on a Damaged Planet," *Environmental Humanities* 8, 1 (May 1, 2016): 24–36; Hugo Reinert, "About a Stone: Some Notes on Geologic Conviviality," *Environmental Humanities* 8, 1 (May 1, 2016): 95–117.

[6] Bennett argues that Thoreau underplays "the role and force of collective ideals, such as community or justice." Bennett, *Thoreau's Nature*, 132. She amends Thoreau (with Kafka) in an attempt to make his sensibility better equipped to engage public affairs. I find Thoreau (sans Kafka) already invested in community-building.

experience of the woods that is full of personality, of alternative society. Beginning with his relationships with animals, plants, and non-living objects, and going on through his knowledge of the "Former Inhabitants" of the woods, whom readers often forget but who were one important example Thoreau had of what independence looked like, the woods as Thoreau described them *were* a society.[7] When we ignore the beings who made up his social world, we get a distorted view of the aim of what he called his "experiment." I use Thoreau's writing about the woods and contemporary history of Concord slavery – which Thoreau's writing has contributed to – to show that his vision of society was broader and deeper than readers often think.

I introduce this chapter with a section on Thoreau's insistence that the center of society could be anywhere. This view was part of Thoreau's lively interest in spatial, scalar, and perspectival questions that I return to throughout the book.[8] His belief that the center of society might be anywhere, depending on your point of view, also meant that whereas the residents of Concord might have seen him as leaving society, he took himself to be joining a society. This spatial play also entailed a commitment to viewing figures that might

[7] In one sense, my reading of Thoreau's time in the woods joins it even more closely to other utopian communities of the period, which interpreters have long compared it to, like those at Brook Farm and Fruitlands. In another sense, in my telling his community was far less utopian than theirs, to the extent it took his own weaknesses into account in the formation of its membership. On Fruitlands and Brook Farm see Richard Francis, *Transcendental Utopias: Individual and Community at Brook Farm, Fruitlands, and Walden* (Ithaca, NY: Cornell University Press, 1997); Sterling F. Delano, *Brook Farm: The Dark Side of Utopia* (Cambridge, MA: Belknap Press, 2004); Richard Francis, *Fruitlands: The Alcott Family and Their Search for Utopia* (New Haven, CT: Yale University Press, 2010). On Walden as a "utopia of one" see Josh Kotin, *Utopias of One* (Princeton, NJ: Princeton University Press, 2017), 17–32.

[8] Similar matters arise throughout this book, especially in Chapter 4.

be coded marginal in one way of thinking about society as in fact central. The first section of the chapter describes Thoreau's recentering of the woods, the second section discusses what to make of the evidence that might suggest Thoreau's retreat to the woods was asocial, and the later sections describe Thoreau's relationships with those who are recentered as "members" rather than "marginal."

The Village and the Woods

One reason that people have an image of Thoreau as avoiding society at Walden is that in *Walden* Thoreau plays with a conceptual pair that has been central to the long tradition of pastoral literature. This is the dynamic tension between the "country" and the "city," or in his case between "the village" and "the woods."[9] When Thoreau describes his life in the woods and its distance from the village, he is not merely insisting on his remoteness. To do so would have been to take for granted that the village was the epicenter of society, which he refused to do. Instead, he was testing the categories themselves, which rely on one another. The woods are wild only *relative* to the village, and the village is civilized only in comparison to the woods. Thoreau thinks the way these concepts are tied together has significance, in that which location is thought primary can be switched. This switch is one of the things that *Walden* tries to do, to make the woods the center of a world and thus test the view that life in the village is somehow primary.[10]

[9] Raymond Williams, a literary critic, is an important expositor of this conceptual pair in pastoral literature. Raymond Williams, *The Country and the City* (New York: Oxford University Press, 1975).

[10] This dynamic play between periphery and center functions in the title of Dipesh Chakrabarty's *Provincializing Europe*. That work treats the indispensability and inadequacy of social science to understanding political and historical life in India.

Thoreau began *Walden* with a paragraph that suggested his home by Walden Pond was remote from society.

> When I wrote the following pages, or rather the bulk of them, I lived alone, in the woods, a mile from any neighbor, in a house which I had built myself, on the shore of Walden Pond, in Concord, Massachusetts, and earned my living by the labor of my hands only. I lived there two years and two months. At present I am a sojourner in civilized life again.
>
> (I, 1)

With this first paragraph, Thoreau introduced the book that would eventually make him famous, and he did it in specifically spatial terms. In three sentences, he implied that the house at Walden Pond had been a retreat from society – he lived there "alone" – and that it had been a retreat to somewhere somewhat desolate – now he is in "civilized life again." What then was his life "in the woods"? The implication is that life in the woods was the opposite of civilized in some way, "a mile from any neighbor." At first, this distance from his closest neighbor reads like an insistence on the way his life in the woods was a retreat from society, the mile between him and the neighbor ensuring that he does not confront other people.

The first sentences of the introduction insist that Europe has already been provincialized – which is to say decentered. Dipesh Chakrabarty, *Provincializing Europe: Postcolonial Thought and Historical Difference* (Princeton, NJ: Princeton University Press, 2000). The decentering of European history and thought is a major theme in postcolonial literature broadly. I am trying to show that Thoreau's conceptual play between center and periphery, which is so central to the Walden project, is conceptually related to the kinds of questions raised by postcolonial efforts to decenter European ways of knowing. Thoreau shared with these more recent philosophical efforts a resistance to European Enlightenment reason's attempt to find a kind of objectivity that required a God's eye view. Every view is a view *from somewhere*. For an example of contemporary postcolonial work that aims to assess the legality of the colonial project from the perspective of Australian Aboriginal law (rather than from the perspective of European law traditions), see Irene Margaret Watson, *Aboriginal Peoples, Colonialism and International Law: Raw Law* (Abingdon: Routledge, 2015).

But this measure, one mile, introduces a perspectival puzzle that Thoreau plays with for the rest of the book. As with the relative significance of "the village" and "the woods," one mile can be very far, as this paragraph implies that it is, or very short, as one mile is when made relative to the "dozen miles" in which Thoreau describes looking for a place to live (II, 1).

The paragraph also has a playful tone, especially at its end. The sentence, "At present I am a sojourner in civilized life again," initiates the reader to Thoreau's sense of humor, which is very dry.[11] It also suggests, as the rest of the book continues to do, that there is a certain play between "the woods" and "civilization." A sojourner is one who visits, and by calling himself a "sojourner in civilized life," the last sentence suggests that Thoreau's time in the woods has accomplished the switch that I have suggested the book aims to make, to take a view of the woods as primary, as the center, as home, and a view of so-called civilized life as a place to visit on the periphery.[12]

[11] I take Thoreau's sense of humor as essential to interpreting *Walden*, and I exposit its centrality in the book further in Chapter 5, "Delight in True Goods."

[12] The philosopher Michel Serres objected to the term "environment" in the early 1990s for a similar reason. In his now classic work on the need for a new peace pact between humans and the world, he wrote, "So forget the word *environment*, commonly used in this context. It assumes that we humans are at the center of a system of nature. This idea recalls a bygone era, when the Earth (how can one imagine that it used to represent us?), placed in the center of the world, reflected our narcissism, the humanism that makes of us the exact midpoint or excellent culmination of all things. No. The earth existed without our unimaginable ancestors, could well exist without us, will exist tomorrow or later still, without any of our possible descendants, whereas we cannot exist without it. Thus we must indeed place things in the center and us at the periphery, or better still, things all around and us within them like parasites." Michel Serres, *The Natural Contract*, trans. Elizabeth MacArthur and William Paulson (Ann Arbor, MI: University of Michigan Press, 1995), 33. Some Indigenous thinkers object, however, to the view of humans as parasites, offering instead a vision of humans

Thoreau demonstrates a similar sense of play between center and periphery at the beginning of the next chapter too. In "Where I Lived, and What I Lived for," Thoreau describes a period in which he searched for a place to live. That chapter begins, "At a certain season of our life we are accustomed to consider every spot as the possible site of a house. I have thus surveyed the country on every side within a dozen miles of where I live" (II, 1). Thoreau was a surveyor; he was hired to measure and map land. He probably referred here both to his professional activities and to his walks around Concord. He describes how he thought about the places he visited.

> Wherever I sat, there I might live, and the landscape radiated from me accordingly. What is a house but a *sedes*, a seat?–better if a country seat. I discovered many a site for a house not likely to be soon improved, which some might have thought too far from the village, but to my eyes the village was too far from it.
>
> (II, 1)

Thoreau insists here, again and explicitly, on a perspectival shift from the one usually taken by those who live in the village, even those who enjoy outings to the woods. When he visited each place, he took *it* as the center, the place from which outings would occur; "the landscape radiated from me" suggests this. And some of the places he visited had much distance between them and the village, too much, even in Thoreau's view. But whereas "some might have thought [it] too far from the village," to Thoreau "the village was too far from it." Here, importantly, he does not suggest that how far away the village is does not matter. Even he thought the

as a "custodial species." Tyson Yunkaporta, *Sand Talk: How Indigenous Thinking Can Save the World* (Melborne, Victoria: Text Publishing, 2019).

distance between them too far. Rather, he insists that any place, no matter how remote from the village, can be a center.

Thoreau's interest in the interplay between the village and the woods takes part in a long tradition of pastoral literature that describes life outside of cities. In that tradition, the dynamic between country and city is always being constructed. In the pastoral imagination, the country is often the seat of rural, agricultural life. The city is the cultural center, where intellectual life and the arts flourish. As Raymond Williams argued in *The Country and the City*, the history of rural and urban settlements is intensely varied – stereotypes will never capture the diversity of actual human settlements. And yet persistent images have grown up around the words "country" and "city."

> On the country has gathered the idea of a natural way of life: of peace, innocence, and simple virtue. On the city has gathered the idea of an achieved centre: of learning, communication, light. Powerful hostile associations have also developed: on the city as a place of noise, worldliness and ambition; on the country as a place of backwardness, ignorance, limitation.[13]

Those images have collected especially persistently in literature. And Williams analyzed this dynamic, between the images of the country and the city, especially but not only in British literature. What he found was that these words, and this dynamic in British literature, had collected images that have to do with the development of capitalism as an economic form. Nostalgia for the country often has to do with transformations of communities because of changed economies. Thoreau's writing is caught up in the tradition that Williams described. Going to the woods was, in part, Thoreau's resistance to the industrial economy he saw overtaking what he

[13] Williams, *The Country and the City*, 1.

viewed as traditional economies of the region.[14] He was seeking a way of, as Williams wrote, "enjoying people and things, rather than using and consuming them." He wanted "to be a member, a discoverer, in a shared source of life."[15]

A second significance of Thoreau's play with location and space has to do with the conceptual issue of center and periphery I have already begun to describe. Cities are often taken to be centers, with country as their surrounding periphery. But where the center is in any field is a completely perspectival question. What is described as center and what as periphery is dependent on what is taken by the describer to be important in the field. Like orthodoxy and heresy, center and periphery are shaped mightily by the position of the person doing the categorization and the purpose of their categories.[16] In *Walden*, Thoreau insisted that where he chose to live, no matter its relation to the village, would be the seat, or center.

Thoreau's play with the concepts of village and woods was shaped by and ought to contribute to philosophical discussion of one of the persistent epistemological problems of the modern period. The problem has only become more pressing,

[14] I discuss Thoreau's worries about industrial economy further in Chapter 2.

[15] Williams thought that, even given the historical diversity of human settlement in fact, the nostalgia of those who longed for the countries of their childhoods was part of something real and important. Writing in 1973, Williams insisted, "Yet what we finally have to say is that we live in a world in which the dominant mode of production and social relationships teaches, impresses, offers to make normal and even rigid, modes of detached, separated, external perception and action: modes of using and consuming rather than accepting and enjoying people and things. . .It is not so much the old village or the old backstreet that is significant. It is the perception and affirmation of a world in which one is not necessarily a stranger and an agent, but can be a member, a discoverer, in a shared source of life." Williams, *The Country and the City*, 298.

[16] For a recent overview of orthodoxy and heresy in the historiography of early Christianity, see David W. Jorgensen, "Approaches to Orthodoxy and Heresy in the Study of Early Christianity," *Religion Compass* 11, 7–8 (July 1, 2017).

and interesting, over the course of the last century. This problem has to do with the dependence of knowledge on the situation of the knower, and the independence of truth from any particular knower's view on it. I take it that all knowledge is, like judgments about center and periphery and orthodoxy and heresy, contextual. This is to say that what we can know depends on where we stand, because where we stand determines what we can see (or hear, or feel, or touch, or taste).

The issue is this: philosophy since Descartes has aimed to secure knowledge against skepticism, to assure us that our knowledge corresponds to an objective world, to achieve certainty. Philosophers with this concern often ask: How can we know that the things we *think* are true, *are actually true*? Descartes wrote that the purpose of the method of doubt he proposed was, "to reach certainty – to cast aside the loose earth and sand so as to come upon rock or clay."[17]

But philosophy that tries to do this, to secure our knowledge against the wonderings of skepticism, has often tried to do so at the expense of our actual relationship to that objective world. It has not generally been concerned with actual earth or sand or rock or clay. To take the most prominent example, Kant insisted that our knowing comes to us through *a priori* conditions, what he tried to enumerate as the categories. This theory suggested that we do, in fact, know, but that our knowing comes to us not from our actual relationships to our objects of knowledge, but via the categories with which knowing knows.

The Kantian doctrine sought, like much philosophy since Descartes, to avoid the problem of relativism. Some responses to skepticism do insist that knowledge comes through the

[17] René Descartes, *Descartes: Selected Philosophical Writings*, trans. John Cottingham, Robert Stoothoff, and Dugald Murdoch (Cambridge: Cambridge University Press, 1988), 34.

relation of the knower to the object of knowledge. But if knowledge works in this relational way, Enlightenment philosophy worried, then it doesn't answer Descartes's challenge to find the rock on which knowledge might be built; it can't secure knowledge against skepticism. Since each person has a different set of relationships, they will therefore have a different view on the truth, and the concern was – the one Kant tried to address – that those views are so relative that knowledge is never secured.

But knowledge *is* relative, as the woods and the village are relative to one another. They only make sense at all in relation to one another. Knowledge is only achieved by knowers, and I can know only things that I can experience in some way, even if that way is – as it so often was for the philosophers of the European Enlightenment – through the fancy books I read. And what I experience, whether it is philosophy in books or raising children or being enslaved, has everything to do with where I am in space and time and in what relations I find myself. This explains what Stanley Cavell described as Thoreau's difference from Kant in *The Senses of Walden*. Like Kant, Thoreau thought that *a priori* conditions for knowledge were a necessity for humans, but, unlike Kant, that they could only be discovered historically. Cavell wrote,

> I am convinced that Thoreau had the Kantian idea right, that the objects of our knowledge require a transcendental (or we may say, grammatical or phenomenological) preparation; that we know just what meets the *a priori* conditions of our knowing anything *überhaupt*. These *a priori* conditions are necessities of human nature; and the search for them is something I think Thoreau's obsession with necessity is meant to declare. His difference from Kant on this point is that these *a priori* conditions are not themselves knowable *a priori*, but are to be discovered experimentally; historically, Hegel had said.

> *Walden* is also, accordingly, a response to skepticism, and not just in matters of knowledge. Epistemologically, its motive is the recovery of the object, in the form in which Kant left that problem and the German Idealists and the Romantic poets picked it up, viz., a recovery of the thing-in-itself; in particular, of the relation between the subject of knowledge and its object. Morally, its motive is to answer, by transforming, the problem of the freedom of the will in the midst of a universe of natural laws, by which our conduct, like the rest of nature, is determined. *Walden*, in effect, provides a transcendental deduction for the concepts of the thing-in-itself and for determination – something Kant ought, so to speak, to have done.[18]

Notice, Cavell makes the point in terms that are relevant to the main thesis of this chapter. He writes that Thoreau's project is a recovery of "the relation between the subject of knowledge and its object." This means that knowledge on Thoreau's picture *requires* relation. And relation defines social life. This means that Thoreau's construction of place in *Walden* has to do with one of the central epistemological puzzles of our time, and opens onto questions about his mistrust of social life and the social life he cultivated in the woods. If knowledge is only found in the relations I have, then what community I take myself to belong to is an epistemological question. It will determine how reliable my knowledge is.

Seeming Asociality/"Solitude"

Thoreau's interest in the self as the seat of knowledge sometimes makes him seem self-centered in a bad way. Like Wordsworth's before him, Thoreau's writing exhibits a focus on self-understanding that some read as selfishness, a fault of

[18] Cavell, *The Senses of Walden*, 93.

his character. Something like this was what Keats criticized in the famous phrase: "wordsworthian or egotistical sublime."[19] An interpretation in this vein would paint a picture of Thoreau as an asocial hermit and a cranky misanthrope. It would say that his loves were impersonal, mostly not for humans to boot. It would conjecture that sharing a room or a life with him would prove difficult, and that this is a bad sign if we are evaluating his character. This interpretation would emphasize Thoreau's insistence on being alone, on his love of solitude.

Many readers take the quintessential description of Thoreau's refusal of society to be in the "Conclusion" when Thoreau famously writes that, "If a man does not keep pace

[19] William Wordsworth was born in 1770, in Cumberland, England. He is a central figure in English poetry of the Romantic period, which is sometimes associated with an understanding of the human person that is radically autonomous, deeply focused on individual emotions, and thus – in a word – selfish. This sense is sometimes applied directly to Wordsworth himself with a phrase, "egotistical sublime," used by John Keats (under the influence of William Hazlitt's disappointment with Wordsworth) in an 1818 letter. Keats was Wordsworth's contemporary and fellow poet, who was, however, a generation younger and wanted to do something different with poetry than he thought Wordsworth had. Keats said, writing to a friend, that his own poetry had no self, no character, no identity. "As to the poetical character itself, (I mean that sort of which, if I am any thing, I am a member; that sort distinguished from the wordsworthian or egotistical sublime . . .) it is not itself – it has no self – it is every thing and nothing – It has no character – it enjoys light and shade; it lives in gusto, be it foul or fair, high or low, rich or poor, mean or elevated . . . A Poet is the most unpoetical of any thing in existence; because he has no Identity." John Keats, *Selected Letters*, Oxford World's Classics (Oxford: Oxford University Press, 2002), 147–48. Keats thought that poets could, if they were good at poetry, remove themselves from it entirely, that they are continually "filling some other body" about which they write. Wordsworth, in Keats's view, practiced a poetry that was overly focused on the poet's self and that saw the world only through his eyes. This is the flip side of the issue about the relativity of knowledge to the position of the knower, and there is a real question – perhaps the most pressing philosophical question of the last centuries – about whether a view that acknowledges the place of the individual in the pursuit of knowledge can avoid falling into the kind of solipsism that Keats worried Wordsworth had.

with his companions, perhaps it is because he hears a different drummer. Let him step to the music which he hears, however measured or far away" (XVIII, 10). The image sometimes seems to suggest that the man who hears a different drummer should take leave from "his companions," which is to say from all other band members. But that reading of this passage misses the point Thoreau is making, as does the contemporary idiom that has sprung from this line: "marching to the beat of your own drum," which is importantly different from what Thoreau actually wrote. Someone who marches to the beat of "a different drummer" is still following "the music which he hears." He is not – as the asocial reading implies and the contemporary idiom makes explicit – drumming his own beat, off on his own.[20] He is following a different bandleader. The metaphor is ambivalent about society. It suggests there is more than one band you might join.

But in some of the most famous portions of *Walden* Thoreau does seem to seek an escape from society. The most straightforward place to find textual evidence that seems to count against my thesis that Thoreau is social is "Solitude," the fifth chapter of *Walden*. Here, Thoreau describes what it is like to be in the woods alone, and he delights in the space he has to himself. "For the most part it is as solitary where I live as on the prairies. It is as much Asia or Africa as New England. I have, as it were, my own sun and moon and stars, and a little world all to myself" (V, 3). Here, Thoreau revels in the distance he has from ordinary New England society. He has "a little world" all to himself, without intrusion except for

[20] Hodder suggests that the drummer passage acquires its full resonance when read in light of the appearance of the night drummer in *A Week*. Hodder, *Thoreau's Ecstatic Witness*, 91. Here, as in other places, Hodder's emphasis on ecstasy pushes his interpretation of this passage toward Thoreau's personal views about individual experience and away from the social and political implications of the passage.

when, in the spring, some people come to fish for pouts in the pond. Even they were always gone by night. He counts this world "all to himself" a good thing. And his description of what he likes about it – being solitary, having his own world – might make him seem asocial. He is avoiding company after all.

Similarly, later in the section he responds to those who ask whether he doesn't get lonely out in the woods. "Men frequently say to me, 'I should think you would feel lonesome down there, and want to be nearer to folks, rainy and snowy days and nights especially'" (V, 5). If Thoreau did want society, you might think, he would sometimes be lonely. But Thoreau dismisses this loneliness question. "Why should I feel lonely? Is not our planet in the Milky Way? This which you put seems to me not the most important question." Instead, Thoreau asks, "What do we want most to dwell near to? Not to many men surely, the depot, the post-office, the bar-room, the meeting-house, the school-house, the grocery, Beacon Hill, or the Five Points, where men most congregate, but to the perennial source of our life." For him, apparently, the woods serve well as a life-source, despite being remote from "where most men congregate." Even more emphatically, he writes, "I find it wholesome to be alone the greater part of the time. To be in company, even with the best, is soon wearisome and dissipating. I love to be alone. I never found the companion that was so companionable as solitude" (V, 12). This quotation supports a reading of Thoreau as departing from society. At Walden Pond, this text suggests, Thoreau found at last the solitude that he thought most satisfying.

These texts (and many others) push against my reading of Thoreau as seeking society at Walden Pond. In them he insists that lacking human society does him no harm. They argue, further, that being alone actually enables him to draw close to the source of his life. And they support Jane Bennett's view that some verison of asociality was required for Thoreau to do the kinds of self-formation he was attempting.

Dwelling on them, however, ignores texts in the same pages that describe another kind of society, the one I argue Thoreau found at Walden. Thoreau may sometimes say he is alone in the woods, but his writing elsewhere tells a different story. Just as Thoreau's spatial descriptions of Walden play with the conceptual pair of country and city, in "Solitude" Thoreau plays with the tension between solitude and society. The very first paragraph of "Solitude" shows a community of creatures and other phenomena in which Thoreau takes delight.

> This is a delicious evening, when the whole body is one sense, and imbibes delight through every pore. I go and come with a strange liberty in Nature, a part of herself. As I walk along the stony shore of the pond in my shirt sleeves, though it is cool as well as cloudy and windy, and I see nothing special to attract me, all the elements are unusually congenial to me. The bullfrogs trump to usher in the night, and the note of the whippoorwill is borne on the rippling wind from over the water. Sympathy with the fluttering alder and poplar leaves almost takes away my breath; yet, like the lake, my serenity is rippled but not ruffled. These small waves raised by the evening wind are as remote from storm as the smooth reflecting surface. Though it is now dark, the wind still blows and roars in the wood, the waves still dash, and some creatures lull the rest with their notes. The repose is never complete. The wildest animals do not repose, but seek their prey now; the fox, and skunk, and rabbit, now roam the fields and woods without fear. They are Nature's watchmen, – links which connect the days of animated life.
>
> (V, 1)

Whereas readers might imagine the woods are empty, might imagine that solitude entails being alone, Thoreau demonstrates the society he finds on the shores of Walden Pond. The trumpets of the bullfrogs announce the coming night, and an announcement implies a community of hearers. Thoreau has "sympathy" with the leaves in the trees, a social feeling. The wind "blows" and "roars." Some creatures sing to lull others to sleep, and other creatures stay awake serving as "watchmen." Thoreau may have been the only human on the shore of the pond that evening, but he was not alone. The days at Walden are full of "animated life."

Even more strikingly, Thoreau himself describes the society he found, even when supposedly alone. After responding to the question about loneliness by describing his "little world all to myself," Thoreau describes the way in which he wasn't, after all, alone. "Yet I experienced sometimes that the most sweet and tender, the most innocent and encouraging society may be found in any natural object, even for the poor misanthrope and most melancholy man" (V, 4).[21] He was sometimes at a remove from other humans, but he found society in objects, and storms, and rain. He goes on to write about "the friendship of the seasons," and then, about the sympathy he received from pine needles. Usually he did not feel lonesome, but there was one time when he did. "I have never felt lonesome, or in the least oppressed by a sense of solitude, but once, and that was a few weeks after I came to the woods, when, for an hour, I doubted if the near neighborhood of man was not essential to a serene and healthy life. To be alone was something unpleasant." But in that one lonesome moment, he was comforted by

> sweet and beneficent society in Nature, in the very pattering of the drops, and in every sound and sight around my house, an infinite and unaccountable friendliness all at once like an atmosphere sustaining me, as made the fancied advantages of human neighborhood insignificant, and I have never thought of them since. Every little pine needle expanded and swelled with

[21] This may be an allusion to Wordsworth's poem, "On the Influence of Natural Objects."

> sympathy and befriended me. I was so distinctly made aware of the presence of something kindred to me, even in scenes which we are accustomed to call wild and dreary, and also that the nearest of blood to me and humanest was not a person or a villager, that I thought no place could ever be strange to be again.
>
> (V, 4)

Thoreau found "society in Nature," where he felt "something kindred." He was sustained by an "unaccountable friendliness" in the "pattering of the drops." This line, "unaccountable friendliness" acknowledges the strangeness of having society with Nature. It participates, too, in Thoreau's play with the language of finance and accounting. The friendliness he experiences is unaccountable in many senses: the friends he finds do not offer an account of themselves and neither can he say what their friendship is or where it comes from. No one can count the value of such friendship in numbers. "The fancied advantages of human neighborhood" were replaced by the sympathy and friendship of the pine needles.

Thoreau sets this society in Nature – "like an atmosphere sustaining" him – against the patterns of other sorts of society. "Society is commonly too cheap. We meet at very short intervals, not having had time to acquire any new value for each other. We meet at meals three times a day, and give each other a new taste of that old musty cheese that we are" (V, 13). Society is cheap when we make it cheap, by meeting too frequently without attention to whether those meetings are good for us or not. But society needn't be that way. In the final pages of "Solitude" Thoreau describes visits from "an old settler" and "an elderly dame." The settler "is thought to be dead" and the dame is "invisible to most persons," but they provide Thoreau with the sort of society he values. Thoreau finds at Walden an alternative way of being in society.

Thoreau did delight in leaving the society that characterizes cities: close neighbors, bustle, and Beacon Hill. But he found another sort of society in the woods, one that nourished his human needs even as it tutored him in the bonds of community we can have with winds, and leaves, and frogs if we will spend time among them.

Thoreau's writing is complicated to be sure. What society, rightly understood, ought to be is a central puzzle in it, and there are certainly some social circumstances he clearly wanted to avoid. This does not make him asocial. My claim is that in going to Walden Thoreau did not retreat from society in general, but left one society and joined another: a spiritual community of exemplary creatures, places, and former inhabitants he thought formed the finest society he could imagine at the time. He sought out the social company of marginal figures who lived in the woods both in the present and the past.

Living People/"Visitors"

Thoreau's description of his retreat to Walden Woods was slightly tongue-in-cheek, in that he did not go very far but still lived and wrote as though he had. Similarly, Thoreau's insistence on his aloneness was also moderated, not only as I have described by his social feeling for beings we do not typically consider part of human community, but also by his relationships to human community. The chapter I have just been discussing, "Solitude," is followed by one called "Visitors." This juxtaposition in itself expresses the dynamic I am trying to describe. "Solitude" offers a description of Thoreau's being alone in the woods that transforms the seeming solitude into society, if admittedly of an atypical sort that includes animals, plants, objects, and weather. Then "Visitors" considers hospitality as a practice, and describes how hospitality is better when there is some distance between the people who come together. You cannot receive a visitor without their having been elsewhere to begin with. Together, these two chapters show Thoreau offering an alternative view of what society should be, how it should work, and what it should be for, but not a rejection wholesale of being with other people.

It is not hard to find evidence in *Walden* of Thoreau's obviously social habits. In "Visitors," Thoreau even wrote about a big party in his tiny house. "It is surprising how many great men and women a small house will contain. I have had twenty-five or thirty souls, with their bodies, at once under my roof" (VI, 2). And later, in "The Village," he writes about his near daily visits to the village.

> Every day or two I strolled to the village to hear some of the gossip which is incessantly going on there, circulating from mouth to mouth, or from newspaper to newspaper, and which, taken in homœopathic doses, was really as refreshing in its way as the rustle of leaves and the peeping of frogs.
>
> (VIII, 1)

Just as the woods offered opportunities for looking, and seeing, and being with, so too the village. Even gossip is good in homeopathic doses. He carries his powers of observation with him from the woods on his outings to town, "to see the men and boys," and "to observe their habits." He shows himself to be an astute ethnographer of his own country: "I observed that the vitals of the village were the grocery, the bar-room, the post-office, and the bank" (VIII, 1).

Thoreau himself was occupied with showing that his life was sociable. "Visitors" begins with Thoreau's own insistence that he is "no hermit."

> I think that I love society as much as most, and am ready enough to fasten myself like a bloodsucker for the time to any full-blooded man that comes in my way. I am naturally no hermit, but might possibly sit out the sturdiest frequenter of the bar-room, if my business called me thither.

> I had three chairs in my house; one for solitude, two for friendship, three for society.
>
> (VI, 1)

Despite his love of solitude, then, Thoreau was not asocial. He had friends who came to see him in the woods, and he welcomed them. The three chairs were a symbol of the fact of sociality in his Walden life, and the sociability of three comes into view in other parts of Thoreau's life in Walden Woods.[22]

"Visitors" is also where we meet Alek Therien, a man whom Thoreau met in his first days living in the woods, in 1845, and with whom Thoreau had an interspecies experience of the sociality among three. In "Visitors," Therien has been translated out of the *Journal* and into *Walden* as a heroic figure, "a true Homeric or Paphlagonian man." I further discuss the significance of the portrait of the woodchopper in *Walden*, the model for whom was Alek Therien, in Chapters 4 and 5. The point at the moment is that if Thoreau had been hoping to enforce a rigorous apartness from other people, we would expect his interactions with Therien to be quite different than they were in those first weeks in the woods. Thoreau moved on July 4, and on July 14 wrote in his journal about meeting Therien as well as the five railroad men I described in the Preface. Then, on July 16, Therien comes to call. The *Journal* describes Therien in detail (which is largely copied into the portrait of the woodchopper in *Walden)*. And then some time after December 23, 1845, and before March 26, 1846, less than a year after Thoreau's moving to the woods, Thoreau and Therien share a social experience that

[22] It also recurs in my description of the sociability of writing in Chapter 4.

includes a bird. It is useful to recall that Therien was Canadian and spoke French. The *Journal* describes it thus:

> Therien the wood chopper was here yesterday – and while I was cutting wood some chicadees hopped near pecking the bark and chips and the potatoe skins I had thrown out – What do you call them he asked – I told him – what do *you* call them asked I – *Mezezence* I think he said. When I eat my dinner in the woods said he sitting very still having kindled a fire to warm my coffee – they come and light on my arm and peck at the potatoe in my fingers – I like to have the little fellers about me –
>
> Just then one flew up from the snow and perched on the wood I was holding in my arms and pecked it and looked me familiarly in the face. Chica-a-dee–dee-dee-dee-dee, – while others were whistling phebe–phe-bee – in the woods behind the house.[23]

This passage strikes me as a vivid example of the sort of society Thoreau cultivated in the woods. In the short interaction, Therien and Thoreau share caring mutual curiosity about one another's languages. Then Therien describes his own relationship to the chickadees he knows in the woods. And then a chickadee joins their circle, speaking its own language (one of the most complex among animals as it happens) and looking "familiarly." In this case, the social occasion included Therien and the bird.[24] It was an interspecies form of the social trinity Thoreau had described when he wrote that he kept three chairs in his house.

[23] Henry David Thoreau, *Journal*, Volume 2: *1842–1848*, 191.

[24] The French scholar of English literature and ecocriticism Thomas Pughe has written about Thoreau in the context of contemporary interspecies studies. Thomas Pughe, "Brute Neighbors: The Modernity of a Metaphor," in *Thoreauvian Modernities: Transatlantic Conversations on an American Icon*, ed. François Specq, Laura Dassow Walls, and Michel Granger (Athens, GA: University of Georgia Press, 2013), 249–64.

Edward Waldo Emerson wrote *Henry Thoreau: As Remembered by a Young Friend*, which was published in 1917. He wrote it in part as a defense, and for this reason it sometimes reads like hagiography more than history. Nonetheless, I think what Edward Emerson wrote about Thoreau's respect for animals suggests that his sociality with living humans and with other living creatures in the woods were related. They were part of the same reverence for created things as part of God.

> He felt real respect for the personality and character of animals, and could never have been guilty of asking with Paul, "Doth God care for oxen?" The humble little neighbors in house or wood whose characters he thus respected, rewarded his regard by some measure of friendly confidence. He felt that until men showed higher behaviour, the less they said about the "lower animals" the better.
>
> For all life he had reverence, and just where the limits of conscious life began and ended he was too wise, and too hopeful, to say.[25]

Edward Emerson describes a man exceptionally attuned to life in the woods, a man who refused standard contrasts between humans and other animals. Further, according to Edward, Henry revered everything alive, and his reverence for created things made him wary of presuming to know which things had consciousness and which did not.[26]

[25] Edward Waldo Emerson, *Henry Thoreau: As Remembered by a Young Friend* (Boston, MA: Houghton Mifflin, 1917), 82–83.

[26] The moral philosopher Mary Midgley would have approved. Her 1978 *Beast and Man* suggested that European philosophy had misconceived human nature by consistently setting it up in contrast to animals, when in fact we learn more about human nature by seeing ourselves as members of the class. She thought this problem in the European philosophical tradition had "distorted arguments in ethics" and might have obscured important human possibilities. She was particularly mad at Existentialism: "The really monstrous thing about Existentialism too is its proceeding as if the world contained only dead matter

Edward seemed to think that Henry's habit of respect for other beings was rare. I can imagine a reader of this book suspicious of my using this moment to characterize Thoreau as sociable; they might think that Thoreau was inventing a society rather than joining one. But the passage about Thoreau, Therien, and the chickadee shows us that Thoreau was not some kind of raving loner who was odd because he thought he could talk to birds. Therien, too, likes "to have the little fellers about." And the chickadee himself, whose language we do not entirely know, gets a word into the account. "Chica-a-dee–dee-dee-dee-dee."[27] All three make a contribution. The trinity of members exhibits mutual investment in the social moment. The important point is that Thoreau's sociability with other people is mutually constituted and not limited to human persons.

It may be, too, that the chickadee's language would have been more familiar to Therien and Thoreau, who spent so much time in the woods, than it is to most readers. Current research, conducted through close observation in controlled settings, has suggested that the "chick-a-dee" call is among the most complex animal communication science has uncovered.[28] Spending time among the chickadees could have

(things) on the one hand and fully rational, educated, adult, human beings on the other – as if there were no other life-forms. The impression of *desertion* or *abandonment* which Existentialists have is due, I am sure, not to the removal of God, but to this contemptuous dismissal of almost the whole biosphere – plants, animals, and children. Life shrinks to a few urban rooms; no wonder it becomes absurd." She did not consider what I take to have been Thoreau's view, that the dismissal of the biosphere was related to the removal of God. For him, the idea that God could be known by humans apart from God's created world was blasphemy. Mary Midgley, *Beast and Man: The Roots of Human Nature*, Revised ed. (London: Routledge, 1995), xiii, 18–19.

[27] The bird's "chic-a-dee" is also quoted in Emerson's poem, "The Titmouse," written and published in 1862, the year Thoreau died.

[28] Christopher N. Templeton, Erick Greene, and Kate Davis, "Allometry of Alarm Calls: Black-Capped Chickadees Encode Information about Predator Size,"

taught Thoreau something about what chickadees mean when they call – when they are far enough away from their fellows that they cannot see one another, but not so far away that they cannot call out, seeking a response. They call to alert their fellows to danger. They call to ask "are you here with me?" They call to encourage others to join them, to resist a threat. This variant of the "chick-a-dee" call is described by contemporary literature as "mobbing calls," and the flock that joins in the harassment of a predator is described as exhibiting "mobbing behavior." Chickadees publish their worries abroad, and they wait for a reply from their friends.[29] Thoreau may have considered the chickadee's call as a model for *Walden*, a call to alert his friends, and a hope they would join his mob.[30] Emerson was struck by the passage, and wrote a poem, "The Titmouse," in response.

This image of Thoreau, Therien, and the chickadee has become, for me, an icon of what Thoreau learned in Walden Woods, what he thought *Walden* might be, and what *Walden* has in fact become. The chickadee of Walden Woods called out, Thoreau and Therien came around to join the bird, *Walden* relayed the call, aiming to alert its readers to the

Science 308, 5730 (2005): 1934–37. See also, Todd M. Freeberg, "Social Complexity Can Drive Vocal Complexity: Group Size Influences Vocal Information in Carolina Chickadees," *Psychological Science* 17, 7 (2006): 557–61. And for a lay description of these studies of chickadee sociality (with reference also to Thoreau) see, Stephen Lyn Bales, *Natural Histories: Stories from the Tennessee Valley* (Knoxville, TN: University of Tennessee Press, 2007), 6–8.

[29] Jeffrey Stout pointed out to me that that there was more for me to learn about chickadees before I assumed that their language was indecipherable (which I had done in a previous draft). He also pointed out that their call ("Can you hear me? Will you join me?") resonated closely with the message of *Walden*. It was characteristically respectful (of the chickadee) and creative on his part.

[30] In Australian Aboriginal English, the term mob often refers to family, linguistic, cultural, or national groups, as in the question, "who's your mob?" It's a lovely way to describe who your people are.

dangers of injustice, and the mob has been gathering ever since. I discuss the significance of this image further in Chapter 4.

Dead People

The respect Thoreau had for living creatures meant that the form of society he lived in was atypical. It included inhabitants of the woods whom other people might exclude from society, like oxen or chickadees. But I think even "living beings" does not properly describe Thoreau's society; he included the now-dead as well. One of the key texts that supports this view is a chapter in the last part of the book, where readers rarely focus attention, entitled "Former Inhabitants; and Winter Visitors." Here, I think Thoreau's attention to the former inhabitants of Walden Woods should suggest to us that they too, though now dead, were among the society Thoreau joined in the woods. Their presence in the woods and in *Walden* also suggests, as I discuss at length in the next chapter, that Thoreau's form of life in the woods was more political than we usually notice.

The first notable thing about this chapter is its doubled title. Only the second chapter, "Where I Lived, and What I Lived For," has a title that includes more than a singular topic. Other chapter titles include "Economy," "Sounds," "Visitors," "Higher Laws," and "Spring." "Former Inhabitants; and Winter Visitors" thus represents the coordination of two seemingly separate topics into one subject. It could be that Thoreau made the choice to include the two topics together because neither had the material for the length of the chapter he planned. But given the variation among chapter lengths in the rest of the book, I do not think this is likely.

It is more plausible to think that Thoreau coordinated these two topics for thematic reasons; the former inhabitants are *among* the winter visitors. *Walden* is organized around the seasons of one year. Thoreau arrives in the woods in July, and the chapters trace seasonal changes. While he lived in the woods for two years, the book collates both years into one seasonal story, so that the major principle of organization in the book is the changing of the weather, and the woods, and the behavior of animals, as well as the work required for Thoreau to live in each of the different periods of the year. The book ends in spring, in part as an emphatic insistence on the promise of morning and associated aim of spiritual awakening that Thoreau weaves through the whole book. The winter months thus appear in the chapters leading up to the end of the book. And in this particular chapter, Thoreau introduces his reflections on the former inhabitants by the fact of his aloneness, especially in that winter period. He wrote, "For human society I was obliged to conjure up the former occupants of these woods" (XIV, 1). In the winter, when he spent more time inside and alone than usual, he conjured the former occupants of the woods in order to enjoy human society that was lacking in that season.

But read the sentence again. "For human society I was obliged to conjure up the former occupants of these woods" (XIV, 1). "For human society" may refer not only to the human society Thoreau found for himself in the woods. It may also signify something like "for the sake of human society," and refer to the society beyond Walden Woods that Thoreau hoped to reach by writing *Walden*. He conjured the former occupants of the woods not only so that he could enjoy their company, but also on behalf of broader human society, a society that did not generally share Thoreau's interest in their lives.

It may be surprising to some readers that Walden Woods, as Thoreau describes his neighborhood, ever had occupants before Thoreau. The popular image of Thoreau's retreat to the woods has him aiming to live outside of society in intense solitude. This was an image Thoreau knew people had, and which he in some sense cultivated, even within the pages where he describes the people who lived there before him.

But against the caricature of Thoreau as living in untouched wilderness, his writing shows that he had historical consciousness and curiosity about the place that he lived, and that he was interested in what had come before.[31] The nineteen-paragraph discussion of the neighborhood *as a neighborhood*, as what had been – as Thoreau wrote – a "small village," shows that the location had a history. It had been a place where people made their homes. Thoreau wrote, "Within the memory of many of my townsmen the road near which my house stands resounded with the laugh and gossip of inhabitants, and the woods which boarder it were notched and dotted here and there with their little gardens and dwellings" (XIV, 1). His knowledge of these former inhabitants suggests that Thoreau had conducted something like what we now call oral history about "the memory" of his "townsmen," as a way to learn what had been before him in the woods he came to occupy. I find it easy to imagine that this may have been one of the things Thoreau liked to gossip about in Concord. In whatever way he came to know what

[31] Treatments of the history of Walden Woods include: Thomas Blanding, "Historic Walden Woods," *The Concord Saunterer* 20, 1/2 (1988): 2–74; W. Barksdale Maynard, *Walden Pond: A History* (Oxford: Oxford University Press, 2005); Elise Lemire, *Black Walden: Slavery and Its Aftermath in Concord, Massachusetts* (Philadelphia, PA: University of Pennsylvania Press, 2009). Maynard's book focuses on the history of the Pond from Thoreau's early life up through the present but briefly mentions the earlier inhabitants of the woods. Lemire concentrates on the history of slavery in Concord, and especially on the free Black people whom Thoreau writes about in "Former Inhabitants." Her book is the most in-depth history of slavery in Concord, and I rely on it not because it is an exemplary history of Northern slavery (there are many fine examples of important new work on Northern slavery), but because it deals in specifics with respect to Concord that are important to my interpretation of *Walden*.

he did, he is one of the key sources for history about the people who had occupied Walden Woods, situated between Concord and Lincoln, in the generation before him.

As it happens, many but not all of these people had been formerly enslaved free Black people, members of the last generation of Concord slavery. This may be one of the reasons so many readers forget that Walden was not a wilderness. US historiography, dominated in the academy by white people, has for too long failed to consider Black society as historically significant society. But this exclusion of the Black people who were always part of Northern history was not a habit of Thoreau's. He describes four free Black people whose homes had been close to where he built his own along the northern shore of Walden Pond. Thoreau's descriptions of the Black people who lived in Walden Woods before him exhibit features of racist thinking deployed among some white people of his period. Stories about the former inhabitants circulating in white Concord gossip must have conveyed these images to Thoreau, and that fact should make us cautious about his representations of them. But all the same, Thoreau never takes the strange tone later white historians did, when they took Concord as the center of society and described these figures as "pariahs or lawless characters," "outcasts and cast-offs."[32]

[32] Thomas Blanding's section on "Walden Woods before Thoreau" offers a glimpse of the strange tone some historians have taken – up through the 1980s – to the people who lived in the woods before Thoreau: "For more than half a century before Thoreau moved to the woods, Walden had harbored the outcasts and cast-offs of the village – freed slaves, drunkards, and, a little later, the shanty Irish. Concord historian F. B. Sanborn records, 'It is curious that the neighborhood of Walden ... was anciently a place of dark repute, home of pariahs and lawless characters, such as fringed the garment of many a New England village in Puritanic times.'" Blanding, "Historic Walden Woods," 7–10. The Sanborn quote comes from the early Thoreau biography, Franklin Benjamin Sanborn, *Henry D. Thoreau* (Boston, MA: Houghton, Mifflin, 1882), 202.

The first of the people whose ruined homes Thoreau describes is Cato.

> East of my bean-field, across the road, lived Cato Ingraham, slave of Duncan Ingraham, Esquire, gentleman of Concord village; who built his slave a house, and gave him permission to live in Walden Woods; – Cato, not Uticensis, but Concordiensis. Some say that he was a Guinea Negro. There are a few who remember his little patch among the walnuts, which he let grow up till he should be old and need them; but a younger and whiter speculator got them at last. He too, however, occupies an equally narrow house at present. Cato's half-obliterated cellar hole still remains, though known to few, being concealed from the traveller by a fringe of pines. It is now filled with the smooth sumach, (*Rhus glabra*,) and one of the earliest species of goldenrod (*Solidago stricta*) grows there luxuriantly.
>
> (XIV, 2)

Three things about this passage are important to note. First, one of the key features of the description has to do with what Cato did in order to live independently. He prepared for his old age (and presumably his current nutritional needs) by growing walnut trees. The text does not make clear whether the walnuts were for food and barter or for lumber, but it was likely both. Walnuts provided important protein and the wood is precious as lumber; it would have made sense for Cato to plan to harvest the trees in his old age.[33] Second, though Cato planned to live independently in Concord through his old age, he never enjoyed the financial proceeds of his labors. "A younger and whiter speculator got them at last." Though the phrase "narrow house" had been used by Thoreau in "Economy" to describe a grave, and therefore might suggest that Thoreau was referring to an unidentified though now dead person, I suspect that the "younger and

[33] Lemire, *Black Walden*, 148.

whiter speculator" was Thoreau, who quite proudly occupied a narrow house himself during his time at Walden, and often used ironic financial puns, like "speculator," to describe his own activities. If the walnuts were for lumber in Cato's old age, and Thoreau was the younger, whiter speculator, then Cato's walnuts – tended in his lifetime both for food and as a financial investment – wound up serving the society of Walden in Thoreau's period.[34] The third thing to note is that the end of the paragraph describes the remains of Cato's house as a ruin being overtaken by plants. There is the "half-obliterated cellar hole" obscured from view by the pines and filled with sumach and goldenrod. These three features – first what Cato did to live independently, second the sense in which the plan did not work out, and third the description of his former home as a ruin – unite Thoreau's descriptions of the first two former inhabitants, first Cato and next Zilpha.

> Here, by the corner of my field, still nearer to town, Zilpha, a colored woman, had her little house, where she spun linen for the townsfolk, making the Walden Woods ring with her shrill singing, for she had a loud and notable voice. At length, in the war of 1812, her dwelling was set on fire by English soldiers, prisoners on parole, when she was away, and her cat and dogs and hens were all burned up together. She led a hard life, and somewhat inhumane. One old frequenter of these woods remembers, that as he passed her house one noon he heard her muttering to herself over her gurgling pot, – "Ye are all bones, bones!" I have seen bricks amid the oak copse there.
>
> (XIV, 3)

[34] I thank one of the anonymous reviewers from the Press for pointing out that Cato may have cultivated the walnuts as lumber and thus that their being handed down to Thoreau – the younger, whiter speculator – makes them members of the society of Walden Woods I am describing.

Like Cato, Zilpha worked to provide for herself, spinning "linen for the townsfolk," and keeping chickens. Nonetheless, her soup was made mostly of bones, and her life was hard, "inhumane" even. Her house and livelihood were destroyed by presumably white arsonists.[35] And now, in Thoreau's time, all that is left is some bricks amid the oak copse, a ruin among the plants that grow around it.[36] Zilpha of Walden Woods also shared a name with Zilpha Elaw, one of a number of early nineteenth-century Black women who defied race and gender hierarchies to preach the Christian gospel.[37] Thoreau could have been alluding to this other Zilpha, as he might have known Zilpha Elaw from her preaching or her autobiography, *Memoirs of the Life, Religious Experience, and Ministerial Travels and Labours of Mrs. Zilpha Elaw, an American Female of Colour*, which was published in 1846.

Next, Thoreau describes Zilpha's brother Brister and his wife Fenda.

[35] Lemire, *Black Walden*, 167.

[36] The figure of the ruin was central to the poetics of the Renaissance, as a figure for the absorption of the past in the making of the future. Andrew Hui, *The Poetics of Ruins in Renaissance Literature* (New York: Fordham University Press, 2016). Describing the ruins of the former village, I think Thoreau is playing with those representations as he so often does, offering a particularly American form of a European classic.

[37] According to Eddie Glaude, preachers like Elaw "challenged directly the idea that the Gospel was the possession of men. Their witness inspired others as they openly rejected – as they preached the word of God – assumptions about the inferiority of black women." Eddie S. Glaude, *African American Religion: A Very Short Introduction* (New York: Oxford University Press, 2014), 46. Womanist theology appeals to their examples. According to Mitzi Smith, Zilpha Elaw and other Black women preachers "named, defined, and legitimized [their experience] as Black women called to preach." Mitzi Smith, "'Unbossed and Unbought': Zilpha Elaw and Old Elizabeth and a Political Discourse of Origins," *Black Theology* 9, no. 3 (June 22, 2011): 287–311.

> Down the road, on the right hand, on Brister's Hill, lived Brister Freeman, "a handy Negro," slave of Squire Cummings once, – there where grow still the apple-trees which Brister planted and tended; large old trees now, but their fruit still wild and ciderish to my taste. Not long since I read his epitaph in the old Lincoln burying-ground, a little on one side, near the unmarked graves of some British grenadiers who fell in the retreat from Concord, – where he is styled "Sippio Brister," – Scipio Africanus he had some title to be called, – "a man of color," as if he were discolored. It also told me, with staring emphasis, when he died; which was but an indirect way of informing me that he ever lived. With him dwelt Fenda, his hospitable wife, who told fortunes, yet pleasantly, – large, round, and black, blacker than any of the children of night, such a dusky orb as never rose on Concord before or since.
>
> (XIV, 4)

Thoreau's description elided two different Bristers: Brister Freeman of Concord, who had lived at Walden, and Brister Sippio of Lincoln whose grave Thoreau had seen.[38] One thing the two Bristers had in common was the burden of their blackness. Racial violence was commonplace in Concord.[39]

[38] Henry David Thoreau, *Walden: A Fully Annotated Edition*, ed. Jeffery S. Cramer (New Haven, CT: Yale University Press, 2004), 249 n20.

[39] Lemire, *Black Walden*, 160–71. The story of one attack is told with chilling nonchalance in the memoir of Peter Wheeler in Edward Waldo Emerson, *The Centennial of the Social Circle in Concord: March 21, 1882* (Riverside Press, 1882), 140–41.

"Mr. Wheeler once had a most ferocious bull to kill. He and his men succeeded with some difficulty in getting the animal into his slaughter-house. They were afraid, however, to go in and encounter his fury, and, while outside conferring upon the safest mode of proceeding, Brister Freeman, the celebrated negro, happened along. Wheeler, giving his men the wink, inquired very affectionately after Brister's health, and told him if he would go into the slaughter-house and get an axe, he should have a little job to do. Brister never suspected mischief, at once opened the door and walked in, when it was quietly shut upon him, and the appalled negro found himself face to face with the enraged bull. It was already a 'case of fight or die,' and after sundry minuets about the house, the celerity of which would have established even a French dancing-master, Brister fortunately spied the axe he had been sent in for, and, seizing it, commenced belaboring his

Another thing the two Bristers had in common was their name. Cato and Brister's names both carried deep significance. Enslaved people were often given names from ancient Greek and Roman history (as Cato had been) or named after places. Brister's name was a common name given to enslaved men in the north, one that carried with it a bitter history. Bristol was England's largest slave port, and "Brister" was a variant of the name of that city.[40] Brister had likely been named after the port in which he had been traded as property.

The former inhabitants, the remains of whose households Thoreau describes, had been part of a small community that had mostly disappeared before Thoreau ever went to the woods. Brister Freeman's grandson, John Freeman, was the last descendent of a person formerly enslaved in Concord and settled in the small village in Walden Woods to die there, which he did soon after his grandfather in 1822.[41] "An Irishman, Hugh Quoil" was the last human inhabitant of Walden Woods before Thoreau, and he died soon after Thoreau moved to the woods (XIV, 11).

adversary, giving him a blow here and there as he had opportunity. All this while stood Peter and his men watching through the dry knot-holes the valiant exploits of Brister, and cheering him on with the most encouraging roars of laughter. Fortune at length decided in favor of the negro; he laid the bull dead upon the floor, and casting down his weapon of fight, came forth unharmed. But imagine the amazement of his tormentors when at length he emerged, no longer the dim, sombre negro he was when he entered, but literally white with terror, and what was once his wool, standing up straight like so many pokers, they could hardly persuade themselves to believe it was Brister; but without waiting for them to identify him, or receive their congratulations for the notable manner in which he had sustained himself, the affrighted and indignant negro turned his back upon them and departed."

Sanborn's biography, published the same year, describes the same occasion. Sanborn, *Henry D. Thoreau*, 206–7.

[40] Lemire, *Black Walden*, 17.

[41] Other formerly enslaved people and their descendants lived in other parts of Concord until the late nineteenth century. Lemire, 171–73.

It is not a coincidence that many, though not all, of the inhabitants of Walden Woods in the generation before Thoreau had been free Black people. People were enslaved in Concord from its founding in 1635 until after the Revolution. One contemporary scholar, herself a child of Concord, was motivated to tell the history of Concord slavery by the fact that even after a surge in studies of Northern slavery, most books about Concord continued to be "more or less about the town's role as the cradle of liberty and literature," almost never acknowledging that "enslaved men and women helped to build what would become New England's most storied town."[42] Thoreau's oral histories of Cato, Zilpha, Brister, and Fenda recorded a Concord that included Black people who had been enslaved in Concord, and in which their continued presence was usually unwelcome by whites except in continued service to white residents in exchange for subsistence.

In the awkward transition from slavery to freedom around the time of the American Revolution, many newly free people understandably chose lives very similar to the ones they lived under slavery. But a few courageous new citizens – some of whom had fought in the Revolution in place of their enslavers – chose to leave lives of domestic service and make their way on their own, to live independently. Because newly free people were usually unable to purchase land, "the abandoned slaves were permitted by their former owners to squat locally, but only on the most out-of-the-way, infertile places."[43] Thus, one of the things we know about the

[42] Lemire, 9. A contemporary museum, The Robbins House, works to raise awareness of the African, African American, and anti-slavery history of Concord from the seventeenth through the nineteenth centuries. See https://robbinshouse.org/about/ (accessed August 20, 2020).

[43] Lemire, 10.

formerly enslaved people who settled at Walden Pond – among them Cato, Zilpha, Brister, and Fenda – was that they refused the new wage economy, in which they would have exchanged labor for wages (or, more likely, subsistence).

Rather than continuing to live by service to others, these courageous people made the difficult decision to eke out an unsteady and harassed, but independent, living on the shores of Walden Pond. There they established a community that endured for four decades (between approximately 1782 and 1822) and at its height seems to have included around fifteen formerly enslaved Black people and some poor white people. Thoreau called it a small village. Brister owned his own land for a time, until he sold it to Rachel Le Grosse, a white widow with whom he commenced a relationship after Fenda died. Because his marriage to Rachel would have been illegal under Massachusetts law, he likely sold Rachel the land as an assurance for her future should he die.[44] Indeed, she sold the land the year after his death.[45] That place, Brister's Hill just north of Walden Pond, still bears his name. Brister's sister, Zilpha, lived independently for forty years, "a feat matched by no other Concord woman of her day."[46]

Walden Woods was not the only such place. Other sites on the outskirts of Concord had also been home to communities of formerly enslaved people and others who were unwelcome in the village. Many such places, where newly free people formed their own communities, often with others who were unwelcome in town, have become – like Walden Woods and the site of Negro Fort near Apalachicola that I discussed in the Preface – icons of wilderness. As Lemire writes, "The history of slavery and its aftermath reveals that at least some of our

[44] Lemire, 163 [45] Lemire, 170–71. [46] Lemire, 137.

nation's cherished green spaces began as black spaces, with Walden Woods a particularly striking case in point."[47] Lemire doesn't elaborate the point, but two other examples begin to fill out this pattern.[48] Contemporary archeological work in Central Park has investigated a community there, Seneca Village, that was razed to build the park.[49] Central Park is now, of course, one of the most famous green spaces in the United States. The Great Dismal Swamp of Virginia and North Carolina, part of which is now a National Wildlife Refuge, was famous as a refuge for people who escaped enslavement and formed new lives for themselves.[50] And of

[47] Lemire, 12.

[48] There are so many individual examples, it seems like there ought to be a book about the pattern. I have not found one. I hope someone else is working on this.

[49] Diana diZerega Wall, Nan A. Rothschild, and Cynthia Copeland, "Seneca Village and Little Africa: Two African American Communities in Antebellum New York City," *Historical Archaeology* 42, 1 (2008): 97–107. Manisha Sinha, *The Slave's Cause: A History of Abolition* (New Haven, CT: Yale University Press, 2017), 356–57.

[50] Thoreau probably alluded to this when he wrote in "Walking": "When I would recreate myself, I seek the darkest wood, the thickest and most interminable, and, to the citizen, most dismal swamp. I enter a swamp as a sacred place,—a *sanctum santorum*." It would have also been an allusion to Longfellow's 1842 poem "The Slave in the Dismal Swamp." Harriet Beecher Stowe went on to set her second novel, published in 1856, in the Great Dismal Swamp: *Dred: A Tale of the Great Dismal Swamp*. On the history of formerly enslaved people in the Great Dismal Swamp see Ted Maris-Wolf, "Hidden in Plain Sight: Maroon Life and Labor in Virginia's Dismal Swamp," *Slavery & Abolition* 34, 3 (September 1, 2013): 446–64; Daniel O. Sayers, *A Desolate Place for a Defiant People: The Archaeology of Maroons, Indigenous Americans, and Enslaved Laborers in the Great Dismal Swamp* (Gainesville, FL: Society for Historical Archaeology, 2014). Shannon Mariotti writes about Thoreau's attraction to swamps, but misses his likely interest in swamp habitation. Shannon L. Mariotti, *Thoreau's Democratic Withdrawal: Alienation, Participation, and Modernity*, Studies in American Thought and Culture (Madison, WI: University of Wisconsin Press, 2010), 141–42. See also Giblett, *Postmodern Wetlands*. For a general treatment of the place of swamps in the nineteenth-century imaginary, see David Miller, *Dark Eden: The Swamp in Nineteenth-Century American Culture* (Cambridge: Cambridge University Press, 2010).

course all of these places had been first dispossessed from the First Nations who occupied them before European settlement.[51]

Thoreau moved to the Pond twenty-five years after Zilpha's death in 1820. He was inspired by the heroism of these 'former inhabitants.' He was drawn for this reason to the neighborhood they had occupied, and they were among the community of spirit he joined while in the woods. Describing the former inhabitants' importance to Thoreau, Lemire writes, "Their experiences after emancipation were one reason Thoreau was drawn to live in Walden Woods himself. He regarded the former slaves' persistence in the face of isolation and harassment as heroic, and like them he sought to live independently."[52] This is one of the main reasons to think that Thoreau was drawn to Walden Woods for social reasons; he sought a community from which he could learn to live well, a community of exemplars.[53]

To the extent that Thoreau was drawn to Walden Woods by exemplars, my interpretation also complicates Alfred Tauber's claim that Thoreau created the following individualist myth: "We each potentially possess the heroic ability to elevate our respective lives by conscious effort, by deliberate

[51] Mark David Spence, *Dispossessing the Wilderness: Indian Removal and the Making of the National Parks* (New York: Oxford University Press, 2000).

[52] Lemire, *Black Walden*, 1.

[53] I thank Andre Willis for drawing my attention to Neil Robert's work on the import of such communities to contemporary political philosophy. Neil Roberts, *Freedom as Marronage* (Chicago, IL: University of Chicago Press, 2015). Roberts argues that "Revolutionary slaves possessed their own political imaginary, an imaginary with its own notions of reason and freedom that developed during the process of struggle against a form of slavery" (21). These notions constitute "theories of freedom from modernity's underside" (21). Roberts elaborates them with more insight and depth than I am capable of. My point is just to say that Thoreau may have been appealing to such theories of freedom in his moving to the woods.

moral choice."[54] Thoreau did make a choice to join the society he found at Walden Woods. It was a heroic effort to surround himself with the spiritual community that would help him improve, and to try to keep something of that community's spirit alive in his period. But he didn't think that he could do it alone. He relied on the community at Walden Woods to elevate his life.

My interpretation of Thoreau's going to Walden to seek society is also supported by the frame Thoreau gives the passage on former inhabitants. The passage comes directly after one of the most moving images of Thoreau's two years in the woods. He writes that when he got a woodstove in his second winter to replace the fireplace he used in his first, "I felt as if I had lost a companion. You can always see a face in the fire" (XIII, 19). The stove is a better technology, it burns less fuel, but it's also less companionable. Having the fire shut up in the stove, where you cannot see it, doesn't provide the same kind of company as watching the flames would. This passage about the fire is followed immediately by the chapter "Former Inhabitants; and Winter Visitors." Instead of the fire, Thoreau says, "For human society I was obliged to conjure up the former occupants of these woods" (XIV, 1). I take it that he is not being coy when he calls this conjuring a provision of society. The face in the fire was a real loss; just so, the former inhabitants – like the elderly dame and old settler of "Solitude" – are real company. This impression is deepened in the tenderness with which Thoreau describes the former habitations of the people he has for company on winter nights.

> What a sorrowful act must that be, – the covering up of wells! coincident with the opening of wells of tears. These cellar dents,

[54] Alfred I. Tauber, *Henry David Thoreau and the Moral Agency of Knowing* (Berkeley, CA: University of California Press, 2001), 9.

> like deserted fox burrows, old holes, are all that is left where once were the stir and bustle of human life and "fate, free-will, foreknowledge absolute," in some form and dialect or other were by turns discussed. But all I can learn of their conclusions amounts to just this, that "Cato and Brister pulled wool"; which is about as edifying as the history of more famous schools of philosophy.
>
> (XIV, 12)

Here, Thoreau expresses sympathy with the loss of the community that had existed before him. He expresses respect for its inhabitants, who were philosophers surely. And when he writes that "all I can learn of their conclusions..." he expresses regret about the problem Lemire came to confront in writing about the formerly enslaved people of Concord – the historical sources on the community at Walden Woods are so thin (though not as thin as most books about Concord would make you think).[55] All of this suggests Thoreau's love for those former inhabitants whose homes welcomed his visits with lilacs, even if they were gone.[56]

[55] The line about pulling wool is apparently a piece of wordplay and a reference to a job that Brister and Cato likely did to earn meat. "Pulling wool referred to a black man pulling his forelock in deference to passing white folks, a way of tipping an imaginary hat. And yet the former slaves may have only acted deferential as a means of covering their tracks or pulling the wool over local people's eyes, making it difficult to know precisely what they did and thought. But even as Henry is indulging his love of word play here, he also means simply that Cato and Brister pulled wool from sheep carcasses for the local slaughtering industry, which grew in Concord from one slaughterhouse in 1791 to eleven in 1801." Lemire, *Black Walden*, 137.

[56] Other readings are, of course, possible. Timothy Powell suggests that Thoreau's treatment of these figures is ambivalent, in that it both insists on the inclusion of Black history in contexts that often ignored it and erases contemporary Black communities of Thoreau's period. "On the one hand, Thoreau's image of the 'covering up of wells' and 'the opening of wells of tears' is a beautifully crafted metaphor of the reservoir of black sorrow that lies hidden beneath the discursive landscape of white 'history,' from which African Americans have been excluded.

Concord lore in Thoreau's time was that the spirits of these people, particularly Zilpha, still occupied the woods.[57] In *Walden* Thoreau receives visitors "thought to be dead" and "invisible to most persons" more than once. In our time, not everyone believes that the spirits of the dead live on among us, but to de-people them from the pages of history is a mistake.[58] The spirits of Cato, Zilpha, Brister, and Fenda, along with the other members of Walden Woods' society – human and animal, vegetable and mineral – were Thoreau's social community and best teachers. Thoreau's insistence that the others in the woods have social standing is part of what I mean by his "nature piety." He thought that due reverence for the woods included reverence for the heroic ones who had lived there before him.

At the same time, Thoreau's descriptions of the former inhabitants also traffic in racialized representations that were part of unfolding patterns of racial thinking in New England. These patterns had themselves developed through the experience of gradual emancipation of which Cato, Zilpha, Brister, and Fenda had been a part. Joanne Pope Melish has argued that the experience of gradual emancipation in New England was central to the formation of ideas about race in eighteenth-

And yet, on the other hand, his insinuation that this revelation can occur only 'when the last of the race departed' implicitly suggests that blacks have somehow already disappeared." Timothy B. Powell, *Ruthless Democracy: A Multicultural Interpretation of the American Renaissance* (Princeton, NJ: Princeton University Press, 2000), 88. Without disputing the horrendous habit of erasure of non-white persons from white-dominated US society, I think Thoreau's reference to when the "last of the race departed" was likely specific to the community in Walden Woods, for which Thoreau had particular piety, rather than the whole of the North as Powell seems to assume.

[57] Lemire, *Black Walden*, 3.

[58] The scholar of American religious history Robert Orsi has tried to grapple with how current historical practice should handle such phenomena. Robert A. Orsi, *History and Presence* (Cambridge, MA: Harvard University Press, 2016).

and nineteenth-century New England. Melish's main object is to undermine a mythology in which New England is viewed as historically free and white, an ahistorical pattern of thought she refers to as "New England nationalism." New England was constructed, in this understanding, as "the antithesis of an enslaved south."[59] In the process, white Northerners developed "a public narrative in which the history of the relations between whites and people of color is rarely if ever glimpsed."[60] Melish argues that Northern "race" was invented during the period of gradual emancipation amid whites' uncertainty about the reasons for enslavement. "Whites' need to resolve post-Revolutionary uncertainty over susceptibility to enslavement and eligibility for citizenship provided a political justification for emerging scientific notions of 'race.'"[61] "New England whites 'racialized' themselves and people of color in response to concerns about citizenship and autonomy posed by emancipation and post-Revolutionary dislocation."[62] The way in which people in Concord felt unsettled by the freedom achieved by Cato, Zilpha, Brister, and Fenda thus also probably contributed to what they would have said about them when they gossiped with Thoreau in town.

Some of the gossip Thoreau reports refers to racialized tropes, and it is difficult to discern (as in so many other places in the book) where Thoreau participates in the tropes he deploys and where he contests them. He is frequently doing both. For example, he reports in significant detail what he heard about the various physical features of these people, especially their coloring, which is not a trait he usually describes. When Thoreau reported that people said Cato

[59] Joanne Pope Melish, *Disowning Slavery: Gradual Emancipation and "Race" in New England, 1780–1860* (Ithaca, NY: Cornell University Press, 2000), xiv.
[60] Melish, 10. [61] Melish, 6. [62] Melish, 5.

was a "Guinea Negro," he likely referred to a usage that indicated Cato had been born in Africa, but the people Thoreau was quoting may also have been describing Cato's coloring, as "Guinea Negro" was sometimes used to describe people of so-called mixed ancestry. When Thoreau described Zilpha, he wrote she was "a colored woman." He wrote that Brister was "a man of color." In the case of Brister, however, Thoreau seems to find the phrase somewhat bizarre; he follows his usage of it with the aside, "as if he were discolored," which I take to imply a criticism of the usage itself. The "as if" insists that Brister's color was entirely wholesome.

Perhaps Thoreau's interest in a more accurate description of color, rather than the euphemistic and vaguely insulting "man of color," was part of what motivated his description of Fenda who was, according to Thoreau's reports of what he heard, "large, round, and black, blacker than any of the children of night, such a dusky orb as never rose on Concord before or since." But while Thoreau may have intended his description as a mark of respect, given that the rising of the sun was one of the main symbols of spiritual awakening in the book, his intense focus on Fenda's physical description marks her, and all of the formerly enslaved people he describes, as different from – for instance – the woodchopper, whose description does focus on his physical traits, but to much different effect. The description of Fenda as a "dusky orb" troubles me in particular. Still, when I look for poetic precedents of the term, I find many in books Thoreau could have read (though I have no evidence that he did): Petrarch's "Triumph of Time;"[63] "Ossian's

[63] Francesco Petrarca, *The Triumphs of Petrarch* (London: Longman, Hurst, Rees, and Orme, 1807), 193.

Apostrophe to the Sun," published in the *American Reader* of 1820;[64] John Dryden's *Oedipus: A Tragedy*.[65] Like Thoreau's other portraits of these formerly enslaved people, his description of Fenda may participate in what Eric Lott described in his landmark history of minstrelsy *Love and Theft* as a "mixed erotic economy of celebration and exploitation."[66] My own appeal to these figures as Thoreau's heroes may participate in a similar dynamic.[67]

New England nationalism, idealized white abolitionist histories, and the general tendency in nineteenth- and twentieth-century historiography to obscure the ongoing relations between whites and people of color hide one of the most important facts of US American history: African Americans enacted their own freedom. One piece of that long history has been told recently in Martha Jones's *Birthright Citizens*, where she argues that the actions of Black Americans – "petitioning, litigating, and actions in the streets – are a record of how people with limited access to legal authority won rights by acting like rights-bearing people. They secured citizenship by comporting themselves like citizens."[68] In the Civil Rights

[64] John Hubbard, *The American Reader Containing a Selection of Narration, Harangues, Addresses, Orations, Dialogues, Odes, Hymns, Poems, &c.* (Bellows Falls: Bill Blake & Co., 1820), 187.

[65] John Dryden, *The Works of John Dryden*, ed. Walter Scott, vol. 6 (London: James Ballantyne and Co. Edinburgh, n.d.), 152.

[66] Eric Lott, *Love & Theft: Blackface Minstrelsy and the American Working Class*, 2nd ed. (New York: Oxford University Press, 2013), 6.

[67] I have become especially attentive to the way in which I may be doing something like this since reading "Coda: Some of Us Are Tired" in Jennifer Nash's *Black Feminism Reimagined*, where she describes and criticizes a contemporary "vision of black women as the saviors of American political life." Jennifer C. Nash, *Black Feminism Reimagined: After Intersectionality* (Durham, NC: Duke University Press, 2019), 134.

[68] Martha S. Jones, *Birthright Citizens: A History of Race and Rights in Antebellum America* (Cambridge: Cambridge University Press, 2018), 10.

Act of 1866, "free men and women of color likely recognized the claims they had already long been pressing."[69]

Some readers fail to see Walden Woods as the alternative place of social life that is was, a place where freedoms that were not yet secure were nonetheless enacted by people without sufficient protections from the nation they inhabited. When those readers forget or suppress that story, they may be doing it because of their failure to understand free Black society as real society. Like New England nationalism, like histories that attribute civil rights gains to growing enlightenment of elites rather than to the work of those coalitions that won the political gains required, the erasure of society from Walden Woods is, bluntly, a feature of white supremacy. It is a problem that has afflicted Thoreau's reception ever since.

This will not be surprising to many US historians. The important point for my purposes here is to point out that the excision from US history of the village Thoreau described distorted interpretations of *Walden*. Readmitting the members of Walden Woods to the story of social life there ought to transform our understanding of Thoreau's experiment and of his book.

Conclusion

This chapter has argued that rather than departing from society when he went to Walden, Thoreau was invested in a neighborhood while he lived at the Pond. By this I mean that he cultivated relationships with a broad array of creatures and other beings. We get the mistaken impression of his departing society when we make two characteristic mistakes that

[69] Jones, 14.

Thoreau's writing challenges: first when we think of "the village" as the center of all sociality, and second when we constrict our understanding of social actors to the particular class to which Thoreau belonged. Thoreau challenges both of these assumptions. First, in response to the view that the village is the center of social life, Thoreau raised a conceptual problem – what we take to be the center of anything depends on where we are and what we think is important. We can make a perspectival switch, and take ourselves to be part of a different field. Such a change in perspective will also, often, transform our understanding of who counts as members of our society. Which leads to the second point. In response to the view that sociality belonged only to the class of which Thoreau was a part, Thoreau insisted that every being participates in social life: frogs, birds, trees, winds, rains, but also foreigners, outsiders, and even the now-dead. His perspectival shift integrated into his society figures otherwise viewed as "outcasts." In this way I have argued that Thoreau's life in the woods was a social life. In the next chapter, I shall argue that Thoreau's cultivation of relationships with the other inhabitants of the woods formed the ground for his political activity.

2

The Politics of Getting a Living

We worship not the Graces, nor the Parcæ, but Fashion.

Walden, (I, 38)

In the previous chapter, I argued that Thoreau's time in the woods was more socially committed than common caricatures of it tend to allow, and that the society it cultivated was one that aimed to recenter itself around figures otherwise seen as marginal. If I am right about this, then that argument should also transform our understanding of Thoreau's politics. Showing that this is so is what this chapter sets out to do.

The first step is to show that the Thoreau of *Walden* is invested in any politics at all. Plenty of readers come away from *Walden* with the impression that Thoreau was unconcerned with the topics and activities we normally associate with political life, that he was apolitical.[1] After all, a central feature of Thoreau's life as represented in *Walden* was withdrawal from practices that seem vital to political life – he thought there were too many newspapers, for example. "I am sure that I never read any memorable news in a

[1] Hannah Arendt expressed this view succinctly when she wrote, of Thoreau's concept of conscience in his essay "On Resistance to Civil Government," that "here, as elsewhere, conscience is unpolitical." Hannah Arendt, *Crises of the Republic: Lying in Politics; Civil Disobedience; On Violence; Thoughts on Politics, and Revolution* (New York: Harcourt Brace & Company, 1969), 60. I think Arendt is wrong about Thoreau, but that she gets Thoreau wrong for interesting reasons that have to do both with the twentieth-century reception of Thoreau and with what she means when she writes "politics."

newspaper" (II, 19). And even in the "political essays," he wrote perfectly contrarian things that seemed to explicitly reject politics: "They who have been bred in the school of politics fail now and always to face the facts" (SM 2). Further, his influence on environmental movements that came after him has – in the eyes of some interpreters – depoliticized them.[2] The sense that Thoreau is seen as apolitical even inspired an essay within the discipline of philosophy about Thoreau's activism, written on the premise that Thoreau's political activity needs to be documented, and without mentioning much of the recent scholarship on Thoreau's politics.[3]

However, insider debates within the discipline of philosophy notwithstanding, there has been burgeoning interest in Thoreau's politics from scholars of political theory and English over the past thirty years.[4] In general, that scholarship has tended to focus on his so-called "political writings."[5]

2 Chaloupka, "Thoreau's Apolitical Legacy for American Environmentalism."

3 Paul Friedrich, "The Impact of Thoreau's Political Activism," in *Thoreau's Importance for Philosophy*, ed. Rick Anthony Furtak, Jonathan Ellsworth, and James D. Reid (Bronx, NY: Fordham University Press, 2012), 218–22.

4 Many of the political theorists doing this work can be found in Jack Turner, ed., *A Political Companion to Henry David Thoreau* (Lexington, KY: The University Press of Kentucky, 2009). Within the discipline of English, recent work on Thoreau's politics includes Michelle C. Neely, "Radical Minimalism: *Walden* in the Capitalocene," *Concord Saunterer* 26 (2018): 144–50; Michelle C. Neely, "Embodied Politics: Antebellum Vegetarianism and the Dietary Economy of Walden," *American Literature* 85, 1 (March 1, 2013): 33–60; James S. Finley, "'Justice in the Land': Ecological Protest in Henry David Thoreau's Antislavery Essays," *The Concord Saunterer* 21 (2013): 1–35; James S. Finley, "A Free Soiler in His Own Broad Sense: Henry David Thoreau and the Free Soil Movement," in *Thoreau at 200: Essays and Reassessments*, ed. Kristen Case and K. P. Van Anglen (New York, NY: Cambridge University Press, 2016), 31–44; James S. Finley, "Pilgrimages and Working Forests: Envisioning the Commons in 'The Maine Woods,'" in *Rediscovering the Maine Woods: Thoreau's Legacy in an Unsettled Land*, ed. John Kucich (Amherst, MA: University of Massachusetts Press, 2019), 141–67.

5 There are of course important exceptions to this over-broad generalization. Twenty years ago, Bob Pepperman Taylor pointed out that understanding Thoreau's politics requires a more holistic reading of his work. Taylor, *America's Bachelor*

Among these political writings, the usual evidence for interpreters of Thoreau's politics are the essays "Resistance to Civil Government" ("Civil Disobedience"), "Slavery in Massachusetts," "A Plea for Captain John Brown," and "Life without Principle." These authors' attention to the political essays is an important part of the reevaluation of Thoreau's politics currently ongoing, but their focus on the political writings to the exclusion of the politics implicit in *Walden*'s ascetic practice has tended to overemphasize a liberal view of democratic theory in accounts of Thoreau's politics.[6]

Uncle. More recently, Shannon Mariotti has shown "how Thoreau's unique politics of withdrawal are best illuminated by exploring his so-called nature writings, not necessarily his more overtly political pieces such as 'Resistance to Civil Government' or other 'reform' essays." Mariotti, *Thoreau's Democratic Withdrawal*, xii. Where Mariotti's work on Thoreau and Adorno interprets the gesture of withdrawal as being for the sake of critique, I am trying to describe something similar, but in a more positive frame: less withdrawal than reinvestment in delight; less critique than establishment of a just economy. The difference is subtle – fundamentally, Taylor, Mariotti and I are agreed that Thoreau's renunciations have important significance for a transformed vision of democratic politics.

[6] Other interpreters of Thoreau's politics take him to be an anarchist. For example, A. Terrance Wiley, *Angelic Troublemakers: Religion and Anarchism in America* (New York: Bloomsbury Academic, 2014), 15–54. The book describes a tradition of religious anarchism articulated by Thoreau, Dorothy Day, and Bayard Rustin. Wiley attaches the following quotation from "Slavery in Massachusetts" as an epigraph to the chapter on Thoreau, "My thoughts are murder to the State, and involuntarily go plotting against her." Wiley distinguishes strong anarchism – which supports the abolition of any form of government – from weak anarchism – which insists that no government is authoritative without the consent of the governed. In this sense, Wiley's weak anarchism, which he attributes to Thoreau, is difficult to distinguish from radical democracy. Wiley writes, "Thoreau advocates for a government that is probably best described as anarchism as government by consent" (8). Wiley and I are agreed that the description of Thoreau as a political liberal has papered over some of the most interesting features of Thoreau's writing and life. But liberals are not the only democrats. My question for Wiley is what we get out of describing Thoreau as an anarchist rather than a democrat. Other interpreters, sharing Wiley's attention to Thoreau's disgust with democratic institutions but taking it in a different direction, separate liberalism from democracy and see Thoreau as a critic of democracy because it threatens liberal

In fact, as I show in this chapter, attention to the form of life Thoreau recommends in *Walden* and the historical context of his practice shows how his theory of politics as reconstructed from the political essays was caught up in his daily practice. I argue that the choices he made about his daily life, especially the renunciatory ones he describes making in *Walden*, were more closely allied to his politics than we usually remember, and that with his practices at Walden in view we get a different picture of what democratic individualism is than we have received from the theorists of political liberalism.[7] Where liberal political theory takes the categories of the sovereign subject, individualism, and rational deliberation as essential to "politics," this chapter argues that *Walden* demonstrated a more relational politics – invested more deeply in common goods – than interpreters of Thoreau's politics usually imagine

values like "free expression, civil disobedience, the liberty to follow one's conscience." Leigh Kathryn Jenco, "Thoreau's Critique of Democracy," *The Review of Politics* 65, 3 (2003): 355–81.

[7] The most prominent of these theorists, and the ones largely responsible for initiating academic interest in Thoreau's politics over the last several decades, are George Kateb and Nancy Rosenblum. Their work has been vital in helping to bring Thoreau into political theory. For Kateb, individualism is an anchoring value for democracy, and the Emersonians (Emerson, Whitman, and Thoreau) are its geniuses. They wrote the richest works we have on this specific form of democratic individualism. He also thinks that individualism without democracy (in Kantianism and English and German romanticism) is incomplete. Thus, he prefers the Emersonians as the geniuses of democratic individualism. For Kateb and other political theorists, individualism does not mean selfishness, as popular usage often indicates. It means respect for the individual as individual, something more akin to human dignity than to individual assertion. It means that individual persons are of utmost value, and that individual human life is a value we should protect. There is nothing wrong with this, as far as it goes, and there are many features of such an individualism I support. But the political theorists go too far (and miss one of the central features of *Walden*) when their concept of individualism obscures – even if unintentionally – the basic relationality and interdependence of human life. George Kateb, *The Inner Ocean: Individualism and Democratic Culture* (Ithaca, NY: Cornell University Press, 1994); George Kateb, *Patriotism and Other Mistakes* (New Haven, CT: Yale University Press, 2006).

that he had.[8] This interpretation also shows ways in which his ethic is more closely related to contemporary relational and care ethics than we usually see.[9]

Neglect of the relational politics of *Walden* is caused by and reinforces the individualist bent of liberal politics. While liberalism's emphasis on individual rights and dignity led to real achievements with respect to democratic justice, this form of politics sometimes has trouble recognizing the political subject as a member of a web. There is thus contemporary backlash against that individualist emphasis now, because people feel they are losing something important, which is a picture of the

[8] Political theorist Nancy Rosenblum sought to describe a wider view of liberalism, expansive enough to hold within it the romanticism she saw expressed by Thoreau and others. Nancy L. Rosenblum, *Another Liberalism: Romanticism and the Reconstruction of Liberal Thought* (Cambridge, MA: Harvard University Press, 1987).

[9] I am thinking here of the wide feminist literature on relationship and care as a basis of ethics. One important account was Gilligan, *In a Different Voice*. Some see much earlier work, for example by Mary Wollstonecraft in the nineteenth century or the example of M and D in Iris Murdoch's *The Sovereignty of Good*, as related to this more recent effort. Mary Wollstonecraft, *A Vindication of the Rights of Woman and A Vindication of the Rights of Men*, ed. Janet Todd (Oxford: Oxford University Press, 1993); Iris Murdoch, *The Sovereignty of Good* (New York: Routledge, 2001). A recent analytic philosophical account is offered in Stephanie Collins, *The Core of Care Ethics* (New York: Palgrave Macmillan, 2015). One explicitly feminist engagement with *Walden* can be found in Laura Dassow Walls, "'Walden As Feminist Manifesto,'" *ISLE: Interdisciplinary Studies in Literature and Environment* 1, 1 (March 1, 1993): 137–44. See also Sarah Ann Wider, "'And What Became of Your Philosophy Then?' Women Reading Walden." *Nineteenth-Century Prose* 31, 2 (2004): 152–171. Wider points out that Thoreau's advocacy of distance can be a boon to already marginalized readers who have sometimes taken it as encouragement that their point of view can challenge more dominant ones.

There is also important work on relational ontologies ongoing in Indigenous thought around the world. One article from Australia – whose lead author is a place – is Bawaka Country, Sarah Wright, Sandie Suchet-Pearson, Kate Lloyd, Laklak Burarrwanga, Ritjilili Ganambarr, Merrkiyawuy Ganambarr-Stubbs, Banbapuy Ganambarr, Djawundil Maymuru, and Jill Sweeney. "Co-Becoming Bawaka: Towards a Relational Understanding of Place/Space," *Progress in Human Geography* 40, 4 (August 1, 2016): 455–75.

rich interdependencies that make our lives. This is especially important in contemporary environmental thinking. Many environmental ethicists and citizens believe that a vision of human life as cut off from the communities on which it is dependent has led to vast indifference to the suffering of communities from which dominant societies have been cut off, whether they are wetland ecosystems or immigrant workers.

Thoreau's time in the woods was invested in the social relationships he cultivated there (and that I described in Chapter 1). But those social relationships also inspired him, I think, to want to set relationships right. Such relational setting right *just is* what justice is.[10] Thoreau's social life in the woods

[10] Jack Turner's *Awakening to Race* makes relinquishment central to its argument and articulates an inspiring vision of democratic individualism, but he endorses relinquishment for typically liberal reasons.

"Democratic individualist character blends playfulness with moral seriousness. The democratic individualist will often interact in an agonistic fashion. But the expansion and flourishing of his character will respect others' moral equality. In the eyes of the democratic individualist, freedom and adventure are finer when constrained by the rights of others. *Domination and exploitation indebt the individual to those he dominates and exploits – making his achievements less commendable and his life less his own.* Achieving personal power on terms of justice and equality, refusing to elevate oneself through the degradation of others, is hard and therefore sweet. The democratic individualist welcomes the challenge fair play imposes." Jack Turner, *Awakening to Race: Individualism and Social Consciousness in America* (Chicago, IL: University Of Chicago Press, 2012), 8; emphasis added.

Who would not want to endorse such a person, who aims for justice and equality over against domination and exploitation? I am agreed with Turner that injustice anywhere is a threat to justice everywhere, as the saying goes, but the way he puts the point raises an important question. Why should debt in itself make an achievement less commendable and a life less one's own? The answer Turner gives, that self-reliance requires that I make my life my own, implies that in order to avoid exploitation and domination I ought not indebt myself to others. It implies that democratic individualists are not dependent on others. But in general we acknowledge that no person can achieve all wholly on his own. We are inclined to cooperation, and in any case we cannot do it all. We will necessarily indebt ourselves to one another. One thing that goes wrong in exploitation and domination is that the dominator or exploiter fails to acknowledge and offer due

thus had a further aim, beyond mere society: justice for the community within and beyond his social world.[11] People sometimes think that Thoreau did his own work while he lived at the pond merely as an end in itself, that he was apolitical or focused only on personal concerns. He certainly did try to provide for himself, to live independently. But he did this for importantly contextual reasons. Thoreau thought self-reliance was a good, but he did not treat it as his only end. He was a seeker of spiritual community, and his efforts to live self-reliantly were his pursuit of the perfection of that society of spirit. One important component of a perfected society of spirit, in his view, would be justice, which obtains when each member of a community receives what they are due, when we distribute rightly all the goods there are: physical, social, and spiritual.

piety to the actual relationships in which he finds himself. It seems strange to characterize the opposite of this as "welcoming the challenge fair play imposes," as though what is good about justice is that it is hard for *me*, rather than that it achieves right relation between *us*.

[11] While I focus in this book on the importance of Thoreau's understanding of his local context in Concord, especially with respect to Concord's history of slavery and contemporary industrialism, I do not do as much as I wish I did to situate Thoreau's view of his context in the broader history of settler colonialism in the region. One interpretive work readers can turn to that describes the everydayness of settler colonialism in Thoreau's context is Mark Rifkin, *Settler Common Sense: Queerness and Everyday Colonialism in the American Renaissance* (Minneapolis, MN: University of Minnesota Press, 2014). Rifkin argues that *Walden* articulates a queer conception of personhood (which Rifkin endorses) while effacing the abjection of the Indigenous peoples of New England (which he does not endorse). He nonetheless thinks that *Walden* can "expose the settler self to its limits" (xxi). For (less critical) treatments of Thoreau's interest in Native American culture, which was extensive especially in his Indian Notebooks, see Robert F. Sayre, *Thoreau and the American Indians* (Princeton, NJ: Princeton University Press, 1977); Suzanne Dvorak Rose, "Tracking the Moccasin Print: A Descriptive Index to Henry David Thoreau's Indian Notebooks and a Study of the Relationship of the Indian Notebooks to Mythmaking in 'Walden'" (PhD, Oklahoma, The University of Oklahoma, 1994); Richard F. Fleck, *Henry Thoreau and John Muir among the Native Americans* (Portland, OR: WestWinds Press, 2015).

Thoreau tried to give up what he could not get for himself partly because he wanted to find an alternative to common ways of life that required the unjust labor of others. And he thought the results of this experiment in "free labor" might serve as an example to encourage other people that abandoning economies of unjust labor would be good for those on both sides of unjust advantage, because it would win them all a kind of flourishing that can only be achieved in common.

While some interpreters see tension between *Walden*'s retreat and Thoreau's more politically explicit writing, I read them together.[12] When we read *Walden* in the context of Concord, we see how the book is both about communion with what Thoreau called "nature" and at the same time an instantiation of his politics. For Thoreau, ethical relations to the material world, on the one hand, and to humans, on the other, are inextricably bound. In this sense, "free labor" in *Walden* is both part of Thoreau's personal religious practice and at the same time political resistance against forces promoting unjust labor.

Clothing, the Factories, and Abolitionist Politics

With respect to unjust labor in the developing industrial North, this section relates Thoreau's ascetic practice to contemporary labor issues in the region around Concord. I take a closer look at Thoreau's own interest in voluntary poverty, especially with respect to clothes, and through the example of clothing his interest in the factories of Concord, and his response to the developing industrial economy of the North.

[12] Lawrence Buell has written on the way in which both *Walden* and "Civil Disobedience" express Thoreau's "ethics of disaffiliation." Lawrence Buell, "Disaffiliation as Engagement," in *Thoreau at 200: Essays and Reassessments*, ed. Kristen Case and K. P. Van Anglen (New York: Cambridge University Press, 2016).

The beginning of *Walden* outlines how Thoreau aimed to live on as little as possible during his time in the woods – to learn what were the "true necessaries of life," the most moderate forms of clothing, shelter, and food he could get by on. The practices of simplicity that Thoreau took up in the woods sought to overcome anxiety by recentering his life on its most basic elements. As represented in the book, these practices are wide-ranging, both negative and positive, active and contemplative. They include moderation in clothing, shelter, and food. They also include hospitality, housework and other labor, bathing, reading, writing, sitting, rowing, fishing, looking, walking, flute-playing, keeping appointments with trees, gossiping, visiting neighbors, and bean-hoeing. All of these practices play a role in Thoreau's form of life, and he hoped that through them he might transform himself, as most ascetic practioners aim to do.

I will just take one of Thoreau's practices as an example: clothing. Thoreau wrote that one way he pursued simplicity was by wearing simple clothes. He thought simple clothing – like simple shelter and simple food – was good for him because it conduced to a life of less "anxiety and strain" (I, 15). He wrote,

> It is desirable that a man be clad so simply that he can lay his hands on himself in the dark, and that he live in all respects so compactly and preparedly that, if an enemy take the town, he can, like the old philosopher, walk out the gate empty-handed without anxiety.
>
> (I, 37)

The old philosopher in this passage is accustomed to dressing so simply that when he wakes in the night and has to flee, he is already wearing the clothes he needs to bring with him. In Thoreau's practices of simplicity, including his insistence on simple clothing, he aimed at personal formation. His asceticism sought to cultivate a life for himself like that of the old philosopher "without anxiety."

But Thoreau's asceticism was also *political*, by which I mean it was aimed not only at his individual formation but also at the radical transformation of the world in which he lived, specifically of emerging industrial capitalism. Thoreau wrote, about why he preferred simple clothes,

> I cannot believe that our factory system is the best mode by which men may get clothing. The condition of the operatives is becoming every day more like that of the English; and it cannot be wondered at, since, as far as I have heard or observed, the principal object is, not that mankind may be well and honestly clad, but, unquestionably, that corporations may be enriched.
>
> (I, 41)

While Thoreau thought that simple clothes would help him live a life of true philosophy, he also had a political reason to prefer simplicity on this count. Life for the mill workers who produced clothing in the period was deteriorating. Thoreau worried that the expanding industrial economy of the North took corporate profit as its central aim rather than providing honest goods, and that it did not offer employees fair conditions.[13]

Though Thoreau doesn't discuss them at length, there were good reasons that the conditions of the operatives would have been on his mind. Textile mills in Lowell, Massachusetts, about 15 miles up the Concord River from Concord, were

[13] Lawrence Glickman has written a history of consumer activism in the United States, which includes a chapter that provides helpful context to Thoreau's own consumer concerns. Lawrence B. Glickman, *Buying Power: A History of Consumer Activism in America* (Chicago, IL: University of Chicago Press, 2009), 61–89. Glickman focuses especially on consumer activists concerned with Southern slavery, and notes, "It is a puzzle of the history of consumer activism that despite the fact that it has been a continuous strand in American politics, each successive generation of consumer activists tends to think it is the pioneering generation" (87).

on the route Thoreau and his brother John travelled in 1839 on a river trip that Thoreau wrote about in his first book, *A Week on the Concord and Merrimack Rivers*.[14] In the five years before John and Henry's river trip, those factories in Lowell were the sites of some of the first labor organizing among industrial textile workers in the United States. The young women who worked in the factories staged "turn outs" or strikes in 1834 and 1836, in an effort to oppose the reduction of their wages. And in 1844, the year before Thoreau moved to his house in Walden Woods, the women workers at Lowell formed a labor reform association, the first US union of women workers. They lobbied to limit the work day to ten hours.

This context suggests that Thoreau's reticence for new clothes was not *merely* oriented toward his own formation. This practice was also aimed at envisioning a radical alternative to the economy of the period, an economy which – Thoreau thought – exploited poor workers.[15]

[14] Thoreau's interest in, attachment to, and knowledge of the Concord River were a central part of his life. Readers interested in Thoreau's life on the water can turn to Robert M. Thorson, *The Boatman: Henry David Thoreau's River Years* (Cambridge, MA: Harvard University Press, 2017). Early in Thoreau's life, he built boats, one of which "he dubbed *Red Jacket* after the Seneca chief whose landmark 'Speech to the U.S. Senate' had insisted on Indians' rights to practice their own religion without interference." Walls, *Henry David Thoreau*, 76.

[15] Readers familiar with debates over the relevance of consumptive choices in the transition away from fossil fuels will notice parallels. I do not intend to say that individual consumptive choices are sufficient to contemporary climate politics. They are not. I agree with Michael Northcott that "discernment about consumption activities in a household in a modern city where energy is supplied through a global energy market will have no impact on the geophysical causes of climate change, since the global market in fossil fuels ensures that as long as they are extracted they will be burned somewhere." Michael Northcott, *A Political Theology of Climate Change* (Grand Rapids, MI: Wm. B. Eerdmans Publishing Co., 2013), 202. This does not acknowledge, however, the importance of personal investment in transformation, which is often manifested through personal choices about consumption and other financial practices. I articulate more about what

Thoreau's mention of the conditions of the women who worked in the factories was not taken merely from what reading he may have done in contemporary newspapers, his protestations against newspapers aside. As with many of the subjects about which he wrote, his observations were made first in intricate, mostly nonjudgmental detail, in his journal. On January 2, 1851 Thoreau wrote in his journal a long passage about a visit he had made to "the Gingham mills" "at Clinton." There, he saw a single room "which covers 1 7/8 acres & contains 578 looms."[16] The tone of the passage is strikingly matter-of-fact, and it is in the voice of one who had more curiosity than worry about the mills. It sounds like its author saw that industrialism might be impossible to stop through acts of resistance. He might even be slightly entranced by the ingenuity of the technology.

Thoreau describes the weaving process from start to finish as he saw it at the mill: the preparation of the raw cotton, the spinning of the thread, the dyeing of the thread, the setting up of the warp, and the weaving of the woof. Then, the quality control: the girls who pick off "inequalities or nubs," the machine that singes off "the fuz," the washing, the drying, the starching, the finishing of the edges, the measuring, folding, and packing. Through all of this, he exhibits the same tone of report that he came to adopt in his observations of the natural world.

Take, for an example of his observational tone, this passage, about the treatment of the raw cotton before its spinning into thread.

Thoreau's political asceticism means for contemporary climate politics in Balthrop-Lewis, "Active and Contemplative Lives in a Changing Climate."

[16] Henry David Thoreau, *Journal*, Volume 3: *1848–1851*, ed. Robert Sattelmeyer, Mark R. Patterson, and William Rossi (Princeton, NJ: Princeton University Press, 1991), 170.

> The cotton should possess a long staple & be clean & free from seed. The sea-island cotton has a long staple and is valuable for thread. Many bales are thoroughly mixed to make the goods of one quality – The cotton is then torn to pieces & thoroughly lightened up by cylinders armed with hooks & by fans. Then spread a certain weight on a square yard – & matted together & torn up & matted together again two or 3 times over.[17]

The process is what seems to interest him, how all the parts fit together. This kind of attention, required for descriptive writing, seems to have been what Thoreau cherished most about being a writer.

The agent, "Forbes," whom he presumably met at the mill, said that that mill was "the best Gingham mill in this country – the goods are better than the imported – The English have even stolen their name Lancaster mills calling theirs 'Lancasterian.'" This passage suggests that Thoreau's line about "everyday becoming more and more like the English" is not merely a throwaway line; he had evidence that suggested that the American mills were like the English in quality, and probably suspected that they were like them in conditions, too.

The journal entry goes on to articulate Thoreau's interest in conducting further research on the mills, especially by visiting "The Coach lace mill – only place in this country where it is made by machinery – made of thread of different materials – as cotton – worsted – linnen – as well as colors – the raised figure produced by needles inserted woof fashion. Well worth examining further."[18]

The one time in the long passage on his visit to the mill that Thoreau adopts a tone that suggests more than mere observation comes at the very end of the passage, where he praises the quality of the work. "I am struck by the fact that no work has

[17] Thoreau, 171. [18] Thoreau, 172.

been shirked when a piece of cloth is produced, every thread has been counted in the finest web – it has not been matted together."[19] We might expect his interest here to lie with the new machines, especially after he mentions in the preceding paragraph the name of the inventor "of what is new in the above machinery." Instead he closes the passage with praise of the operator's virtue: "the operator has succeeded only by patience perseverance and fidelity."[20] This suggests, I think, that though Thoreau took great interest in the mechanical processes adopted in the mills, he attributed the value of the work in the end to those workers who operated the machines.

Thoreau's ascetic politics of clothing in *Walden* – and, I think, his interest in the factories – was not cut off from wider political discourse but was an intervention into political debates of the period, in particular among abolitionists.

Thoreau thought the enslavement of Black people was an affront to justice, he aligned himself with those who opposed it, and he worked actively for its abolition. But in his critique of the economy of the North he also dissented from some of the most famous proponents of abolitionism. The controversy was over whether to analogize conditions of Northern workers to those of Southern slaves. The labor activism of the women in the factories at Lowell – the operatives to whom Thoreau may have referred when he wrote about the factory system – sometimes analogized their plight with slavery. Songs they sang during strikes said, for example, "I cannot be a slave."[21] They were part of a broader labor movement in which wage-workers resisted their unjust subjection to the arbitrary power and will of employers.

[19] Thoreau, 172–73. [20] Thoreau, 173.

[21] Quoted in Thomas Dublin, *Women at Work: The Transformation of Work and Community in Lowell, Massachusetts, 1826–1860* (New York: Columbia University Press, 1979), 98.

But abolitionists like Wendell Phillips and William Lloyd Garrison refused the analogy between Southern slavery and Northern wage labor. Garrison wrote that the term "wages slavery" was an "abuse of language." And that "we cannot see that it is wrong to give or receive wages."[22] Abolitionists had good reasons to insist on a sharp distinction between wage labor in the developing industrial North and slave labor in the South. For anti-racists (clearly an anachronism, but a useful one given how much racist anti-slavery there was) among abolitionists, the term "wage slavery" may have seemed to use racism as a political tool. Indeed, the white women at Lowell may have been using white racist portrayals of slavery to their political advantage. Their song, "I cannot be a slave," might have played on the desires of many white people to draw distinctions between white and Black, and appealed to advantages that (in a racist imagination) white women ought to have over Black people.[23]

Further, laborers in the North may have been paid poorly and subject to terrible conditions, but they were party to a voluntary contract and thus (in one, voluntaristic sense) free

[22] Quoted in Eric Foner, *Free Soil, Free Labor, Free Men: The Ideology of the Republican Party before the Civil War* (New York: Oxford University Press, 1995), xxiii. The quotation is from *The Liberator*, "Chattel Slavery and Wages Slavery," October 1, 1847. See also Marcus Cunliffe, *Chattel Slavery and Wage Slavery: The Anglo-American Context, 1830–1860* (Athens, GA: University of Georgia Press, 1979).

[23] Anti-slavery and women's rights movements were tightly tied to one another in the nineteenth century, but the story of their relationship is complicated. Kathryn Kish Sklar and James Brewer Stewart, *Women's Rights and Transatlantic Antislavery in the Era of Emancipation* (New Haven, CT: Yale University Press, 2017); Ana Stevenson, *The Woman as Slave in Nineteenth-Century American Social Movements* (Cham, Switzerland: Palgrave Macmillan, 2019). On white women's importance in the maintainance of white supremacy in the twentieth century, see Elizabeth Gillespie McRae, *Mothers of Massive Resistance: White Women and the Politics of White Supremacy* (New York: Oxford University Press, 2018).

to leave their work. In addition, some abolitionists felt that the comparison of wage labor to slave labor would undermine the argument against the enslavement of Black people. In their view, abolitionism's moral urgency meant it had to be prioritized and the sharp distinction between slave labor and wage labor upheld.

For their part, labor activists in the North thought that the abolitionist emphasis on Southern slavery to the neglect of labor reform at home stank of hypocrisy. George Henry Evans, the editor of the National Reform Association's publication *Young America*, promoted the view that landless employees were unfree because dependent on employers, and that only land reform in the form of redistribution would create a just economy.[24]

Thoreau refused the standard abolitionist contrast between wage labor and Southern slavery, and the voluntaristic conception of freedom that underwrote it. While remaining committed to the abolition of slavery, he sided with the labor activists about the problems of wage labor. He also went beyond either group in what is one of *Walden*'s most easily misunderstood passages. Thoreau wrote,

> I sometimes wonder that we can be so frivolous, I may almost say, as to attend to the gross but somewhat foreign form of servitude called Negro Slavery, there are so many keen and subtle masters that enslave both North and South. It is hard to have a Southern overseer; it is worse to have a Northern one; but worst of all when you are the slave-driver of yourself.
>
> (I, 8)

[24] For details on the dispute and on the voluntaristic conception of freedom that underlies abolitionists' objections to labor activists' use of the term "wages slavery," see Alex Gourevitch, *From Slavery to the Cooperative Commonwealth: Labor and Republican Liberty in the Nineteenth Century* (Cambridge, UK: Cambridge University Press, 2014), 41–46.

Thoreau agreed with Garrison: "It is hard to have a Southern overseer." But then he also agreed with the labor activists: "it is worse to have a Northern one." And finally, he insisted that worse than either of these subjections was "when you are the slave-driver of yourself." The passage might offend us, in its dismissiveness of chattel slavery. How could Thoreau say that a Northern overseer was worse than a Southern one? Or that any form of self-rebuke was worse than actual oppression? It should shock us. The horrors of Southern slavery ought not be subject to such comparison.

The shock we experience at the comparison may be a rhetorical effect Thoreau sought. The passage was likely intended to shock Thoreau's audiences. Thoreau lectured from the manuscript of *Walden* about 12 times in the four years between 1848 and 1852, and many of these lectures were taken mostly from "Economy," which became the first chapter of *Walden*. Audiences to which he lectured would have been largely sympathetic to abolitionism; some of them would have been invested in labor reform. The abolitionists would have been opposed to comparing the factory system to slavery; the labor reformers would not have known what to make of the claim that you could be a slave-driver of yourself.

The rhetoric of shock positioned Thoreau awkwardly with respect to both abolitionists and labor reformers, and did so in order to intervene in the debate among abolitionists about what a just economy requires. Thoreau's claim that having a Northern overseer is worse than having a Southern one is, I think, his response to abolitionists like Garrison who viewed Northern industrial capitalism as the improved economic alternative to slavery. Thoreau was not so sanguine about industrialism or Northern claims to virtue. He wanted to hold together the critique of slavery with the critique of wage labor and to fight for a politics that would seek a radically different economy for both the South and the North. Such a politics rested most basically on a freedom that could only be achieved by the renunciation of slave-driving of every kind, including of the self, a freedom achieved through what I call in this book political asceticism.

Still, it is also likely true that Thoreau's willingness to make a claim we find, and ought to find, quite shocking – that Northern wage labor was worse than Southern slavery – reflected his own privileged position relative to the labor systems he was criticizing. He was, of course, distant from the abuses of Southern slavery, if deeply dismayed by them. Many Black abolitionists, perhaps especially those who had experienced enslavement, knew Northern industrialism was a kind of unfreedom but were clear that chattel slavery was a horror.[25]

Through the limited example of Thoreau's restraint with respect to clothes, I have tried to show that Thoreau's asceticism was invested in a radical politics against industrial capitalism. I also suggested that his ascetic politics of clothing was not cut off from the wider political context but was responsive to political debates among abolitionists, especially about what a desirable economy would look like.

As in all else, Thoreau's interests in politics were deeply informed by his immediate contexts. Recall the "Former Inhabitants" of Walden Woods discussed in Chapter 1, Concord's formerly enslaved Black men and women who, upon gaining freedom around the time of the American Revolution, made their way as they could in the woods.

[25] "To African Americans comparing the condition of slaves and the working classes was like comparing apples and oranges." Sinha, *The Slave's Cause*, 351. The quote comes from a section that details relations between labor activists and abolitionists. Sinha contests the view that Garrison was overly sanguine about Northern labor.

In moving to the woods, these people left behind *both* the slavery to which they had previously been subject *and* the wage labor many Black people in the North – without inheritable wealth in land for farming or capital for trade – transitioned to upon gaining freedom. Thoreau moved to the Pond twenty-five years after Zilpha's death. He was inspired by the heroism of the former inhabitants. He was drawn for this reason to the neighborhood they had occupied.

I interpret Thoreau's *Walden* as taking these people as inspiration to a form of economy that no one had yet imagined – an economy that would submit neither to the domination of slavery nor to the exploitation of industrial capitalism.

Civil Disobedience

The articulation of Thoreau's politics presented in the previous section insists that his everyday, mundane practices represented in *Walden* were not mere eccentricities but were integral to his vision of just society. However, the political theorists are of course right to focus attention on Thoreau's political essays when interpreting his politics, and especially to focus on the essay now known as "Civil Disobedience." The essay was published under the title "Resistance to Civil Government" in 1849, in a collection edited by Elizabeth Palmer Peabody called *Aesthetic Papers*, and it has had enduring influence on politics all over the world.[26] It considered, in

[26] This may be an opportune place to point out the distinction between "ascetic" and "aesthetic," which struck me as not worth mentioning until the similarity in pronunciation of these words raised an intriguing discussion at a public lecture given by Mark Jordan. During the discussion following the lecture, some of us were talking about asceticism and some of us were talking about aestheticism, but we all thought we were talking about the same thing for quite a long time. Why is that? My instinct is that the confusion arose because both words refer to form – in

its way, another of the main issues facing – and dividing – abolitionists of Thoreau's period: the question of whether forcible resistance was ever justified, either by injustice or aggression.[27]

William Lloyd Garrison upheld the view that force was never justified and insisted that abolitionism and pacifism could be held together. In "Resistance to Civil Government" Thoreau, typically, answered the question by refusing it.[28] Instead, he argued that conscience should inspire citizens to resist unjust government in which they are complicit by breaking the law. If the injustice "is of such a nature that it requires you to be the agent of injustice to another, then, I say, break the law. Let your life be a counter friction to stop the machine. What I have to do is to see, at any rate, that I do not lend myself to the wrong which I condemn" (CD, 18). The problem was that too many people who *claimed* to be against war and slavery continued to support a government that waged war and justified slavery. "Practically speaking, the opponents to a reform in Massachusetts are not a hundred thousand politicians at the South, but a hundred thousand merchants and farmers here, who are more interested in commerce and agriculture than they are in humanity, and are not prepared to do justice to the slave and to Mexico, *cost what it may*" (CD, 10, emphasis original). Thoreau insisted that what made a good man good was his willingness to pay the price for doing

the ascetic case to a form of life focused on the good, and in the aesthetic case to forms of beauty.

[27] On "Civil Disobedience" as a response to "non-resistance" – or abolitionist pacifism – see Richardson, *Henry Thoreau*, 176.

[28] Thoreau's place in controversies over nonviolence was always complicated and remains contested. While he has been a major influence on the tradition of nonviolent civil disobedience in the United States, he was a fiery supporter of John Brown. Larry Reynolds examines the appeal of the martial in Thoreau's life in Larry J. Reynolds, *Righteous Violence: Revolution, Slavery, and the American Renaissance* (Athens, GA: University of Georgia Press, 2011).

right. Such men were rare. "There are nine hundred and ninety-nine patrons of virtue to one virtuous man" (CD, 10).

Another reason interpreters tend to focus analysis of Thoreau's politics on "Resistance to Civil Government" is that it turned Thoreau into a political figure for the twentieth century. The essay was given new life in politics when it confirmed for Gandhi the ideas he was working out in his own thinking about what he came to call *satyagraha*.[29] Thoreau had been inspired toward his own view by Indian literature and philosophy, and Gandhi was able to take from Thoreau's "Civil Disobedience" (as he knew the title) the idea that individual conscience should stand between an unjust government and the injustices that it perpetrates. But the story of "Civil Disobedience" did not stop there.

Gandhi's movement for Indian home rule at the outset of the twentieth century became itself an example in America during the 1960s, when Martin Luther King, Jr. took "the Gandhian method of nonviolent resistance" as the method for enacting "the Christian doctrine of love."[30] For King, the method of nonviolence just was "Thoreau's and Gandhi's civil disobedience," as he wrote in the *New York Times Magazine* on September 10, 1961.[31]

The force and importance of Thoreau's essay, then, is not only what it did in its own period. It has also – through

[29] An early, in-depth look at this influence is George Hendrick, "The Influence of Thoreau's 'Civil Disobedience' on Gandhi's Satyagraha," *The New England Quarterly* 29, 4 (December 1, 1956), 462–71.

[30] Martin Luther King, Jr., *Strength to Love* (Philadelphia, PA: Fortress Press, 1980), 150.

[31] Martin Luther King, Jr., "The Time for Freedom Has Come," *New York Times Magazine* (10 September 1961): p. 25ff. On one feature of Thoreau's influence on King, and King's import for ecology, see Nathaniel J. Van Yperen, "'The Fierce Urgency of Now': The Ecological Legacy of King's Social Ethics," *Journal of the Society of Christian Ethics* 36, 2 (September 2016): 159–72.

Gandhi, King, and so many others – become an icon of resistance to injustice around the world.[32]

The essay's topic is the conscience of the citizen as a motivation for resistance to government, and it takes as its central example the night that Thoreau spent in Concord's jail for refusing to pay the poll tax.[33] That story is told also in *Walden*, briefly, but it is given its most vivid articulation in this essay and used as an illustration of the resistance that

[32] Readers interested in the history of the nonviolent wing of American civil disobedience can turn to Ira Chernus, *American Nonviolence: The History of an Idea* (Maryknoll, NY: Orbis Books, 2004). For a broader history of American civil disobedience, that starts earlier than most, see Lewis Perry, *Civil Disobedience: An American Tradition* (New Haven, CT: Yale University Press, 2013). Thoreau's praise of John Brown complicates his reception among practitioners of nonviolent resistance. I look forward to John Kelsay's forthcoming book on violent political resistance, including John Brown. On John Brown, religion, and violence in politics: Ted A. Smith, *Weird John Brown: Divine Violence and the Limits of Ethics* (Stanford, CA: Stanford University Press, 2014).

[33] Some interpreters of Herman Melville's "Bartleby, the Scrivener: A Story of Wall-Street" see echoes in it of Thoreau's "Resistance to Civil Government." Egbert S. Oliver, "A Second Look at 'Bartleby,'" *College English* 6, 8 (1945): 431–39; Michael Rogin, *Subversive Genealogy: The Politics and Art of Herman Melville* (Berkely, CA: University of California Press, 1985), chapter 6. Bartleby also became an icon for some strands of leftist politics in the mid-2000s and during Occupy Wall Street. Slavoj Žižek, "Notes towards a Politics of Bartleby: The Ignorance of Chicken," *Comparative American Studies: An International Journal* 4, 4 (December 1, 2006): 375–94; Nina Martyris, "A Patron Saint for Occupy Wall Street," *The New Republic*, October 15, 2011, https://newrepublic.com/article/96276/nina-martyris-ows-and-bartleby-the-scrivener (accessed August 20, 2020); Jonathan D. Greenberg, "Occupy Wall Street's Debt to Melville," *The Atlantic*, April 30, 2012, www.theatlantic.com/politics/archive/2012/04/occupy-wall-streets-debt-to-melville/256482/ (accessed August 20, 2020); Lauren Klein, "What Bartleby Can Teach Us about Occupy Wall Street," ARCADE, https://arcade.stanford.edu/blogs/what-bartleby-can-teach-us-about-occupy-wall-street (accessed August 20, 2020). My interpretation of Thoreau should make clear that his withdrawal is decidedly more committed to the good pursued by way of withdrawal than comparisons to Bartleby would imply. It can thus also have a place in correcting contemporary enthusiasm for Bartleby's "I would prefer not to." My interpretation of Thoreau should thus challenge and assist contemporary resisters to articulate just what it is they *would* prefer.

Thoreau takes to be required of citizens whose consciences conflict with the government to which they are apparently subject.[34] In Thoreau's case, the refusal to pay the tax was inspired by the feeling that paying the tax constituted collusion with a government that supported the enslavement of human persons and that waged imperial war against Mexico, both grave injustices. What we now call the Revolutionary War, Thoreau called "the Revolution of '75" and he suggested that the revolution was *less* justified than the resistance to slavery and resistance to wars of conquest he was presently promoting. This was strong rhetoric. He wrote that he would likely not have participated himself in the Revolution of '75.

> All men recognize the right of revolution; that is, the right to refuse allegiance to, and to resist, the government, when its tyranny or its inefficiency are great and unendurable. But almost

[34] The account as told in *Walden,* in the chapter on Thoreau's outings to the village: "One afternoon, near the end of the first summer, when I went to the village to get a shoe from the cobbler's, I was seized and put into jail, because, as I have elsewhere related, I did not pay a tax to, or recognize the authority of, the state which buys and sells men, women, and children, like cattle at the door of its senate-house. I had gone down to the woods for other purposes. But wherever a man goes, men will pursue and paw him with their dirty institutions, and, if they can, constrain him to belong to their desperate odd-fellow society. It is true, I might have resisted forcibly with more or less effect, might have run 'amok' against society; but I preferred that society should run 'amok' against me, it being the desperate party" (VIII, 3). In *Walden* then, the justification for resistance does not refer to consent but rather to the unjust treatment of men, women, and children. This reframing of the "Civil Disobedience" story in the *Walden* account lends further credence to my argument here in this chapter that Thoreau's politics as articulated by *Walden* is more focused on relational justice and common goods than on typical liberal values of consent, rights, or fairness. Where I press on Thoreau's investment in relational justice and common goods, Christian Maul has argued that Thoreau offers a synthesis of two typical modern political theories that are often seen in conflict: liberalism and communitarianism. Christian Maul, "'A Sort of Hybrid Product': Thoreau's Individualism between Liberalism and Communitarianism," in *Thoreauvian Modernities: Transatlantic Conversations on an American Icon*, ed. François Specq, Laura Dassow Walls, and Michel Granger (Athens, GA: University of Georgia Press, 2013), 157–70.

> all say that such is not the case now. But such was the case, they think, in the Revolution of '75. If one were to tell me that this was a bad government because it taxed certain foreign commodities brought to its ports, it is most probable that I should not make an ado about it, for I can do without them. All machines have their friction; and possibly this does enough good to counterbalance the evil. At any rate, it is a great evil to make a stir about it.
>
> (CD, 8)

Here, Thoreau describes the instigation of the Revolution of '75 as the taxation of "certain foreign commodities." He suggests that he would not have supported such a revolution, because those commodities are ones that he could have done without, by way of asceticism, and avoided paying the tax that way. Then, he begins a confusing analogy when he writes, "All machines have their friction." The machine may be the government, the taxes the friction. Or the machine may be the unjust taxes and Thoreau's refusal to pay them the friction. "At any rate," to "make a stir about" such a case, in which you can avoid the tax through abstemiousness, "is a great evil." In this, Thoreau suggests not all civil disobedience is justified. The American Revolution might not have been.

Then he makes the case that his present resistance is *more* urgent than the Revolution had been.

> But when the friction comes to have its machine, and oppression and robbery are organized, I say, let us not have such a machine any longer. In other words, when a sixth of the population of a nation which has undertaken to be the refuge of liberty are slaves, and a whole country is unjustly overrun and conquered by a foreign army, and subjected to military law, I think that it is not too soon for honest men to rebel and revolutionize. What makes the duty the more urgent is the fact, that the country so overrun is not our own, but ours is the invading army.
>
> (CD, 8)

Thoreau argues that the present case is decidedly different from that of the Revolution of '75. The urgency is partly due to the fact that the country being overrun by a foreign army is not *ours*, but is in fact *theirs*, which means that *we* are the perpetrators of injustice. In the Revolution of '75 the colonists resisted another occupying army; now it's *our* army that is doing the robbery. Thoreau ignores the fact that the colonists' complaint was that the power exercised through arbitrary taxation was the moral equivalent of slavery. He thinks that unlike then, when there was friction in the machine, now it is not just friction in the machine but a whole machine of friction, a machine whose sole purpose is friction: "oppression" in the case of slavery and "robbery" in the case of the war against Mexico.

The machine against which citizens were obliged to act as a counter friction, the machine that was a friction machine, good for nothing else, was a metaphor in "Resistance to Civil Government." But, like the illustration of resistance in his own night spent in prison, the imagery of machinery was not abstract to Thoreau – he wrote about it concretely in those journals about the textile mill quoted above.

What "Civil Disobedience" does not make clear is how, for Thoreau, chattel slavery was not the only pressing labor issue. Thoreau was an abolitionist, aided people on the run from slavery, and participated in abolitionist politics.[35] He hosted the anti-slavery society's annual meeting in commemoration of West Indian Emancipation at his house at Walden Pond in the summer of 1846.

But he also thought that too often abolitionists told a self-satisfied story about the North, locating the problem of unjust

[35] One important primary source about Thoreau's assistance to enslaved people seeking freedom, beyond Thoreau's own writings, is Edward Waldo Emerson, "Interview with Ann Bigelow (Transcribed from the Manuscript Notes of His 1892 Interview)," Concord Free Public Library, https://concordlibrary.org/special-collections/antislavery/68 (accessed August 20, 2020).

economy in the faraway South. As he wrote in "Resistance to Civil Government," "I quarrel not with far-off foes, but with those who, near at home, co-operate with, and do the bidding of, these far away, and without whom the latter would be harmless" (CD, 10). Where most Republicans of the North, including the most prominent white abolitionists, promoted "free labor" as the alternative to slave labor, Thoreau implied that the only "free" labor was that at which you are employed by yourself By doing so he took a jab at the regnant political ideology of the North. In this sense, his retreat to the woods to do the labor his own life required was the instantiation of his central political ideal.

His critique of Northern economy is strongest in "Economy," the first chapter of *Walden*, and in my reading Northern economy is the problem to which the whole of the rest of the book responds. Thoreau seemed especially emphatic about the injustice of Northern economy, perhaps in part because he knew that Concordians were not that far removed from slavery themselves. In the next section, I show that Thoreau's ascetic practice in *Walden* has a radically different political significance when read in light of Concord's slave-owning history.

Political Significance of Concord Slavery and the Rhetoric of *Walden*'s Politics

Elise Lemire's research about the formerly enslaved inhabitants of Walden Woods helped me to show, in Chapter 1, that Thoreau's time in the woods was more invested in his neighborhood and its community than people usually notice. Lemire's research also offers important context for Thoreau's practices of simplicity by describing the uses of slavery by white people in Concord in the generation before Thoreau. *Black Walden* tells the story not only of Concord's freed people and their lives in the woods, but also of the men who were the so-called owners of those slaves and who, under political pressure from the enslaved people themselves during the Revolution, granted them freedom. John Cuming was the former owner of Brister Freeman, and "he and the town's other gentlemen residents were afforded the time to practice their professions and rule the town's and eventually the nation's civic affairs by the slaves, servants, and hired hands who did the necessary work of raising food for their owners."[36]

In the context of the previous generation's reliance on enslaved labor to support their lives and to support the establishment of the republic that claimed to be a bastion of liberty, Thoreau's insistence on doing his own work and on the simplification of his personal economic affairs takes on a different, less cranky, hue. Thoreau's pursuit was not only to do his own work because it would build his character, though he did seem to think that it would. It was also a necessary part of disentangling himself from systems that relied on the unjust labor of others. Doing the work his own life required was also his pursuing the good of others. The labor practices of Concord's recent past and ongoing present may have haunted him. He hoped to practice more just labor himself.

This comes through most clearly in the critique of philanthropy at the end of "Economy," where Thoreau begins by acknowledging that some people will see his retreat to the woods as selfish and asocial in the sense discussed in Chapter 1. "But all this is very selfish, I have heard some of my townsmen say" (I, 102). In reply, Thoreau suggests that philanthropy often works against its own aims. He says that he would not want anyone else coming to do him good. And

[36] Lemire, *Black Walden*, 12.

at the end of this long critique of philanthropy, he says that the philanthropist himself needs healing.

> I believe that what so saddens the reformer is not his sympathy with his fellows in distress, but, though he be the holiest son of God, is his private ail. . .If you should ever be betrayed into any of these philanthropies, do not let your left hand know what your right hand does, for it is not worth knowing. Rescue the drowning and tie your shoestrings. Take your time, and set about some free labor.
>
> (I, 109)

I discuss the critique of philanthropy at greater length in Chapter 3, but the two most important things about this passage at the moment are that Thoreau suggests philanthropy is caused by a deeper illness and that his cure for it is free labor, that is, labor that withdraws from the unjust economies that require philanthropy in the first place.

In this context, each person's responsibility is to heal himself from the deeper illness and to free himself from reliance on the unjust use of any other's labor; or, if he is the one providing unjust labor, to stop, as those formerly enslaved inhabitants at Walden Woods had done. In the grandest vision of this effort, it means not only doing the work your own life requires, but also making the way you do the work worthy of your highest aims. Accomplishing this requires the simplicity that Thoreau preached.

> To affect the quality of the day, that is the highest of arts. Every man is tasked to make his life, even in the details, worthy of the contemplation of his most elevated and critical hour. . .Still we live meanly, like ants;. . . Our life is frittered away by detail. An honest man has hardly need to count more than his ten fingers, or in extreme cases he may add his ten toes, and lump the rest. Simplicity, simplicity, simplicity! I say, let your affairs be as two or three, and not a hundred or a thousand; instead of a million count half a dozen, and keep your accounts on your thumb nail.
>
> (II, 15-17)

Thoreau's famous call to "simplicity, simplicity, simplicity" is a spiritual pursuit by which Thoreau aims to heal his "private ail." But it is also, as we can see in the context of the slavery to which the former inhabitants of Walden Woods had been subject, resistance against injustice.

Elite households in the generation before Thoreau had relied on the labor of enslaved people. *Black Walden* tells the story of Brister Freeman's former owner, John Cumings. John was well-educated and owned land, which made him eligible in principle to join Concord's elite. He was married in 1753 to Abigail Wesson. In order to enable John to join Concord's elite, which would require both the status he already had and time away from household labor, Abigail's father gave him Brister as a slave. This wedding gift enabled John to achieve his gentlemanly ambitions. With Brister growing the family's food and harvesting its fuel, John was free to practice medicine, become a military officer, and otherwise join the ranks of gentlemen. In this context, Thoreau's admonition to simplify is not only a pursuit to clear your mind for contemplation; it is also, and as importantly, a refusal of standard class politics that rely on unjust labor. In this sense, the simplicity of Thoreau's life in the woods is an act against slavery and the social stratification it supported.

Thus, *Walden* articulates some of the most vivid features of Thoreau's politics, especially his insistence on just labor as a condition for any flourishing society. However it does this via an uncommon political rhetoric. Whereas the story the book tells is of a seemingly private affair, the book itself, which Thoreau revised through seven drafts in eight years, is evidence of Thoreau's effort at *public* reasoning.[37] And there is a

[37] The most in-depth study of Thoreau's process for writing *Walden* is found in J. Lyndon Shanley, *The Making of* Walden, *with the Text of the First Version.* (Chicago, IL: University of Chicago Press, 1957). See also Robert Sattelmeyer,

reappearing figure in the book, one that helps to dramatize the rhetorical situation Thoreau took himself to be participating in. The figure refers to his neighbors in Concord; Thoreau calls them his "townsmen."

The second paragraph of *Walden* makes it plain that Thoreau was interested in the way the book made his own personal life a public document and explained – jokingly – why he did it. This is the first time the "townsmen" arrive on the scene. Thoreau wrote, "I should not obtrude my affairs so much on the notice of my readers if very particular inquiries had not been made by my townsmen concerning my mode of life" (I, 2). For the sake of his nosy townsmen, he went to great efforts to turn the life he had led in the woods into its public form. This account for his townsmen required an effort at public reasoning.

The townsmen remain central characters in the book as it goes on. They work too hard, to pay for the farms they have inherited (I, 4). They meet Thoreau on the road to Boston, coming back from his walks before dawn (I, 25). They raise what has – apparently from before the drafting of the book – been among the most virulent criticisms of Thoreau, that he was selfish (I, 102). They judge Thoreau's willingness to sit doing nothing mere idleness (IV, 2). They wonder how he can stand to give up so much to live the way that he does, all while they force themselves to work too hard (V, 5). They have heard the stories of the American Indians Thoreau recounts (IX, 12). They remember the formerly enslaved men and women who lived in Walden Woods before Thoreau (XIV, 1). In "Civil Disobedience," they say they would never serve in an unjust war, and yet they "sustain the unjust government that makes the war" (CD, 13). Finally, and most amusingly to

"The Remaking of *Walden*," in *Writing the American Classics*, ed. James Barbour and Tom Quirk (Chapel Hill, NC: University of North Carolina Press, 1990), 53–78.

me, they fail to appoint Thoreau to his dream office as Concord's sinecure of tree peeing.

> For many years I was self-appointed inspector of snow-storms and rain-storms, and did my duty faithfully; surveyor, if not of highways, then of forest paths and all across-lot routes, keeping them open, and ravines bridged and passable at all seasons, where the public heel had testified to their utility.
>
> I have looked after the wild stock of the town, which give a faithful herdsman a good deal of trouble by leaping fences. . .I have watered the red huckleberry, the sand cherry and the nettle-tree, the red pine and the black ash, the white grape and the yellow violet, which might have withered else in dry seasons.
>
> (I, 30)

Thus, the townsmen have a key role in Thoreau's thought and writing – whether as accusers, neighbors, conversation partners, informants, objects of critique, or features of and audience for Thoreau's jokes – they function to enmesh Thoreau in his civic context.

Further, Thoreau's political rhetoric in *Walden* demonstrates that Thoreau took political persuasion to be about more than logical argumentation. *Walden*'s politics is premised on a different hypothesis: that persuasion requires a seduction to the good through images and narrative.

The beginning and ending of *Walden* do trade in the discursive presentation of the kinds of reasons that the philosophers of public reason seem to have in mind as the central feature of democratic persuasion. But the long middle of the book does something entirely different. It offers images and experiences from the life Thoreau found in the woods, and it does this to demonstrate the goods that his townsmen could find in more just living.

The deeper, political point of the pleasure was that the life Thoreau found in the woods, the one he thought the abolition of slavery in all its forms would require, was going to yield a better life for everyone, including the ones who would have to renounce many of their privileges.

I believe Thoreau wrote the book for this purpose partly because of the history of the construction of the book itself. Lyndon Shanley's *The Making of Walden* traces the history of the manuscript's construction and suggests that the intensive composition of *Walden* was motivated by Thoreau's own delight. Shanley wrote,

> The manuscript thus gives us information that is essential to a just interpretation of Thoreau's work and life, as well as an insight into his craft and art. It emphasizes the importance to Thoreau of his Walden experience. We know, as we did not before, how long [Thoreau] dwelt upon his life in the woods, going back again and again, solicitous that his story should be fully told, and constantly moved to recapture for his readers more of the delights he had sought and found in living.[38]

The work required to make the book was itself motivated by the delight Thoreau found in living in the woods.

Conclusion

In *Walden*, Thoreau was concerned that people may think the way of life that relies on unjust labor is bad but nonetheless unavoidable.

> When we honestly consider what, to use the words of the catechism, is the chief end of man, and what are the true necessaries and means of life, it appears as if men had deliberately chosen the common mode of living because they preferred it to any other. Yet they honestly think there is no choice left.
>
> (I, 10)

[38] Shanley, *The Making of* Walden, 6–7.

To this despair in the face of the sort of radical change in the economic system that would be required by giving up unjust labor – whether as laborer or labored for – Thoreau replies, "It is never too late to give up our prejudices" (I, 10). He not only wants to show himself that his experiment in living simply is possible. The main point of *Walden* as I see it is to show its reader that they too can work against systems of unjust labor. Thoreau was "trying to hear what was in the wind, to hear and carry it express!" (I, 26).

I think this interpretation of *Walden* as the evidence required to truly believe that a way of life was possible without slavery and other forms of unjust labor can also help us understand Thoreau's increased political activity after his time at Walden, as his time there, living simply, gave him evidence to think that the kind of life required by a reformed economy would be both possible and good. All of Thoreau's central political commitments – his abolitionism, his anti-industrialism, and his anti-imperialism – are married to his commitment to the form of society he developed in the woods and that I sought to describe in Chapter 1. That society in the woods was one that aimed to justly recognize every member. Whether bird or enslaved man on the run or ox or bean or child or pauper or poet or railroad man, in the Walden Woods of Thoreau's experiment, you were at home. In the generation before his, the place had been home to those who, for whatever reason, chose to squat on land apparently owned by others. Thoreau thought such a society should be normative. He was convinced that slavery was a great evil, that the factory system was unjust, and that citizens should not support war-making for the purpose of territorial expansion, which he called – frankly – robbery.

Even when political theorists attend to *Walden*, they tend for understandable reasons to focus on the more blatantly political bits and less on the parts that are characteristic of the book, the passages that describe Thoreau's piety for the natural world, his time in the woods, and his work and leisure on the land.[39] But the fact that they have done so has sometimes obscured the tight relationship between Thoreau's capacious understanding of the society he joined in the woods, his piety toward that community, and his insistence on justice for all.

Thoreau's insistence on the renunciation of affairs sometimes looks like cranky miserliness, or the asociality people seem to have attributed to him even in his own time. But when we read *Walden* in the context of Concord's slave history and developing industrial present, which is the context in which he wrote it after all, when we contrast Thoreau's thumbnail accounts with those of John Cuming – enslaver of a previous generation – we see that for Thoreau, simplicity is not only self-cultivation. With it, Thoreau resisted both slavery and exploitative industrialism.

Thoreau's account of his life in the woods is not simply a description and commendation of religious asceticism for the sake of religious virtue. Thoreau also thought the results of his experiment in what he called "free labor" could serve as an example, as a way to persuade his readers – who he worried faced political despair and hopelessness – that renouncing slave-driving of all kinds and abandoning present economies would be not only good for our world and good for our fellows, but also good for us.

[39] Another important exception to this generalization is George M. Shulman, *American Prophecy: Race and Redemption in American Political Culture* (Minneapolis, MN: University of Minnesota Press, 2008). Shulman articulates the central place of prophecy in American political life, including in the authorship of Thoreau, but, in his analysis of Thoreau, he does not only focus on Thoreau's jeremiads. Shulman argues that Thoreau revises American prophecy in *Walden*, by putting the poet in the office of the prophet.

3

Thoreau's Theological Critique of Philanthropy

Humility is still a human virtue.

Thoreau, *Journal*, Fall 1846[1]

Chapters 3 and 4 will argue that Thoreau's sociality and politics, as described in Chapters 1 and 2, are part of something broader, a tradition of thinking and doing and living – a religion you might say – that Thoreau received through diverse sources and that, through Thoreau, had diverse impacts after him.[2] This may be surprising for some readers, as many interpreters of Thoreau's attitudes toward religion have focused on the resentments he carried toward the Christianity of his milieu.[3] These readers see Thoreau preferring a more idiosyncratic, non-dogmatic, self-styled spirituality, and they thus have tended to interpret him as at least somewhat areligious.

[1] Thoreau, *Journal*, Volume 2: *1842–1848*, 350.

[2] Among the most useful sources for those interested in Thoreau's intellectual biography is Robert Sattelmeyer, *Thoreau's Reading: A Study in Intellectual History with Bibliographical Catalogue* (Princeton, NJ: Princeton University Press, 2014).

[3] Bron Taylor expresses the common view that Thoreau "made it clear that he was post-Christian." Bron Taylor, *Dark Green Religion: Nature Spirituality and the Planetary Future* (Berkeley, CA: University of California Press, 2009), 51. On the one hand, this is an understandable view, since Thoreau expressed such strong judgments against the Christianity of his period. On the other, it neglects the sense in which many of Thoreau's *reasons* for his rejection of Christianity were theological, and it decides in advance – without offering supporting theological argument – whether Christianity admits the pagan, pantheistic views Taylor ascribes to Thoreau.

In response to those views of Thoreau as areligious, Chapter 3 shows Thoreau to be a theological interpreter of Christianity. It does this by focusing on his critique of the practice of philanthropy. Thoreau condemns philanthropy in the first chapter of *Walden*, on specifically theological grounds. In my interpretation, his condemnation of it is the motivation for the rest of *Walden*. If the philanthropists were wrong about how to be good, *Walden* was an answer to the logical next question: How then shall I live? Chapter 4 describes in more detail what Thoreau thought of as the alternative to philanthropy. It describes his answer to that next question, which he spent the rest of *Walden* articulating. I call this Thoreau's "political asceticism." *Thoreau's Religion* as a whole suggests that asceticism may be political more often than we usually notice. Chapter 4 explains what political asceticism is, how Thoreau practiced it, and to what ends.

The present chapter argues that while Thoreau's critique of philanthropy in "Economy" is clearly motivated by his social and political commitments as I described in Chapters 1 and 2, a close reading of the section demonstrates essential Christian theological motivations for the critique. Against a picture of Christian goodness as unidirectional giving in the form of philanthropic charity, a picture Thoreau thought most Christians of his period held, he preferred a more mutual ethic. I use a close reading of Thoreau's critique of philanthropy to describe the contrast between the picture of goodness Thoreau saw others promoting and the – perhaps surprisingly – more relational understanding of theological ethics he pursued himself. This more relational ethics required (1) diverse practices of attention which he cultivated especially through his writing life in order to achieve (2) self-understanding and (3) humble knowledge of others that was open to correction.

Thoreau and the Christian Milieu

Concord's little intelligentsia, which came to be seen as the finest of American intellectual culture in the period, took from Weimar Germany, and perhaps especially from Goethe, an interest in the development of the self, *Bildung* in German and self-culture in English. Emerson and Thoreau's mutual interest in the ascetic discipline required for self-culture was in keeping with the mood of the period.[4] As I described in the Introduction, Thoreau took Emerson's metaphorical description of scholarly life as a sort of asceticism very literally, perhaps more seriously than Emerson himself took it, and then Thoreau set out to establish his own rule of life, like the ancient monks and hermits to which Emerson had appealed.

For both Emerson and Thoreau, as well as for the larger Transcendentalist circle, interest in self-culture was partly a response to the sense that contemporary Christian churches were shortchanging the Christian tradition's promise. Emerson's 1838 "Divinity School Address" had expressed dissent against what some Unitarians took to be orthodox Christian doctrine, as well as chastised local clergy for offering an emaciated understanding of the tradition. The address had caused a fracas among Boston clergy and intellectuals.[5]

And the disagreements over doctrinal matters persisted among Transcendentalists themselves. The Transcendental Club met only twice more after the first time Thoreau

[4] Richardson, *Henry Thoreau*, 55.

[5] Philip F. Gura, *American Transcendentalism: A History* (New York: Hill and Wang, 2008), 101–16. Gura's is one of the best histories of Transcendentalism as a religious movement. "It answers the question of how a movement whose roots were so catholic and universal eventuated in a discourse that promoted an American exceptionalism based on self-interest," Gura, xv.

attended in May 1840. And the cessation of the meetings was caused for the most part by a failure to agree among themselves about what the identity of a church they would establish should be. Some of the members thought that the church would be Christian, insisting on its continuity as a reform of Unitarianism. Others thought it ought to articulate a post-Christian, universalist view, basically conceding the point to those who sneered at Transcendentalism as a Christian heresy.[6] Transcendentalism was born and buried in a debate over how to locate the spirit of God in the world.

Thoreau spent the rest of his life considering the same question, in a far less institutional way. For him, the fascination with self-culture and asceticism was at least partly a response to the sense that contemporary Christianity was failing at one of its most central callings, which, he wrote in the summer of 1840, was to joy. "The age is resigned. Everywhere it sounds a retreat, and the word has gone forth to fall back on innocence. Christianity only *hopes*. It has hung its harp on the willow and cannot sing a song in a strange land. It has dreamed a sad dream and does not yet welcome the morning with joy."[7] The passage complained that Christianity "only *hopes*," and does not fulfill its obligation to "welcome the morning with joy." Like much of the rest of Thoreau's writing, the passage was full of biblical allusion. These few sentences alluded to at least three passages from the Old Testament.

[6] "That September, defiant in the face of growing national hostility, they held two more meetings to discuss organizing a new and more liberal church of their own. The split in their ranks opened wider: Would such a church be Christian? Or would it articulate new, post-Christian, universal principles? The deepening fractures destroyed what was left of their common ground, and the Transcendentalists never met again." Walls, *Henry David Thoreau*, 116.

[7] Thoreau, *Journal*, Volume 1: *1837–1844*, 167.

First, Thoreau wrote, "the word has gone forth." This phrase may have alluded to Isaiah 55:10-11.

> For as the rain cometh down, and the snow from heaven, and returneth not thither, but watereth the earth, and maketh it bring forth and bud, that it may give seed to the sower, and bread to the eater: So shall my word be that goeth forth out of my mouth: it shall not return unto me void, but it shall accomplish that which I please, and it shall prosper in the thing whereto I sent it.[8]

The passage from Isaiah suggests that God's word operates like rain that waters the earth. Thoreau's worry is that contemporary Christianity is rejecting such nourishment.

The sentences after the condemnation of Christianity for mere hope contain two more allusions, these to the Psalms, prayers from the Hebrew Bible that are often recited during Christian daily prayer, especially the liturgy of the hours that is prayed in monastic contexts. Thoreau wrote that Christianity had "hung its harp on the willow and cannot sing a song in a strange land." And he wrote that Christianity "does not yet welcome the morning with joy." These are allusions to Psalms 137 and 30. I cite Psalm 30:5: "For his anger *endureth but* a moment; in his favour *is* life: weeping may endure for a night, but joy *cometh* in the morning." The psalm was close to Thoreau's heart. *Walden* was a sustained meditation on the meaning of morning and awakening, a sort of echo of Psalm 30. The book responded to the dejection that the British Romantics had worried about ("weeping may endure for a night"), by suggesting that life is joy.[9]

Thoreau's complaint is a critique of Christianity. It is one among many such critiques he made, especially in his early life. *A Week on the Concord and Merrimack Rivers* was even

[8] Biblical citations are to the King James Version, since Thoreau knew it best.

[9] I discuss the centrality of awakening to the themes of *Walden* further in Chapter 4, where I also connect it to Thoreau's political hopes.

more explicit about his disappointments with Christianity. But here the critique of Christianity is made specifically on *biblical* grounds. Those grounds include Thoreau's own sense that one of Christianity's central messages is good news, joyous news. His point was that if Christianity does not sustain joy, joy that is central to its own gospel, it needs to be critiqued precisely in order to sustain Christianity. This is one good reason to view Thoreau as invested in Christian reform.

In this passage, however, Thoreau's evidence for joy does not come from the story of Jesus, but rather from the natural world – from the fish, and insects, and frogs that show something particular about what life *is*.

> Surely joy is the condition of life. Think of the young fry that leap in ponds – the myriads of insects ushered into being of a summer's evening – the incessant note of the hyla with which the woods ring in the spring. the *non chalance* of the butterfly carrying accident and change painted in a thousand hues upon his wings – or the brook-minnow stemming stoutly the current, the lustre of whose scales worn bright by the attrition is reflected upon the bank.[10]

Thoreau took the doings of such creatures to be evidence for the thing he thought Christianity was failing to offer more than mere hope of – that life is in some important way joy, that resignation and retreat are not required nor accurate to the world as it is.

In addition to praising joy, however, the passage had also alluded to Psalm 137, which describes the experience of the people of Israel while enslaved in Egypt. It offers an instance in which the joy Thoreau took to be the condition of life is remote.

[10] Thoreau, *Journal*, Volume 1: *1837–1844*, 167.

> By the rivers of Babylon, there we sat down, yea, we wept, when we remembered Zion. We hanged our harps upon the willows in the midst thereof. For there they that carried us away captive required of us a song; and they that wasted us *required of us* mirth, *saying*, sing us *one* of the songs of Zion. How shall we sing the Lord's song in a strange land? If I forget thee, O Jerusalem, let my right hand forget *her cunning*. If I do not remember thee, let my tongue cleave to the roof of my mouth; if I prefer not Jerusalem above my chief joy. Remember, O Lord, the children of Edom in the day of Jerusalem; who said, Rase it, rase it, even to the foundation thereof. O daughter of Babylon, who art to be destroyed; happy shall he be, that rewardeth thee as thou hast served us. Happy shall he be, that taketh and dasheth thy little ones against the stones.

They wept when they remembered Zion. The Israelites – weeping – had hung their harps on the willows by the rivers of Babylon, far from home. And their enslavers had asked them to sing songs of Zion. The Israelites' question, "How shall we sing the Lord's song in a strange land?" spoke to the connection between the people and God and the land, and the cruelty of the enslavers asking for songs of joy in the condition of captivity. The final disturbing verse about dashing the little ones against the stones suggests that those who can enact cruelty against the cruel will take pleasure in it.

In alluding to this psalm, Thoreau accuses contemporary Christianity of playing the part of the Israelites, but in bad faith. The Israelites could not sing songs of Zion in a strange land because the songs enacted the good relation that obtained between the people, God, and the land. Without that relation, their songs could not be sung, truly. But unlike the actually enslaved Israelites, coercively held captive by dominative power, Thoreau's contemporary white settler Christianity was pretending as though it were held captive, and thus could not sing songs of Zion in a strange land, even though – unlike the Israelites – they were enslaved only by themselves.

These allusions to the Bible demonstrate the depth at which the Christian scriptures occupied Thoreau's imaginative, writerly, theological life. They also show us some of the sources with which Thoreau found his way to criticize one of the most prominent Christian practices of the period: philanthropy.

Suspecting Philanthropy

The end of the first chapter of *Walden* is an emphatic tirade against philanthropy. Many of his readers have taken this as an indication that he was disinclined to care about other people. Thoreau himself begins these paragraphs with the recitation of a charge he had apparently heard against his experiment at Walden, and what appears to be a confession to the charge. "But all this is very selfish, I have heard some of my townsmen say. I confess that I have hitherto indulged very little in philanthropic enterprises" (I, 102). It thus begins by giving the impression that it is an apology for his own unwillingness to participate in charity, to "undertake the support of some poor family in the town," which is what the townsmen in question seem to have thought he should do. But, you will notice, the confession does not match the accusation. The accusation is of selfishness; the confession is that he has not "indulged ... in philanthropic enterprises." This disjuncture sets up the ten-paragraph ending of "Economy," the first chapter of *Walden*, in which Thoreau argues there is a difference between being good and doing philanthropy. Philanthropy is, on Thoreau's telling, an indulgence. It does not turn out looking very good.[11]

[11] Readers interested in some of the examples Thoreau could have had in mind of self-serving philanthropy can turn to a matter that appears in the historiography of Concord abolitionism. Sandra Petrulionis has done all who study Thoreau and Transcendentalism a tremendous service by writing the history of Concord abolitionism as a story of a whole community. Before her book, too often scholars writing about Concordian abolitionism "focused on the political ideals of Thoreau

A shift begins, already at the end of the first paragraph, and the apology with which Thoreau began becomes ironic. "When I have thought to indulge myself in this respect, and lay their Heaven under an obligation by maintaining certain poor persons in all respects as comfortably as I maintain myself, and have even ventured so far as to make them the offer, they have one and all unhesitatingly preferred to remain poor." Coming as it does at the end of "Economy," the reader has in mind here the meager style of life that Thoreau has just described – his own attempts to live on as little as possible in terms of clothing, shelter, and food. The implication is that his offer to "certain poor persons" was refused because what was on offer was not better than what they already had. The

and Emerson rather than on the civic context in which their abolitionism evolved and took place." Petrulionis, *To Set This World Right*, 3. Her work has exposed the abolitionism of Concord as a communal project, often led by women. However, as Elise Lemire pointed out in her review of Petrulionis's book, the evidence for specifically interracial activism – which Petrulionis suggests there was – is scanty. Lemire wrote, "to assume that antislavery was motivated by antiracism is to avoid the question of what compelled local white women to embrace the abolitionist cause." And this avoids the issue of what kind of racism might have actually motivated some of the benevolence of Concord's philanthropic societies. The example Lemire points to is illustrative. "Certainly it is difficult to determine what part kindness and what part paternalism, or worse, motivated these and other charitable gestures, such as when Concord's abolitionist women outfitted Susan's daughter Ellen [Garrison] for a life of domestic servitude in Boston. Petrulionis concludes that 'the Thoreaus, Emersons, and Alcotts worked in tandem' with Susan and her husband Jack (p. 4), but it would have been more accurate to conclude that the impoverishment of the Garrisons and other local blacks left them vulnerable to the machinations of elite white women intent on managing town affairs, no matter how benevolently. Ellen Garrison went on to lead a life of social activism in Boston, as evidenced by the many petitions she signed there. But she never returned to Concord. And as other scholars have documented, plenty of white Concordians were happy to have rid their town of blacks and immigrants in the name of benevolence." Lemire went on, "How antislavery activism, racism, and segregation intersected in Concord and other New England towns is a question still to be answered." Elise Lemire, review of *To Set This World Right: The Antislavery Movement in Thoreau's Concord*, by Sandra Harbert Petrulionis, *The New England Quarterly* 80, 2 (2007): 338–40.

further implication is that the townsmen who are so enthusiastic about "Doing-good," are giving in charity something that does not have value.

Indeed, what "good" is becomes a main point of contention in the second paragraph, where Thoreau makes clear that his own view of what is good is rather different from that of the neighbors he has in mind. In the first two occurrences of "good" in that paragraph, its meaning is in question. "At doing something, – I will not engage that my neighbors shall pronounce it good, – I do not hesitate to say that I should be a capital fellow to hire; but what that is, it is for my employer to find out. What *good* I do, in the common sense of that word, must be aside from my main path" (I, 103). The first of these two sentences is quite confusing, with a subordinate clause inside dashes breaking up the significance of the sentence as a whole. But the impression it gives is that Thoreau expects to do some things. In fact, if what you want is for just "something" to be done, Thoreau would "be a capital fellow to hire." But the "something" he has in mind is not something he thinks his neighbors will call good. Whether it is good or not "it is for my employer to find out." "Good" according to his neighbors is not necessarily good. Given Thoreau's insistence on economic independence, it is very difficult to imagine that the "employer" he has in mind in this passage would be one who offered him wages for "doing something."[12] It may

[12] Christian ethicist Jonathan Malesic has argued that Thoreau had an "anti-work spirituality," one that can inform contemporary Christian thinking about labor, especially the ways that thinking has been informed by the so-called Protestant ethic, which Malesic renders as "pro-work." Jonathan Malesic, "Henry David Thoreau's Anti-work Spirituality and a New Theological Ethic of Work," *Journal of Religious Ethics* 45, 2 (June 1, 2017): 309–29. Though Malesic and I share an appreciation for Thoreau's asceticism, I worry that Malesic's formulation neglects the extent to which *just* labor was essential to Thoreau's proposal. Thoreau was not anti-work – he was for just labor. Malesic wants to acknowledge that work is related to divinity (322), and thus not essentially bad. But his anti-work

be that the "employer" refers to himself. But I think the best reading is that it is a tongue-in-cheek reference to God's judgment. Thoreau's neighbors won't pronounce his doings good, but he insists that what his doings are "is for my employer to find out," that is, a judgment reserved for God. Many of Thoreau's readers take it as obvious that Thoreau did not believe in God, but his writings suggest that while somewhat apophatic with respect to what could be said of God, he did not refuse the category itself.[13] As Terrance Wiley has pointed out, Thoreau once wrote to a friend, "God Reigns! I say God. I am not sure that is the name. You know who I mean."[14]

formulation limits his ability to do so. In my view of Thoreau's thought, labor has the "power to deform the person" not because it is work, but because of the unjust economic systems in which it is often embedded (313). Work in itself can of course be good, and often is, when it is situated in a more just economy. Kathryn Tanner also appeals to the phrase "anti-work" when she says she aims to provide a "Protestant anti-work ethic." Tanner, *Christianity and the New Spirit of Capitalism*, 30. I worry that formulations like this concede too much to the unjust labor systems they are trying to resist by implicating all work in the unjust economic regimes that make labor unjust to begin with.

[13] David Newheiser has argued that the dynamic between saying and unsaying things about God, *apophasis*, is an ethical discipline oriented toward politics. "In my view, the discipline of *apophasis* is paradigmatically political, for its aim is to open possibility." David Newheiser, *Hope in a Secular Age: Deconstruction, Negative Theology, and the Future of Faith* (Cambridge: Cambridge University Press, 2019), 149. Newheiser's view suggests that Thoreau's apophatic view of God was part of the way in which his asceticism was oriented toward his politics.

[14] The quote can be found in Henry David Thoreau, *Letters to a Spiritual Seeker*, ed. Bradley P. Dean (New York and London: W. W. Norton & Company, 2005), 53. Wiley quotes it in Wiley, *Angelic Troublemakers*, chapter 1, section I. I discuss Thoreau's apophaticism somewhat further in Alda Balthrop-Lewis, "Thoreau's Woodchopper, Wordsworth's Leech-Gatherer, and the Representation of 'Humble and Rustic Life,'" in *Theology and Ecology across the Disciplines: On Care for Our Common Home*, ed Celia Deane-Drummond and Rebecca Artinian-Kaiser (London: Bloomsbury, 2018). There it applies not only to speech about God but also to knowledge of human character.

Next, Thoreau suggests that it is better to try to become good than to try to do good.[15] The next sentence follows from the idea that what is good is a judgment reserved for God. "What *good* I do, in the common sense of that word, must be aside from my main path, and for the most part wholly unintended." Though Thoreau refrains from pronouncing his doings good, he nonetheless continues doing, and there may be some good in those doings, even if unintended.[16] It is not that Thoreau avoids doing good.[17] Rather, he finds the way people take for granted what is good disturbing. They think they know. "Men say, Begin where you are and such as

[15] Michael Fischer put the point differently in an essay on how Thoreau challenges the instinct to critique that is common in some literary theory: "Thoreau is thus constantly challenging us to ... not let changing the world excuse us from changing ourselves." Michael R. Fischer, "*Walden* and Contemporary Literary Theory," in *New Essays on* Walden, ed. Robert F. Sayre (Cambridge: Cambridge University Press, 1992), 110.

[16] Hodder suggests that Thoreau is criticizing "a charity drained of its spontaneous goodness and converted to the interests of the religious and social status quo," and "reduced to routinized expressions of individual and social coercion." Hodder, *Thoreau's Ecstatic Witness*, 149–50. Hodder here again focuses on the individual ecstatic experience ("spontaneous goodness") over against the obviously political implications that also pertain, such as those raised by Lemire in the note about racist motivations for benevolence, which Hodder does not mention.

[17] Of course many interpreters do see Thoreau withdrawing from social and political life. Among these, Jonathan McKenzie has argued that Thoreau "uses his writings to shape a philosophical personality that can withstand the seductions of democratic political participation." In this view, which McKenzie places in a long tradition going back to Socrates, philosophy is for avoiding the personal dangers of democracy. Jonathan McKenzie, *The Political Thought of Henry David Thoreau: Privatism and the Practice of Philosophy* (Lexington, KY: University Press of Kentucky, 2016). This interpretation is directly contrary to my own to the extent it suggests that Thoreau abandons the concept of justice whereas I insist that justice is central to his concern. But McKenzie's view has become more appealing to me over the last five years, as my own disappointments with democratic life have forced me to ask what personal practices I must adopt in order to resist my own unhelpful obsessions with the day-to-day intrigue of what currently goes by the name "democratic politics" in the societies I know best in the United States, Australia, and Europe.

you are, without aiming mainly to become of more worth, and with kindness aforethought go about doing good. If I were to preach at all in this strain, I should say rather, Set about being good" (I, 103). Here, Thoreau likens his own speech to a sermon, suggesting what he might preach, and he expresses a worry about the instruction to "go about doing good." This "doing good" is an activity that worries Thoreau. He suggests that "being good" would be a better thing to aim at. What the difference consists in is not clear in this passage, but the sentence is followed by a reference to Phaeton, the son of the sun in Greek mythology, who caused great harm in his attempt to show off his goodness.

> When Phaeton, wishing to prove his heavenly birth by his beneficence, had the sun's chariot but one day, and drove out of the beaten track, he burned several blocks of houses in the lower streets of heaven and scorched the surface of the earth, and dried up every spring, and made the great desert of Sahara, till at length Jupiter hurled him headlong to the earth with a thunderbolt, and the sun, through grief at his death, did not shine for a year.
>
> (I, 103)

Thoreau does not spell out the moral of the story. The implication seems to be that Phaeton's wish to prove his beneficence leads to destruction on a grand scale. That is to say, whereas at the beginning of the paragraph Thoreau registered doubt that what his neighbors pronounce good is actually good, at the end of the paragraph he suggests – through appeal to the story of Phaeton – that the attempt to do good causes harm.

Thoreau does not explicitly describe the difference between doing good and being good, but I think it likely that the difference is in what actions are inspired by these two aims. Thoreau's concern is that ethical life ought not be the doing of a certain set of prescribed good deeds. Ethics is relational, the working out together of what our relationship and our world ought to be like. Someone who *does* good without thinking about whether he *is* good enforces *his view* of the good on the recipients of his charity, which – if he does not have justified authority to discern the good for them – is an act of arbitrary power over them. Someone who *is* good can do good, but only unintentionally, through the working out of his relationships.

Thoreau writes that being the recipient of philanthropy is suffocating, and that he himself hopes to avoid being the object of the philanthropist's efforts.

> If I knew for a certainty that a man was coming to my house with the conscious design of doing me good, I should run for my life, as from that dry and parching wind of the African deserts called the simoom, which fills the mouth and nose and ears and eyes with dust till you are suffocated, for fear that I should get some of his good done to me, – some of its virus mingled with my blood. No, – in this case I would rather suffer evil the natural way.
>
> (I, 104)

This passage is strange, because it makes the do-gooding man into a natural force, a wind, and then says that instead Thoreau would rather suffer evil the natural way. This leaves unresolved a confusion about which is the natural way Thoreau would prefer. It seems like both ways – the wind Thoreau would avoid and natural evil – are natural. But "that dry, parching wind" of do-gooding may refer back to the passage about Phaeton above, in which Phaeton's beneficence made the Sahara, and thus the natural way is the evil that one suffers without the help of the philanthropist.

The example Thoreau offers next of what evil can come of the attempt to do good is a disturbing one taken from the history of Christian colonial violence against First Nations people, a classic example of the dangers of doing the good *I perceive* for someone else without establishing a just relationship *between us*. The example is of Jesuits burning at the stake American Indians who would not convert to Christianity. Thoreau says the Jesuits "were quite balked" when the Indians being burned "suggested new modes of torture to their tormentors." Thoreau praises the spiritual superiority of the Indians. The last clause of the paragraph suggests that the Indians were more Christian than the missionaries: "the law to do as you would be done by fell with less persuasiveness on the ears of those, who, for their part, did not care how they were done by, who loved their enemies after a new fashion, and came very near freely forgiving them all they did" (I, 105). Thoreau takes "the law to do as you would be done by" to be one central message of Christianity, along with the love and forgiveness of enemies. In this example, the missionaries tried to do what they thought was good for the Indians, to share the gospel. But the gospel, "the law to do as you would be done by," did not persuade the Indians – Thoreau suggests because they were spiritually superior. The missionaries burned them at the stake, and in that a great evil came of the missionaries' attempt to do good.

Even aside from violent missions to Indigenous peoples, which is an example of the evils of do-gooding on a grand scale, one of the more mundane dangers of a philanthropy based on doing good – good according to the philanthropist – is that do-gooders do not always have the clearest sense of what aid the poor most need. "We make curious mistakes sometimes" (I, 106). When we make judgments about the needs of others without consulting them, we are liable to get it wrong. Thoreau writes, "Often the poor man is not so cold and hungry as he is dirty and ragged and gross." Where the philanthropist would assume that the poor are cold and hungry, and try to provide for those needs, Thoreau says the philanthropist's taste may be what makes him think that, rather than the actual needs of the poor. I think, in this sentence, Thoreau is not describing "the poor man" as "dirty and ragged and gross" in his own voice. Coldness and hunger are real problems in Thoreau's thinking, they relate to the essential heat he described as necessary in the beginning of the chapter. But "dirty and ragged and gross" are judgments of taste, ones he thinks the philanthropist is likely to make of someone poor, whether they are hungry and cold or not. Thoreau is setting up a contrast for the philanthropist, who takes the dress of the poor man to indicate that he is cold and hungry, when it may be that what the philanthropist calls "dirty and ragged and gross" is just the way the poor man sees fit to dress. "It is partly his taste, and not merely his misfortune" (I, 106). Where the philanthropist sees misfortune, he should look more carefully at whether he is simply seeing a different fashion.

Thoreau provides an example of a mistake he made in his own judgments about what another person needed, in an instance in which he himself took the dress of another to indicate his misery.

> I was wont to pity the clumsy Irish laborers who cut ice on the pond, in such mean and ragged clothes, while I shivered in my more tidy and somewhat more fashionable garments, till, one bitter cold day, one who had slipped into the water came to my house to warm him, and I saw him strip off three pairs of pants and two pairs of stockings ere he got down to the skin, though they were dirty and ragged enough, it is true, and that he could afford to refuse the *extra* garments which I offered him, he had so many *intra* ones. This ducking was the very thing he needed. Then I began to pity myself, and I saw that it would be a greater charity to bestow on me a flannel shirt than a whole slop-shop on him.
>
> (I, 106)

The example is an everyday one. Thoreau found himself pitying the workers he saw laboring on the frozen pond, because their clothes were ragged. When he had the chance to interact with one of these laborers, whom he welcomed into his home to get warm, he offered the man what his pity suggested the man needed. But the man refused the clothes Thoreau thought the man needed, and for good reason; the man's clothes were sufficient to the job. Thoreau's pity did not match the man's actual needs. In fact, Thoreau could have shivered less himself in clothes more like those of the man he pitied. The most effective charity, in the circumstance, would have been for someone else to give Thoreau a warmer shirt.

The everyday example of how we easily misperceive the needs of others has a deeper, troubling significance with respect to what philanthropists are doing when they provide for the needs they think the poor have. If it is the case that the philanthropist just wants everyone to have the goods that he, the philanthropist, values, then philanthropy is the enforcement of a set of values that may not be (likely are not) shared. The philanthropist may never find out. This seems a paltry pastime.

And, furthermore, if philanthropy acts to enforce the fashions cherished by the philanthropist, then it neglects the evil that people actually suffer. It does not even aim at true problems. Thoreau wrote, "There are a thousand hacking at the branches of evil to one who is striking at the root" (I, 106). The philanthropist is so busy making sure that everyone gets to enjoy the things he likes that he ignores the reason he is the philanthropist and they are the poor to begin with.

Indeed, Thoreau thought it likely that those with money to give away in philanthropic enterprises had likely been a cause of the problems any philanthropy they "indulged in" would aim to ameliorate. He wrote, "it may be that he who bestows the largest amount of time and money on the needy is doing the most by his mode of life to produce that misery which he strives in vain to relieve." He went on to use a striking analogy. "It is the pious slave-breeder devoting the proceeds of every tenth slave to buy a Sunday's liberty for the rest" (I, 106). "Slave-breeder" is, of course, a polite euphemism for a person who perpetrated sexual violence upon enslaved people and then enslaved and sold their children. The enslaver Thoreau describes practices a form of historical Christianity (as opposed to true Christianity) when he takes the proceeds of the tenth child he sells to allow the remainder of those enslaved to practice the Christian sabbath. Readers who shared Thoreau's abolitionist leanings would have recognized and rejected the hypocrisy of "the pious slave-breeder." Many of them had "come out" of their own churches over those churches' failures to denounce slavery.[18] Thoreau's point to them was that the capitalist's philanthropy wasn't much better than the slave-breeder's hypocrisy.

What would be better than philanthropy, in Thoreau's account, is justice. "I would not subtract any thing from the praise that is due to philanthropy, but merely demand justice for all who by their lives and works are a blessing to mankind" (I, 108). The sentence is complicated. In the context of the analogy to slave-breeding, Thoreau's admitting the "praise that is due to philanthropy" is a rather sarcastic concession. Having already established that philanthropy is like the slave-breeder's giving Sundays off by selling an enslaved person's child, what praise could possibly be due to philanthropy? Only the negative sort these final paragraphs of economy render. "Justice" just means a relationship set right, in which each gives and receives according to what is due, and

[18] "Come-outism" as a term for withdrawing from churches over the politics of slavery comes from 2 Corinthians 6:17. "Wherefore come out from among them, and be ye separate, said the Lord, and touch not the unclean thing; and I will receive you." Albert J. Von Frank, *The Trials of Anthony Burns: Freedom and Slavery in Emerson's Boston* (Cambridge, MA: Harvard University Press, 1998), 25, 267.

thus establishes jointly a good shared between them: right relation. The second half of the sentence demands for all what Thoreau has already given the philanthropist. Where the philanthropist has likely exploited the poor and stolen from society at large to obtain the excess wealth he gives, "those who by their lives and work are a blessing to mankind" are the opposite of the philanthropist, in that their lives and work give true good, and bless the community to which they belong. To demand justice for them is to say that they are due something they have not yet received. But their due will not likely be a form of praise. They, the truly good, do not seek praise and rarely even know they offer blessing: "His goodness must not be a partial and transitory act, but a constant superfluity, which costs him nothing and of which he is unconscious" (I, 108).

Philanthropy's Spiritual Failures

What ultimately motivates Thoreau to denounce philanthropy, however, is not its practical failures, its difficulty identifying and treating true problems, or its papering over of the exploitation on which wealth is so often built. The main issue, and the one with which Thoreau closes the ten-paragraph critique of philanthropy, is spiritual.

In paragraphs seven and eight Thoreau diagnoses the philanthropist's motivation. "If any thing ail a man, so that he does not perform his functions, if he have a pain in his bowels even, – for that is the seat of sympathy, – he forthwith sets about reforming – the world" (I, 108). The philanthropist, or the reformer whom Thoreau figures in a similar way, is motivated by his own ailing. And rather than identifying the pain as coming from a problem within himself, and reforming – his diet, he "sets about reforming – the world." The dash represents comic timing. The sentence is supposed to be funny; audiences who heard Thoreau lecture apparently did find him hilarious. A review of Thoreau's lecture on "Economy" to the Salem Lyceum in November 1848 (an early version of *Walden* material) reported that the lecture was done in "a strain of exquisite humor, with a strong undercurrent of delicate satire against the follies of the times." Thoreau kept "the audience in almost constant mirth."[19] Emerson wrote in a letter of 1850 about one of Thoreau's Concord lectures on material from *Cape Cod*: the audience "laughed till they cried."[20]

But Thoreau's story of the reformer with a bellyache is not a mere joke. The passage goes on from "he forthwith sets about reforming – the world," continuing to suggest that the philanthropist's personal ailing motivates him to save the world.

> Being a microcosm of himself, he discovers, and it is a true discovery, and he is the man to make it, – that the world has been eating green apples; to his eyes, in fact, the globe itself is a great green apple, which there is danger awful to think of that the children of men will nibble before it is ripe; and straightaway his drastic philanthropy seeks out the Esquimaux and the Patagonian, and embraces the populous Indian and Chinese villages; and thus, by a few years of philanthropic activity, the powers in the mean while using him for their own needs, no doubt, he cures himself of his dyspepsia, the globe acquires a faint blush on one or both of its cheeks, as if it were beginning to be ripe, and life loses its crudity and is once more sweet and wholesome to live.
>
> (I, 108)

[19] "Salem Lyceum," *Salem Observer*, November 25, 1848. See also David S. Reynolds, *Beneath the American Renaissance: The Subversive Imagination in the Age of Emerson and Melville* (New York: Oxford University Press, 2011), 500.

[20] Kent P. Ljungquist, "Lectures and the Lyceum Movement," in *The Oxford Handbook of Transcendentalism*, ed. Joel Myerson, Sandra Harbert Petrulionis, and Laura Dassow Walls (New York: Oxford University Press, 2010), 339.

On this telling, philanthropy is not a response to the needs of the world, but rather to the needs of the philanthropist. The philanthropist sees the whole world as "a microcosm of himself," and, in his egomania, he even mistakes his own eating green apples (which caused the bellyache to begin with) for the world's having done it. Then he sets off around the world to make sure "the Esquimaux and the Patagonian," and "the populous Indian and Chinese villages" will not eat green apples. Never mind if they do not have any. In "a few years of philanthropic activity," "he cures himself of his dyspepsia." After he cures himself through philanthropy, "life loses its crudity and is once more sweet and wholesome to live." The condemnation is that the reformer has to "save the world" to save himself, when both he and the world would be better off if he saved himself first. "The philanthropist too often surrounds mankind with the remembrance of his own cast-off griefs as an atmosphere, and calls it sympathy. We should impart our courage, and not our disease" (I, 108). All of *Walden* is aimed at addressing the despair that Thoreau worries motivates the philanthropist, and that he senses is a temptation to many, even – perhaps especially – himself.

The basic problem is that seeing the world as the microcosm of our own problems is a spiritual failure, and Thoreau's motivation for the critique of philanthropy, and I think for the whole of *Walden*, is religious. In paragraphs nine and ten, Thoreau stakes his theological claim against the "drastic philanthropy" of the reformer. Paragraph nine begins, "Our manners have been corrupted by communication with the saints. Our hymn-books resound with a melodious cursing of God and enduring him forever. One would say that even the prophets and redeemers had rather consoled the fears than confirmed the hopes of man" (I, 110). This is a critique of the contemporary church on theological grounds. A superficial reading might assume Thoreau meant to say that saints, prophets, and redeemers are corrupting, and therefore that he objects to religion itself.[21] But Thoreau's objection to philanthropy is a theological one based on a specific understanding of who God is.

Thoreau takes exception to the portrayal of God in the hymns he cites, the ones that curse God. And he writes, "There is nowhere recorded a simple and irrepressible satisfaction with the gift of life, any memorable praise of God" (I, 110). Thoreau's religiosity requires first and foremost satisfaction with the gift of life and the praise of God that follows. "There is nowhere recorded..." is an overstatement. Thoreau's engagement with scripture demonstrates that he found the imagery of the Psalms did offer memorable praise of God (along with expressions of lament). But the point is that philanthropy failed most basically on a spiritual plane, by spreading the disease of despair. And what was wrong with this was that it neglected the most basic religious duty of praise. Philanthropy was a sort of idolatry. It worshiped the wrong things.

[21] My understanding of Thoreau as motivated by Christian theological commitments contrasts with a common reading of radical abolitionists as prioritizing morality over Christianity. For example, Molly Oshatz has argued that abolitionists took one of two main tacks with respect to biblical Christianity. They either presented the Bible as having decided against slavery (with pretty shaky exegesis), or they suggested that the Bible was not authoritative on questions of morality. Her work uncovers moderate antislavery Christians who took a third route, to develop liberal, historicist hermeneutics of the Bible. But Thoreau shows a different strand of radical abolitionism than the usual options admit. Oshatz writes that "Radical abolitionists believed that morality was prior to religion and its holy texts." Thoreau remained faithful that holy texts were central to human understanding of morality, and especially faithful to the idea that human attitudes toward God were central to living good lives. Oshatz might argue that his interpretation of scripture is so unorthodox as to belong beyond even those moderate antislavery Christians her work treats, but I think that denies the faithfulness Thoreau shows to the role of scripture and tradition in living well against slavery. Molly Oshatz, *Slavery and Sin: The Fight against Slavery and the Rise of Liberal Protestantism* (New York: Oxford University Press, 2011), 126.

The place wherein God's gift of life was most obvious to Thoreau was, as he wrote, "Nature." And thus, his response to the spiritual shortcoming of the philanthropy of the period was there. "Let us first be as simple and well as Nature ourselves, dispel the clouds which hang over our own brows, and take up a little life into our pores. Do not stay to be an overseer of the poor, but endeavor to become one of the worthies of the world" (I, 110). In likening the philanthropists of the North to overseers of the poor, Thoreau again analogized conditions in the North to Southern slavery.[22] Then, in case there was any doubt about the theological claim Thoreau was staking, the final paragraph of "Economy" quoted a story from the *Gulistan*, a Sufi poem that is a landmark of Persian literature. In the translation he quotes, the cypress is called "free" because it never blooms nor withers, and the tree carries a religious message. Those praised in the passage are called "religious independents."

> I read in the Gulistan, or Flower Garden, of Sheik Sadi of Shiraz, that "They asked a wise man, saying: Of the many celebrated trees which the Most High God has created lofty and umbrageous, they call none azad, or free, excepting the cypress, which bears no fruit; what mystery is there in this? He replied; Each has its appropriate produce, and appointed season, during the continuance of which it is fresh and blooming, and during their absence dry and withered; to neither of which states is the cypress exposed, being always flourishing; and of this nature are the azads, or religious independents. – Fix not thy heart on that which is transitory; for the Dijlah, or Tigris, will continue to flow through Bagdad after the race of caliphs is extinct: if the hand has plenty, be liberal as the date tree; but if it affords nothing to give away, be an azad, or free man, like the cypress."
>
> (I, 111)

[22] See Chapter 2.

The story explains why the cypress, which bears no fruit, is called free, or azad. The answer is that rather than suffering seasons of blossoming and withering, the cypress always flourishes. Like the cypress, the religious independents (also called azad) flourish always, never fruiting and never withering, and never with anything to give. This is the religious alternative to philanthropy – to embrace poverty and become a "free man, like the cypress."[23] This kind of independence is not merely for its own sake; it is true sainthood rather than the corrupting kind. And it does not succumb to the spiritual temptation of the philanthropist to exploit for profit and then enforce her vision of goodness.

A Quieter, More Relational Goodness

I find this account of philanthropy both accurate and in many places frustrating. I think it says something true about what motivates many people to do-gooding: the need to feel that they are helping others as a balm for their own guilt and despair. And I believe when unexamined this need has led many to harm. But I also have a feeling that Thoreau is too hard on the instinct to help. Isn't there something good about wanting to help one another? Even if we shouldn't force our vision of the good onto one another, shouldn't we cherish generosity?

[23] Though Thoreau's engagement with Asian religions was central to the development of his political asceticism, I do not focus closely in this work on his interpretation of Asian religions. Readers looking for such engagement can turn to Arthur Versluis, *American Transcendentalism and Asian Religions* (New York: Oxford University Press, 1993); Hodder, *Thoreau's Ecstatic Witness*. There is one story from the *Mahābhārata* that seems to have been important to Thoreau and remains under-discussed in the literature. I discuss that story and its resonances with *Walden* in Balthrop-Lewis, "Active and Contemplative Lives in a Changing Climate."

I suppose one issue with this complaint against him is that it is an exaggeration to say that he thinks wanting to help is a problem. "If you should ever be betrayed into any of these philanthropies, do not let your left hand know what your right hand does, for it is not worth knowing. Rescue the drowning and tie your shoe-strings. Take your time and set about some free labor" (I, 109). This, I take it, is one of the mottos of *Walden* as a whole, in which Thoreau aims to pursue reform by other means. At the moment, I am interested in the admonition, "Rescue the drowning," because it suggests there are some helping activities that are important, and even good. And it implies a distinction between the activities of philanthropy and the activity of rescuing the drowning. (An obvious instance of Thoreau giving help is the situation in which he welcomes the Irish worker who was just dunked in the pond to warm himself in Thoreau's house. Rescue the drowning.)

What is the difference to Thoreau between philanthropy and rescuing the drowning? Is it a matter of motivation? Much of what Thoreau denounces in these pages is the self-satisfaction of philanthropic enterprises. Perhaps the problem with philanthropy is that it makes a show of charity. This is also a theological claim. When Thoreau writes "do not let your left hand know what your right hand does," he echoes a biblical injunction about almsgiving. The line comes from the gospel of Matthew 6:1–4, during the middle of the three-chapter Sermon on the Mount. Jesus says,

> Take heed that ye do not your alms before men, to be seen of them: otherwise ye have no reward of your Father which is in heaven. Therefore when thou doest *thine* alms, do not sound a trumpet before thee, as the hypocrites do in the synagogues and in the streets, that they may have glory of men. Verily I say unto you, They have their reward. But when thou doest alms, let not they left hand know what they right hand doeth: That thine alms

> may be in secret: and they Father which seeth in secret himself shall reward thee openly.

The giving of alms is supposed to be so secret that your left hand does not know when your right hand gives. This teaching suggests that doing good should be neither a show enacted for "glory of men" nor to persuade myself that I am good.[24]

This biblical echo may explain Thoreau's disdain of philanthropy but support for rescuing the drowning. Philanthropy sounds a trumpet before it and seeks the glory of men. The form of charity that Thoreau thinks we ought to offer one another is quieter. In paragraph seven, Thoreau writes, of the form of goodness he values, "His goodness must not be a partial and transitory act, but a constant superfluity, which costs him nothing and of which he is unconscious" (I, 108). This is why becoming good rather than doing good is the aim that Thoreau endorses. Only someone who *is* good can do good in this quiet way.

But there are other features of the critique of philanthropy that are troubling, in particular ones that make Thoreau seem self-important, or simply callous. One passage occurs in paragraph three, right after the analogy to the windstorm. Thoreau suggests that philanthropy's focus on some over others sets him against it.

> Philanthropy is not love for one's fellow-man in the broadest sense. Howard was no doubt an exceedingly kind and worthy man in his way, and has his reward; but, comparatively speaking, what are a hundred Howards to *us*, if their philanthropy do not help *us* in our best estate, when we are most worthy to be helped?

[24] This, in addition to the danger associated with record-keeping about illegal activities, could go some way to explaining why Thoreau seems to have written a lot less about helping enslaved people on the run than he did about, say, huckleberrying.

> I never heard of a philanthropic meeting in which it was sincerely proposed to do any good to me, or the like of me.
>
> (I, 104)

Thoreau seems to take exception to the fact that philanthropists like John Howard, a prison reformer who worked to ameliorate conditions for prisoners in Britain in the eighteenth century, focus their efforts to do good on other people besides people like Thoreau. The passage suggests that they do not love broadly enough. The evidence for this is that they never help him out. "I never heard of a philanthropic meeting in which it was sincerely proposed to do any good to me, or the like of me." This can read as selfish. No one can love abstractly. We always love particulars. Howard loves the prisoner. Thoreau looks pouty when he complains philanthropists don't help him.

Thoreau must have known, however, that the passage could be read this way, and used to charge him (again) with selfishness. Why would he have written ammunition for those townsmen he addressed just a few paragraphs earlier, the ones whom he has heard say that "all this is very selfish"? These paragraphs are not a confession to the charge. They try to explain why a person who cares about justice would act as Thoreau does.

So, consider another alternative, that the townsmen's understanding of selfishness itself is a mistake at which the critique of philanthropy takes aim. In this case, the problem with philanthropists is not that they do not help Thoreau specifically, but that without the relational understanding of good Thoreau is promoting, they have a false picture of who doing-good does good for. They assume that what makes an act good is pure altruism, a complete renunciation of egotism, and a unidirectional movement of good from the giver to the receiver. On this picture, one I think Thoreau means to contest, altruism and egotism are the only options, and they are mutually exclusive. Actions are either motivated by the good of another or by one's own good. The philanthropist endorses those actions I aim at another's good and condemns those I aim at my own good. The philanthropist does his philanthropy because he means to help another, selflessly, unidirectionally, and in so doing win the title "good." Anyone who acts to his own good is "selfish."[25]

But most truly good things, and especially the goods with which justice is concerned, are not the sorts of things that belong either to you or to me. The things we value most are goods held in common, that can only be held between us. Right relation is among the most important of these things. When my relation to you is right, that is a good that redounds to both of us. When I am unjustly related to you, the unjust relationship harms both of us, even if one of us receives some advantages from the injustice. Injustice works its evil on both sides of advantage. I may exploit your labor, and yield an economic benefit, but my life is worse for having done so. I have lost the opportunity for good living our just relationship would have provided. The Thoreau of Walden Woods – who cherished relation to the woods, and his neighbors, and the now-dead former inhabitants – was preoccupied with

[25] Of course, this description recalls current controversies within ethics over deontic, duty-based approaches to ethics, in which – following Kant – morality is what I do based on duty or obligation over against self-interest. Current ethicists who think that you can act morally to your own good are sometimes called eudaimonist, in an appeal to the ancient philosophies of *eudaimonia*, or what is often translated as happiness. It may be obvious, but I should just say here that I don't believe morality requires agents to act out of duty or obligation. One major theme of this book is the way in which moral action, even moral action that I experience as sacrificial, is often driven by delight in good things. I must sometimes sacrifice lower goods to higher ones, but moral acts on my view are actions oriented to the good, which can include my own good. Jennifer Herdt defends eudaimonism from the charge of egoism in Jennifer A. Herdt, "Excellence-Prior Eudaimonism," *Journal of Religious Ethics* 47, no. 1 (2019): 68–93.

these sorts of goods, common goods. The philanthropist's altruism fails to acknowledge the good of which he himself is deprived by the injustices in which he is implicated. And he fails to account for the good he would receive should those relationships be set right. He thinks only self-sacrifice will make him good, and in this he misinterprets the significance of sacrifice.

When Thoreau writes, "I never heard of a philanthropic meeting in which it was sincerely proposed to do any good to me, or the like of me," he may write this not because he feels jilted by Concord's charitable societies, but because the picture is wrong when it leaves out the good of either party to a relationship. "Love for one's fellowman in the broadest sense" must include the good of *all*, including the supposedly needy *and* the philanthropist. The philanthropist should also care for his own good because he may sometimes be the recipient of a benefit he fails to examine, one that may or may not be moral. Think, for example, of the philanthropists who helped Concord's Black people leave Concord, and got the (from their racist perspective) benefit of an almost entirely white Concord. They ought to have examined more closely the impact of their philanthropy on their own lives.[26]

Another passage makes Thoreau seem grabby but is probably further reason to think that Thoreau wants to undermine the picture of goodness that motivated other philanthropic efforts. In the previous passage he complained that philanthropists don't help people like him. But in this second passage he seems to resent that people who do receive help from philanthropists like it because it helps them. In paragraph six of the critique, Thoreau seems to condemn a man for praising someone who was kind to him.

[26] See the note in "Suspecting Philanthropy" for the passages from Lemire about Concord philanthropy that whitened the town.

> Philanthropy is almost the only virtue which is sufficiently appreciated by mankind. Nay, it is greatly overrated; and it is our selfishness which overrates it. A robust poor man, one sunny day here in Concord, praised a fellow-townsman to me, because, as he said, he was kind to the poor; meaning himself.
>
> (I, 107)

Thoreau seems to take exception to the robust poor man's valuing the townsman's generosity to the poor. Thoreau implies that it is the man's own selfishness that overrates it. But again, why should Thoreau criticize generosity, or the appreciation of generosity, especially when in the previous passage he complained that the philanthropists did not want to help *him*? I think the answer must be that Thoreau means to undermine the moral picture that suggests actions are either motivated by selfishness or by altruism. Philanthropists *and* the recipients of their charity err when they assume that doing good means delivering kindness, unidirectionally, to the needy. Doing good, Thoreau insists, is something entirely different.

The "Complemental Verses" (authored by Thomas Carew) that appear at the end of "Economy" seem to purposefully denigrate the "poor needy wretch" to whom they are addressed and to speak in the voice of an enlightened "we." Thoreau titled the poem "The Pretensions of Poverty."

> Thou dost presume too much, poor needy wretch,
> To claim a station in the firmament,
> Because thy humble cottage, or thy tub,
> Nurses some lazy or pedantic virtue
> In the cheap sunshine or by shady springs,
> With roots and pot-herbs; where thy right hand,
> Tearing those humane passions from the mind,
> Upon whose stocks fair blooming virtues flourish,
> Degradeth nature, and benumbeth sense,
> And, Gorgon-like, turns active men to stone.
> We not require the dull society
> Of your necessitated temperance,

Or that unnatural stupidity
That knows nor joy nor sorrow; nor your forc'd
Falsely exalted passive fortitude
Above the active. This low abject brood,
That fix their seats in mediocrity,
Become your servile minds; but we advance
Such virtues only as admit excess,
Brave bounteous acts, regal magnificence,
All-seeing prudence, magnanimity
That knows no bound, and that heroic virtue
For which antiquity hath left no name,
But patterns only, such as Hercules,
Achilles, Theseus. Back to thy loath'd cell;
And when thou seest the new enlightened sphere,
Study to know but what those worthies were.

(I, 112)

The beginning of the poem evokes the pastoral imagination, in which virtue is won through simple living, in a "humble cottage" in the shade near a spring. The voice of the poem chastises the "you" of the poem, the "poor needy wretch," and contrasts it with the "we" that interrupts, a we that does not require "the dull society of" the you's "necessitated temperance." Read in one way, with the "you" identified as some particular poor person, and the "we" with some class of not poor people, the poem seems to succumb to the worst stereotypes about poverty: that it makes people stupid and abject, that the poor are satisfied by mediocrity, and that they have servile minds. But the poem does not identify the "you" and the "we" in this way. It may be that the poem's pronouns tempt us to the condescension of the philanthropist that Thoreau has just condemned. Another set of subjects could be in play.

Imagine, instead, that the "you" of the poem is a kind of poverty itself, that pretends to virtue. And imagine the "we" is those *among the poor* who reject "passive fortitude" preached by pretentious poverty for a life of action and true virtue. Think of the poem as addressed to the figure of Thoreau that often annoys people – the Thoreau who "claims a station in the firmament" because he lives in a "humble cottage." That is, readers sometimes think of Thoreau as nursing "some lazy or pedantic virtue," virtue that is not real virtue. He presumes too much about what his voluntary poverty can accomplish for his own goodness. But the poem condemns such a person and offers him an alternative prescription: "advance such virtues only as admit excess." The charge made at Thoreau, that his simplicity pretends to virtue, succumbs to the emaciated picture of goodness that Thoreau means to contest, a picture in which what goodness requires is the fulfillment of certain set of prescribed actions. The poem is a rebuke to those who think that mere poverty *or* philanthropy can win them virtue. True good, including justice among us, is something I must care about *for the sake of both of us*, and something I cannot accomplish without being good myself, which will help me give what is due to others and receive what is due to me. This is a more relational understanding of what goodness consists in, one in which morality is always situated in a specific relational context, and in which what is good is always responsive to that context.

What You Should Do with Money

You might admire Thoreau's tirade against philanthropy for its insistence on relational justice over mere charity but still think that it leaves something important out. What should people who *do* have wealth do *with* that wealth? Thoreau himself did not, in fact, have much to give away, though evidence suggests he was generous with what he had. But it was easy enough for him to condemn charitable activities that consisted largely of giving money; he wasn't rich. There was his family home and business, which gave him advantages of course: the resources most philosophers need – a place to live (in the family boarding house where he paid rent his whole adult life after Walden) and a job to work (in the pencil business) when he needed one.[27] But those things did not belong to him when he was writing *Walden*. He always shared them with his family. He could not give them away.

Still, he would have known some people who did have wealth that was their own. He thought that what they did as charity was a pittance. He wrote, in paragraph five of the critique of philanthropy, "Some show their kindness to the poor by employing them in their kitchens. Would they not be kinder if they employed themselves there?" (I, 106). The kindness of employing yourself in your kitchen is somewhat strange to us, who live in an era where "job creators" are blessed saints. But it is important to recall that this was a period in which wage labor was only just beginning and was in fact controversial. The industrial revolution was underway, which meant that whereas people had once been employed in their own and others' homes – in kitchens, growing food for their families, making things for barter and sale – now, they were being employed for wages in industrial jobs with set hours. Thoreau's own employment was in trades in which you were usually paid by the job, not by the hour, and thus had the freedom to set your own hours and pace.[28] The

[27] For details on the economics of the Thoreau family life in Henry's childhood see Walls, *Henry David Thoreau*, 31–49.

[28] The philosopher Elizabeth Anderson has argued that the current workplace and the unfreedom workers experience there is a threat to democratic tradition. Elizabeth Anderson, "Liberty, Equality, and Private Government," in *The Tanner Lectures in Human Values* (Princeton University, 2015), https://tannerlectures.utah.edu/Anderson%20manuscript.pdf (accessed August 20, 2020). The anthropologist David Graeber has recently argued that this situation is also deeply unproductive. David Graeber, *Bullshit Jobs: A Theory* (New York: Simon & Schuster, 2018).

cultural shift that this entailed was enormous and, Thoreau thought, problematic for his understanding of just labor. Better, he thought, to leave a man (as he would have said) free to pursue his own business than to trap him with wages.

I don't mean to offer an overly romantic picture of life before industry. There were many ways in which it was difficult and dangerous. And I certainly don't want to say that industrialism brought with it only evil. The history of democratic progress, especially with respect to the extension of the franchise far beyond property-owning white men, suggests otherwise. But the social and economic transformation that ensued with the transition of labor out of the household is one we now take for granted, and one which makes this line about the kindness of employing yourself in your own kitchen somewhat difficult to understand.

The context it appeals to and relies on is one entirely outside the economy of wages. The way in which it is kinder to employ yourself in your kitchen, rather than someone else, is that it leaves the person who would have been employed free to pursue some other thing, whether that is employment in his own kitchen or something else; the point is, he gets to decide. When I employ someone in my kitchen, Thoreau thinks I make him subject to my will, which is an unjust relation. For us, this sounds like nonsense. Now, you have to have wages to do anything at all. But I think we hear it as nonsense in part because we have been thoroughly conducted out of any forms of subsistence and into a wage economy. Hardly any of us can live, now, without concern for wages. We would rather be employed than not. We've been persuaded that we will work for a meager wage and be grateful.

Thoreau wrote in a time when the justice of this system as it emerged was under dispute.

Employing yourself in your own kitchen was Thoreau's kind of philanthropy; Thoreau's kind of charity was similarly radical. "You boast of spending a tenth part of your income in charity; may be you should spend the nine tenths so, and done with it" (I, 106). If philanthropists were going to boast, in Thoreau's view, about the money they gave in charity, if they were not going to follow the biblical injunction to not let the left hand know what the right hand is doing, they ought to do more than the standard Christian practice of a 10 percent tithe; they ought to just give it all away. Doing so would keep the philanthropist out of a position of power over the receiver, and it would prevent the recipient from being at the mercy of the philanthropist. Without giving it all, philanthropists short-changed society. When the philanthropist gives a tenth as a tithe, "Society recovers only a tenth part of the property then" (I, 106).

This line condemned the individualist (in the sense of non-relational) picture of society Thoreau meant to undermine, and it also raised complicated associated issues about property and ownership. Thoreau's insistence that life was essentially relational meant that Thoreau was often suspicious of the practice of private property. "Society recovers" suggests that the property given in charity always belonged in some sense to society, and thus that charity, rather than being supererogatory, is the restoration of communal property to the community. He called again for justice over charity. "Is this [the philanthropist's tithing] owing to the generosity of them in whose possession it is found, or to the remissness of the officers of justice?" The line, in which the "this" seems to refer back to "spending a tenth part of your income in charity," suggested that giving a tenth part of your income has two possible interpretations. The first is that you are generous. This was the one the philanthropists adopted. The second interpretation, which Thoreau wanted to raise, is that because they have been remiss, the officers of justice have left nine tenths of your income with you. True justice would entail giving it all away. Further, it would entail thinking of my ethical responsibilities in terms of, first, acknowledging and, second, righting the relationships in which I live – as the officers of justice ought to have done – rather than asking the question the philanthropists ask: How can I relieve the suffering of another a little by giving away things I don't need?

In calling for the philanthropist to give everything away, Thoreau suggested (though never made quite explicit) that wealth itself was an offense against justice, in that it had been stolen from society. As a previous sentence had put the point: "it may be that he who bestows the largest amount of time and money on the needy is doing the most by his mode of life to produce that misery which he strives in vain to relieve" (I, 106). On Thoreau's view, most wealth was earned through exploitation, indeed on his calculus profit could likely *only* be earned through exploitation. Thus the appropriate form of recompense would not be the restitution of a tenth of the income made off of such exploitation, but rather the ceasing of the exploitation in the first place. "I would not subtract anything from the praise that is due to philanthropy, but merely demand justice for all who by their lives and works are a blessing to mankind" (I, 108).

As in Thoreau's advice to not let your left hand know what your right hand does at the end of paragraph six, this recommendation, to give all of your money as charity, has a famous biblical warrant. A rich man came to Jesus and said, as Luke's Gospel has it, "Good Master, what shall I do to inherit eternal life?" (18:18). The first thing Jesus did was take exception to being called good. Jesus's reason for the objection is that there is only one good, and that is God. Perhaps this is part of the reason for Thoreau's suspicions about philanthropy, that it is called good. Thoreau *says* there that the problem with philanthropy is that it fails to notice the good. But it seems clear that a failure to notice the good is related to confusion about what the true good is.

Then, Jesus says that the man knows what to do: "Thou knowest the commandments, Do not commit adultery, Do not kill, Do not steal, Do not bear false witness, Honour they father and thy mother." These were written in the law of Moses and well-known commands of God. The man responds that he has followed the commandments. He says, "All these things I have kept from my youth up." Then Jesus issues a charge that Christians have only very rarely taken up. "Yet thou lackest one thing: sell all that thou hast, and distribute unto the poor, and thou shalt have treasure in heaven: and come, follow me." This one sentence, the "one thing" Jesus says the rich man lacks, describes three acts: selling everything, giving the proceeds to the poor, and following Jesus.

Jesus's description of what the man can do to make up for the one thing he lacks constitutes a triumvirate of difficulties, ones that are quite different from the commandments in the law of Moses. The commandments in the law of Moses are commands of God and also socially sanctioned. In the biblical world, it is good for your wife when you do not commit adultery; it is good for your community when you do not kill; it is good for your economy when you do not steal; it is good for your legal system when you do not bear false witness; it is good for your father and mother when you honor them.

The instructions from Jesus, on the other hand, detail actions that are not socially sanctioned, actions that purposefully set you apart from your social and economic community by declaring that old relational models no longer obtain (mother, child, wife, husband, slave, master, etc.) and that the new model for relation is children of God and siblings of one another in the kingdom of God. This is a radical and unsettling view, since some of the models it rejects (for example, mother and child) are places that people learn to make any relationship at all. The point, however, it to undermine unjust social structures that are taken for granted (including some familial ones) in order to restructure all relationships according to the justice of God's kingdom. For the rich man, selling everything involves giving up the social position he had in the world in which his wealth was achieved and mattered. Giving the proceeds to the poor entailed renouncing the security that his wealth had provided and the dominant class position he previously held over them. And following Jesus meant leaving the place that he lived, and likely the family that he lived with and found some comfort among. The man's response is thus not too surprising: "he was very sorrowful: for he was very rich."

> And when Jesus saw that he was very sorrowful, he said, How hardly shall they that have riches enter into the kingdom of God! For it is easier for a camel to go through a needle's eye, than for a rich man to enter into the kingdom of God. And they that heard *it* said, Who then can be saved? And he said, The things which are impossible with men are possible with God. Then Peter said, Lo, we have left all and followed thee. And he said unto them, Verily I say unto you, There is no man that hath left house, or parents, or brethren, or wife, or children, for the kingdom of God's sake, Who shall not receive manifold more in this present time, and in the world to come life everlasting.

The three-part instructions from Jesus for the rich man do not fit precisely onto but do fit closely with the traditional vows of Christian monastics to obedience, poverty, and chastity. By selling everything, the rich man would renounce his social position in a hierarchy and claim a different social model than the one in which he was at the top; this coincides with the obedience that religious life requires. By giving the money to the poor, the rich man would make his life among the poor; this coincides with the poverty that religious life requires. By following Jesus, the man would leave traditional kinship associations in favor of the community of Jesus's followers; this coincides with the chastity that religious life requires.

Thoreau's recommendation to the philanthropist that he should give it all away is a theological claim about what Christian goodness is: relational justice that is only achieved through the renunciation of unjust advantage, a renunciation that is required to enable a community of mutuality.

Conclusion

I framed the first three chapters of this book as responses to readers of Thoreau who interpret him as asocial, apolitical, and areligious. In Chapter 1, I described the society Thoreau joined in Walden Woods. In Chapter 2, I explained that Thoreau's ascetic practices were aimed at the imagination and enactment of just political and economic life.

Against a view of Thoreau as areligious, Chapter 3 has argued that he was an interpreter of Christianity. Further, I have suggested that he was not merely a disinterested interpreter of Christianity, removed in some way from the conclusions of his own interpretations. He was, instead, personally invested in a theological interpretation of Christianity that was a part of the religious motivation for his writing life and the rest of *Walden*. I demonstrated that Thoreau's criticism of philanthropy was based on a Christian theological argument about what is actually good and was invested in what Thoreau saw as a key feature of the theological tradition: its insistence on the good gift of God's creation and the joyful, relational, spiritual life that this goodness can enable. Thoreau went to Walden in part to enact a more relational ethic than the one he saw other Christian reformers pursuing in their philanthropic lives. And in the rest of *Walden* we can see him offering a whole lifeway, a form of what I will call political asceticism, as a response to the theological problems he identified in the critique of philanthropy.

Chapter 4 aims to make explicit how the interpretive work of the first three chapters contributes to an understanding of Thoreau's religion, and to show why Thoreau's religion might be interesting to readers who don't already care about Thoreau. I argue that Thoreau's life in the woods – including its social, political, and theological ends as described in Chapters 1, 2, and 3 – exemplifies what I call political asceticism. There I will explain what political asceticism is, how Thoreau practiced it, and to what ends.

4

Political Asceticism

> The finest qualities in our nature, like the bloom on fruits, can be preserved only by the most delicate handling. Yet we do not treat ourselves nor one another thus tenderly.
>
> *Walden*, (I, 6)

Thoreau's perspective on time and its utility was contrarian in the context of New England society. Poking fun at forms of economic thinking in which work could not be sacrificed for leisure, Thoreau wrote, about his life at Walden: "There were times when I could not afford to sacrifice the bloom of the present moment to any work, whether of the head or hands" (IV, 2). In this, he reversed a piece of economic wisdom common in the work ethic of the culture in which he lived – that work should always be the first priority, and that other ways of using time were only available if they could be "afforded." As I discussed at the end of Chapter 2, the long, descriptive middle of the book puts forward another hypothesis. Thoreau described in those chapters the pleasures he found in a form of life that rejected the common economy of the townsmen. "My days were not days of the week... nor were they minced into hours and fretted by the ticking of a clock... This was sheer idleness to my fellow-townsmen, no doubt; but if the birds and flowers had tried me by their standard, I should not have been found wanting" (IV, 2). In this, Thoreau rejected one standard of time and took up another, that of the birds and the flowers. Such an attitude toward time allowed the forms of observation with which Thoreau wrote, for example, about the sounds that filled Walden Woods. "Regularly at half past seven, in one part of the summer, after the evening train had gone by, the whip-poorwills chanted their vespers for half an hour, sitting on a stump by my door" (IV, 16). In his attention to the whippoorwills and his living on their time, Thoreau was practicing political asceticism.

Whereas many people assume that asceticism is oriented toward spiritual, interior, individual experience, and does not contribute to political ends, the burden of this book is to show that there are some forms of asceticism whose function is to transform self, community, and broader political conditions. These forms are the ones I call, in this chapter, political asceticism. Thoreau's retreat at Walden is a form of political asceticism.

It could seem strange to describe Thoreau's ascetic practice as political in this sense. Scholars in English, history, politics, and philosophy have tended to ignore Thoreau's interest in religion, and scholars in religious studies and theology are only beginning to notice the ways in which Thoreau participated in and shaped theological traditions that came before and after him. Scholars who do treat Thoreau's religion often describe it as individual and interior, thus neglecting the ways that it was related to his political commitments. My work on Thoreau demonstrates that Thoreau's religious, ascetic practice was conceptually and practically tied to his politics against slavery, industrial capitalism, and wars for territorial expansion. Voluntary poverty, he thought, could contribute to new forms of just economy and government. Thoreau was thus a political ascetic, not a quietist one.

The argument of this chapter goes something like this. Thoreau's political asceticism begins with practices of renunciation. This is a complicated starting point for a practice that aims to effect political change for the better. Many people are justifiably suspicious of religious practices of renunciation. In fact, Thoreau was too. The first section discusses the asceticism of Thoreau's townsmen. Its failures made him suspect they were renouncing the wrong things, so he aimed to articulate an alternative practice. The second section describes what he pursued instead, which he called – with much of the Christian tradition – voluntary poverty. He thought voluntary poverty was important to wisdom, because it made space for positive practices of self, social, and political formation. The third section explains one of the practices that Thoreau's voluntary poverty was aimed at making space for: his writing. It articulates the ways in which Thoreau's writing practice was sociable and political. The fourth section articulates what kind of politics follows from seeing writing and the pursuit of knowledge more broadly in these social terms. The final section explains how all of this constitutes Thoreau's religion.

Renunciation

Scholarly neglect of the broader, political significance of ascetic life is in some ways understandable, because some forms of asceticism are solipsistic, which is to say oriented only inward rather than outward toward community and political life. Other forms of asceticism are self-denying in a way that neglects the good of the practitioner. Not all forms of ascetic practice contribute to the flourishing of individuals or communities, and for some people the fact that asceticism involves renunciation makes it suspicious from the start. Letting go of good things is a counterintuitive way to live a good life. And indeed, many Christian theologies have been too negative about human needs, pleasures, and relationships, and this posture has contributed to forms of ascetic practice that are degrading and perverse.[1] My work aims to participate in a thriving feminist literature that emerges from the acknowledgement that Christian theologies of self-sacrifice have often gone wrong. This literature raises an important question that follows from such acknowledgment: Under what circumstances might asceticism and other practices of personal sacrifice contribute to social liberation?[2]

For those who are suspicious of every form of renunciation, Thoreau will not assuage their complaint. Thoreau's political asceticism begins with practices of renunciation. *Walden* recommends voluntary poverty. But – and this is a key idea in my thinking about asceticism – describing the practices Thoreau recommends as renunciation can lead to a distortion of the central point of them. When we renounce some things, the logic of this thinking goes, we do it *for the sake of others*. Renunciative, negative gestures – for instance, Thoreau's

[1] Which forms of theology are "too negative" and which ascetic practices should count as "degrading and perverse" are of course contested questions. I do not intend to take a position on those questions here, only to raise the fact that mistakes of this kind exist and that those mistakes explain suspicion of ascetic practice. I have in mind debates about classic theological texts that are negative about human embodied life and contemporary practical examples of renunciative practices gone wrong. With respect to classic texts, Augustine's denigration of embodied life in *The City of God* has been a site of much Christian theological contestation over how human needs, pleasures, and relationships ought to figure in Christian practice. With respect to contemporary practical examples, I have in mind the enforced celibacy of Catholic clergy, a practice that can certainly be life-giving for many, but that too often neglects human needs and in this way contributes to diminished flourishing.

[2] Much of the most interesting contemporary work in Christian theology addresses questions that arise about Christianity's calls for self-giving. For example, Anna Mercedes, *Power For: Feminism and Christ's Self Giving* (London: Bloomsbury, 2011). I focus on Christianity because that is my field of expertise. Other religious traditions face other dynamics having to do with individual renunciation and relationship. One feminist response to a common Buddhist focus on individual liberation is Hsiao-Lan Hu, *This-Worldly Nibbana: A Buddhist-Feminist Social Ethic for Peacemaking in the Global Community* (Albany, NY: SUNY Press, 2012).

voluntary poverty – can almost always be redescribed in positive terms. Often, they should be. Giving up some things necessarily makes space for other things. Renunciation is never complete; one cannot renounce everything. Even the martyrs could not renounce the lives they had lived before their deaths or the ideals for which they sacrificed their lives. It is a condition of existence that there is no nothing. In the best cases, practices of renunciation are oriented toward making time and space for *better* things. The key question then is not *whether* we will renounce; we are always choosing for some goods and against others. The key questions are (1) *what* will we renounce? And (2) what do we stand to *gain* from our renunciations?

Thoreau would have been sympathetic, however, to people who thought asceticism didn't do enough to value human needs, desires, and relationships. Thoreau himself was worried that his neighbors in Concord were practicing an asceticism that was too harsh. Many of his neighbors renounced the wrong things, for the sake of the wrong things. He wrote, to those who lived in New England, "I would fain say . . . something about your condition, especially your outward condition or circumstances in this world, in this town, what it is, whether it is necessary that it be as bad as it is, whether it cannot be improved as well as not" (I, 3). The book is addressed first of all to Thoreau's townsmen, and he wants to tell them that they can tutor themselves to take pleasure in the right things (which is a really hard thing to do) by simplifying their lives, which is to say, by giving up some things. Counterintuitively, however, the giving up will yield, according to Thoreau, both a better life for them and more just relations with those among whom they live. In this way, renunciation will issue in a more just society.

In the first paragraphs of *Walden*, Thoreau describes the "trouble and anxiety" he sees around him in Concord, and he suggests that life might be otherwise (I, 16). Trouble and anxiety are not necessary, he insists. In one passage, he suggests that his neighbors are suffering their trouble and anxiety as a form of penance. "I have travelled a good deal in Concord; and every where, in shops, and offices, and fields, the inhabitants have appeared to me to be doing penance in a thousand remarkable ways" (I, 3). Penance is a Christian practice through which one who has sinned expresses penitence or regret, and the desire to make the sin right again. After a Christian seeks absolution for her sins, she may be encouraged to do penance for them, usually through some act appropriate to the sin, thus regaining right relation to the one sinned against and to God.

But the penance Thoreau sees around him does not appear to be righting the relevant relationships. Thoreau compares the "penance" he sees his townsmen doing to severe "Bramin" practices he has read about: "sitting exposed to four fires and looking in the face of the sun; or hanging suspended, with their heads downward, over flames; or looking at the heavens over their shoulders" until their necks are permanently twisted, "or dwelling, chained for life, at the foot of a tree" (I, 3). Those practices, which Thoreau seems to assume his readers will believe are overly harsh, were "hardly more incredible and astonishing than the scenes which I daily witness." When Thoreau compared his Concord townsmen's penance to the practices of "Bramin" ascetics, he used his readers' suspicion of Indian ascetic practice to suggest that the townsmen were succumbing to their own misconceived asceticism. Thoreau thought his townsmen were working harder than they really needed to or should. They were sacrificing better things for worse ones.

The Concordian asceticism Thoreau witnessed was the ceaseless labor and debt he saw his neighbors caught up in (and had been himself to some extent). I argued in previous chapters that Thoreau's practice in Walden Woods was oriented toward finding alternatives to slavery and industrial economy. He also wrote *Walden* because he thought there ought to be an alternative to the economy of endless labor and debt he saw around him in Concord. Even land-owning, white Concordians were subjects of a vicious financial economy. Those who had inherited large farms and were trying to maintain them often faced the problem of debt. This happened when they had to mortgage the farm seasonally to afford the costs of farming. They also faced interminable labor to pay back the debt. Such work was harder than the twelve labors of Hercules, Thoreau wrote. At least for Hercules there were only twelve; Hercules found rest at the end of his labor, as these men never do. Such men would have been better off, Thoreau claimed, if they had been born with nothing, because then "they might have seen with clearer eyes what field they were called to labor in" (I, 4). One of the problems with the anxiety and strain that Thoreau sees these men suffering is that it blinds them to their callings. Being called is hearing a summons, often a divine one, to a form of life and often an associated occupation. The farms these men inherited gave them the capacity to grow their wealth but took away from them the opportunity to reflect on what God might be calling them to do.

Thoreau suggested that in trying to maintain their property, such men were both subject to an unjust economy and ignoring the call of the gospel. He wrote that their ceaseless toil was oriented toward an aim that was ultimately, religiously, worthless.

> But men labor under a mistake. The better part of the man is soon ploughed into the soil for compost. By a seeming fate, commonly called necessity, they are employed, as it says in an old book, laying up treasures which moth and rust will corrupt and thieves break through and steal. It is a fool's life, as they will find when they get to the end of it, if not before.
>
> (I, 5)

The labor these men do is part of a mistaken understanding of the purpose of human life. "The better part of man is soon ploughed into the soil for compost." There are two senses of better implied by the sentence, a quantitative one and a qualitative one. The line implies that most, though not all, of a man is composted when he dies. It also suggests that the part of a human person that is buried when he dies has more value than the part that survives death. Laying up treasures, the aim of these men's labor, is futile not only because you die and you cannot take them with you when you do, but also because even before you die you have a tenuous relationship to them: they may disappear before you if the moths or the rust or the thieves get them. The allusion to "an old book" is the first biblical allusion in *Walden*, and it, like the line about how to give alms that I discussed in Chapter 3, points to the Sermon on the Mount in the Gospel of Matthew, again from Chapter 6, this time, verses 19–20. I quote here Matthew 6:19–24:

> Lay not up for yourselves treasures upon earth, where moth and rust doth corrupt, and where thieves break through and steal: But lay up for yourselves treasures in heaven, where neither moth nor rust doth corrupt, and where thieves do not break through nor steal: For where your treasure is, there will your heart be also. The light of the body is the eye: if therefore thine eye be single, thy whole body shall be full of light. But if thine eye be evil, thy whole body shall be full of darkness. If therefore the light that is in thee be darkness, how great *is* that darkness! No man can serve two masters: for either he will hate the one, and love the other; or else he will hold to the one and despise the other. Ye cannot serve God and mammon.

Here, Jesus says that it is better to lay up treasures in heaven than treasures on earth. This is, in part, because you can lose the treasures you lay up on earth – the moth can eat them, rust can corrupt them, thieves can steal them. But more importantly, "where your treasure is, there will your heart be also."

The treasure that you can lay up on earth will keep you from God, in that it will hold your heart. "Ye cannot serve God and Mammon." Thus, when the farmers who have inherited large lands spend their lives serving the labor their farms require, they follow what is "commonly called necessity," but is in fact a dire religious mistake. It is a mistake that risks turning them away from God. "It is a fool's life, as they will find when they get to the end of it, if not before." The labor it requires does not leave time for the most important parts of life. "The finest qualities in our nature, like the bloom on fruits, can be preserved only by the most delicate handling. Yet we do not treat ourselves nor one another thus tenderly" (I, 6). The asceticism of young farmers sacrifices the finest qualities of their nature to a life of ceaseless labor without benefit.

Thoreau's aim is to persuade the reader that there is another form of life she may pursue, one that will preserve the finest qualities of her nature. It must be tenderer than the overly rigorous penance Thoreau sees among young farmers.

Those who have inherited farms, the relatively wealthy who work too hard to maintain what they have, are not the only ones Thoreau addresses. His audience is local – he's writing to those in New England – and his local audience includes mixed classes. From the beginning of the chapter he identifies another audience among those who are poor. "Perhaps these pages are more particularly addressed to poor students." Having identified at least two classes of people who might read the book, Thoreau suggests that all who read it should take from it only what applies to them. Some readers will find that particular parts are more useful to them than others. Other readers might find nothing relevant to their circumstances. It is for the reader to discern. "As for the rest of my readers, they will accept such portions as apply to them. I trust that none will stretch the seams in putting on the coat, for it may do good service to him whom it fits" (I, 2). Thoreau knows that the renunciation he describes will not be good advice for everyone.

Indeed, a few paragraphs later, after describing those with inherited wealth, he writes to those who have no such fortune. "Some of you, we all know, are poor, find it hard to live, are sometimes, as it were, gasping for breath" (I, 7). To these readers, Thoreau offers sympathy in the face of constant poverty. His own experience has helped him to see how hard such a life is.

> I have no doubt that some of you who read this book are unable to pay for all the dinners which you have actually eaten, or for the coats and shoes which are fast wearing or are already worn out, and have come to this page to spend borrowed or stolen time, robbing your creditors for an hour. It is very evident what mean and sneaking lives many of you live, for my sight has been whetted by experience . . .
>
> (I, 7)

The passage goes on in one, long, sixteen-line sentence joined by semicolons. It describes what it's like trying to earn enough money to get out of debt, the number of methods "you" employ to get work, and the deepest irony of all, that you work yourself sick to protect yourself for when you become sick:

> It is very evident what mean and sneaking lives many of you live, for my sight has been whetted by experience; always on the limits, trying to get into business and trying to get out of debt, a very ancient slough, called by the Latins *æs alienum*, another's brass, for some of their coins were still made of brass; always promising to pay, promising to pay, tomorrow, and dying to-day, insolvent; seeking to curry favor, to get custom by how many modes, only not state-prison offenses; lying, flattering, voting, contracting yourselves into a nutshell of civility, or dilating into an atmosphere of thin and vaporous generosity, that you may persuade your neighbor to let you make his shoes, or his hat,

> or his coat, or his carriage, or import his groceries for him; making yourselves sick, that you may lay up something against a sick day, something to be tucked away in an old chest, or in a stocking behind the plastering, or, more safely, in the brick bank; no matter where, no matter how much or how little.
>
> (I, 7)

The form of this one long sentence adds emphasis to its message: those in Concord who are poor are – in a breathless, ceaseless way, like the sentence itself – desperate to pay their debt and save just a little, no matter how much.[3] They are doing all that they can (even voting!) to seek advantage in the world of commerce. But as with the overly rigorous labor of the farmers, the work never ends. It is in this sense that it is desperate, and it is in this context that Thoreau writes what is one of the most famous lines of the book. "The mass of men lead lives of quiet desperation" (I, 9). They are caught up in ceaseless labor, sacrificing their wellbeing to a false security. But such desperation is the opposite of the wisdom that Thoreau pursues. "It is characteristic of wisdom not to do desperate things" (I, 9).

Thoreau has described a form of life in which labor is incessant and pointless. The feats of penance he sees being done every day in Concord, those that are as incredible and astonishing as the overly rigorous forms of the "Bramin" practice he had read about, risk turning people away from God and causing harm to "the finest qualities of our nature." This way of life is itself a form of asceticism, in that it runs on disciplined practices, especially of renunciation, but it gives up all the wrong things in pursuit of all the wrong things. We have to treat ourselves and one another more tenderly.

[3] Thoreau himself borrowed from Emerson when Thoreau was jobless and fruitlessly job searching. Dann, *Expect Great Things*, 36.

Voluntary Poverty

Thoreau offers an alternative to what he sees as Concord's citizens' unnecessarily rigorous economic lives, what he calls their practices of "penance" in paragraph 3 of "Economy," and what he characterizes as their self-slavery in paragraph 8. Such lives misjudge their aim: "Men labor under a mistake" in their pursuit of what they think of as necessity but is, actually, luxury (I, 5). Luxuries are "hindrances to the elevation of mankind," which we know, he thinks, by the fact that "the wisest have ever lived a more simple and meagre life than the poor" (I, 19). The quintessential example of wisdom for Thoreau is the practice of "the ancient philosophers, Chinese, Hindoo, Persian, and Greek" (I, 19). The alternative they demonstrate from the one he sees around him in Concord is a life of what Thoreau calls "voluntary poverty," whose fruit is wisdom. Such a life fulfills, "to use the words of the catechism, the chief end of man" (I, 10). The first question of the Westminster Catechism, a seventeenth-century document articulating Christian doctrine for the purposes of teaching, is "What is the chief end of man?" The words of the catechism, which Thoreau had been taught by Ezra Ripley as a member of First Parish Church of Concord, still articulates Thoreau's most important aim.[4] Thoreau presents his life in *Walden* as the tenderer asceticism his townsmen could adopt, rather than their overly punishing penance. Its practice is a form of life that would – if we take the reference to the catechism seriously – "glorify God" and enable the ascetic to "enjoy God forever."

[4] Sargent Bush, Jr. argued that the first question of the Westminster Catechism provided the essential shape and direction of *Walden*. "His method and his conclusions are both somewhat different from those of the fathers at Westminster, but, like them, he has kept the primary question uppermost." Sargent Bush, Jr., "The End and Means in *Walden*: Thoreau's Use of the Catechism," *ESQ: A Journal of the American Renaissance* 31, 1 (1985): 1–10.

The practice Thoreau recommends, of conscientiously living on only what you need, was related to a sense he had, which was theologically motivated, that the practice of property ownership – especially of land – was idolatry. The idea was something like this: God gave creation to all in common, partly as a way of giving God's self to them. Land and the communities that inhabit it thus represent important features of God's life with humanity. For me to take permanent ownership of a part of that for myself was therefore to act as though God's grace was mine alone.[5] This was, ultimately, the reason to resist slavery, which was a particularly unjust instantiation of ownership because of the special status of human beings. But slavery was only the worst form of the in-any-case dubious practice of ownership. One of the reasons that the rigorous labors of his townsmen are desperate is that they are pursuing ownership, especially of land. In Thoreau's view, such ownership is a form of relation that fails to give the things considered "owned" what they are due as gifts from God and members of the community.

Thoreau discussed his views about property with Emerson, as Emerson recorded in his journal in November of 1838. "My brave Henry Thoreau walked with me to Walden this afternoon and complained of the proprietors who compelled him, to whom, as much as to any, the whole world belonged, to walk in a strip of road and crowded him out of all the rest

[5] Thoreau may be participating in a tradition of critique of the practice of private property ownership that was vigorously advanced in English theology and philosophy around the time of the English Revolution in the seventeenth century, especially by figures such as Gerrard Winstanley. For a view of the English Revolution from a popular perspective, see Christopher Hill, *The World Turned Upside down: Radical Ideas during the English Revolution* (London: Temple Smith, 1972). For a study of Winstanley, see George M. Shulman, *Radicalism and Reverence: The Political Thought of Gerrard Winstanley* (Berkeley, CA: University of California Press, 1989).

of God's earth."[6] Thoreau seems to have been in a rather contrary mood. He hated when property owners' fences got in the way of his wandering, and he resented the way they acted like God's earth was theirs. Thoreau insisted that God's prior gift was still in force. God's having gifted creation entailed conclusions about how each person ought to relate to the places she inhabited.

Thoreau described the practice of ownership as a habit, by which he likely meant a cultivated disposition. Such dispositions contribute to both attitudes and actions, and the habit of ownership deforms them both. The habit of relating to others as owner was not only an injustice to those it kept out, as it did Thoreau on his walks, or to that which was considered owned. Unjust relations of ownership pervert the lives of all parties to them. Take, for example, the habit "of regarding the soil as property." "By avarice and selfishness, and a groveling habit, from which none of us is free, of regarding the soil as property, or the means of acquiring property chiefly, the landscape is deformed, husbandry is degraded with us, and the farmer leads the meanest of lives" (VII, 16). The groveling habit of regarding the soil as property does deform the landscape and degrade husbandry, but it also leads would-be owners to lives that are mean, by which Thoreau means something like abject or ignoble. This habit makes the lives of those who practice it worse.[7] In "Walking," Thoreau suggested that such relational habits interfere with true enjoyment of the goods at stake. "To enjoy a thing exclusively is commonly to exclude yourself from

[6] Ralph Waldo Emerson, *Journals of Ralph Waldo Emerson, with Annotations*, vol. 5 (New York: Houghton Mifflin company, 1914), 129.

[7] Another example from the very beginning of the book: "How many a poor immortal soul have I met well nigh crushed and smothered under its load, creeping down the road of life, pushing before it a barn seventy-five feet by forty, its Augean stables never cleansed, and one hundred acres of land, tillage, mowing, pasture, and wood-lot!" (I, 4).

true enjoyment of it."[8] The idea is that the habit of exclusive ownership interferes with the enjoyment of the goods purportedly owned, whose true enjoyment – as gifts given to all – can only be shared in common.

Crucially, Thoreau includes himself in this critique of the habit of property by saying "none of us is free" of it. Habits like these, ones that are everywhere all the time, ones that are particularly hard to overcome, these are the habits at which asceticism takes aim.[9] Ascetics cultivate disciplined practices in order to learn new habits, new dispositions, especially when the old habits (for instance, regarding soil as property) are very hard to unlearn. Habits like those cannot be simply willed away. It doesn't do us any good to change our *minds* about the soil if we have not changed our *lives*.[10] Thoreau's

[8] Henry David Thoreau, Walden, *Civil Disobedience, and Other Writings*, 3rd ed. (New York: Norton, 2008), 267.

[9] The environmental philosopher Bryan Norton once wrote that mainstream economists' acceptance of consumer preferences as "givens" contradicts a major credo of Thoreau's – that our preferences can and often should be transformed. Norton thought that this difference with respect to whether consumer preferences are viewed as subject to transformation accounts for the dissatisfaction among environmentalists – who think we must transform from a consumer society to a conserver society – with mainstream economics. Norton described Thoreau's view as "blatantly moralistic," which he meant not as a slur but as acknowledgment of Thoreau's commitment to moral transformation. Norton did not associate Thoreau's commitment to transformation with his religious asceticism. Bryan G. Norton, "Thoreau's Insect Analogies: Or Why Environmentalists Hate Mainstream Economists," *Environmental Ethics* 13, 3 (1991): 235–51.

[10] Eddie Glaude once asked me whether the renunciation by white people of whiteness was a form of political asceticism. I took the question to rest on a premise, one that I share with Glaude: whiteness is not a natural feature of the human species. It is a socially constructed racial identity whose main function is to confer unjust advantages on some over others. I said that renouncing whiteness would be political asceticism on my understanding to the extent that it rectified the relationships that are deformed by the unjust advantages whiteness delivers. It is clear, however, that working out what actual practices could effect such rectification in the case of whiteness and other unjust advantages is very difficult to discern. Because I think such discernment must happen in particular contexts, I do

critique of the habit of property ownership is radical, as it suggests that the corruption is not only in the means of acquiring property. He is not merely worried about poor land management or the exploitation of labor. He is not only concerned that the land has been stolen from those who inhabited it before. He is criticizing the practice of property ownership itself because he thinks that the proprietary way of constructing the relevant relationships is vicious.[11]

I consider the first five chapters of *Walden* a first movement of the book, where Thoreau introduces the reader to the reasons he went to the woods and some of what it was like there. The second movement of *Walden* begins with "The Bean-Field," which is where Thoreau describes his own experiments in agriculture on land he was borrowing. Thoreau's bean field is cultivated differently from the desperate farms of the beginning of the book. In "The Bean-Field" Thoreau integrates the more economic focus of "Economy," the first chapter of *Walden*, and the more social focus of

not attempt to do anything like it here. One important feature of such discernment for white people, however, would be determining which advantages ought to be renounced and which ought to be made more widely available, and thus marshalled in the struggle for greater justice rather than made subject to renunciation. I've also been taught by conversation with Sarah Stewart-Kroeker and Molly Farneth that calling the renunciation of unjust advantage "sacrifice" is often a tempting way to cover over the fact that the advantage renounced was never due to begin with. It is not a sacrifice to renounce something that is not actually due to you.

[11] Denial of the right to property is another point of resonance with Jack Turner's interpretation of James Baldwin, who, Turner claims, refuses "the right to exclude, a right essential to property as an institution." Jack Turner, *Awakening to Race: Individualism and Social Consciousness in America* (Chicago, IL: University of Chicago Press, 2012), 101. But, again, Turner purveys a liberal view of rights that my relational Thoreau would not quite know what to make of. The problem with "owning the soil" is not that you have usurped the right to exclude over and against the rights of others to the soil. The problem is that you have misconceived what the soil is (you have reduced it to a thing that can be owned) and in so doing have corrupted your relationship to it and your neighbors.

"Solitude," which I described in Chapter 1. He does this by showing ways in which his labor itself has a social aspect. He describes an alternative model of relation to soil and plants. He becomes intimate with the object of his labor. "What shall I learn of beans or beans of me? I cherish them, I hoe them, early and late I have an eye on them" (VII, 1). This kind of relation is not proprietary. It is a kind of watchfulness aimed at intimacy. "Consider the intimate and curious acquaintance one makes with various kinds of weeds" (VII, 10). This social way of doing the work of raising beans appeals to ancient poetry and mythology. "Ancient poetry and mythology suggest, at least, that husbandry was once a sacred art." Thoreau contrasts this sacred, artful husbandry with the way husbandry is usually practiced. "It is pursued with irreverent haste and heedlessness by us, our object being to have large farms and large crops merely" (VII, 16). Agriculture, like all practical life in Thoreau's view, ought to be an act of reverence for the sacred.

Thoreau takes the critique of property to its fullest extent in *Walden* at the very end of "The Bean-Field," where he suggests that farmers should renounce their expectations of any yield at all. "The true husbandman will cease from anxiety, as the squirrels manifest no concern whether the woods will bear chestnuts this year or not, and finish his labor every day, relinquishing his claim to the produce of his fields, and sacrificing in his mind not only his first but his last fruits also" (VII, 17). Thoreau's instruction for the true husbandman alludes to a biblical command to sacrifice first fruits to God, which appears in Proverbs among other places. Thoreau's recommendation to sacrifice the last fruits, in addition to the first, goes beyond the biblical command.[12] In this way, it echoes

[12] Joshua Nunziato points out that the passage adapts Christ's "lilies of the field" (Matthew 6:25–34; Luke 12:22–34). Joshua Nunziato, *Augustine and the*

Thoreau's insistence that the 10 percent tithe was insufficient, which I discussed in Chapter 3. Thoreau endorses living like a squirrel, one who does not worry whether the woods will produce chestnuts but instead works every day without expecting the fruits of his work to be solely his own.

But none of this is very practical advice, and a reader – or, this reader – suspects Thoreau can't quite have meant it. He was doing some of it as myth-making, a way of expressing a spiritual truth that might never be achieved in life. Despite his suspicion of ownership, and his insistence on sacrificing both first and last fruits, Thoreau did not think that humans could just live on a wing and a prayer. There are some things that each person does need to have securely in her possession, for her use, even if she ought not consider her relation to those things one of ownership. Thoreau does not think you can be free without the necessities. There are basic material prerequisites to freedom.[13] Thoreau's voluntary poverty did not reject things that are truly necessary. Discerning what those things were was a big part of the Walden experiment. This was because freedom was impossible without them. "Not till we have secured [the necessities] are we prepared to entertain the true problems of life with freedom and a prospect of success" (I, 17). The point of voluntary poverty was to entertain the true problems of life, which is to say to live a life of wisdom, and such a life could not be achieved without material necessities. In this, Thoreau contests the voluntarist account of freedom that underwrites the standard abolitionist acceptance of Northern economy.

Economy of Sacrifice: Ancient and Modern Perspectives (Cambridge: Cambridge University Press, 2019), 207.

[13] This is a commitment he shares with mid-twentieth century American author James Baldwin, at least in the interpretation of Baldwin offered by Jack Turner. Turner, *Awakening to Race*, 101.

Walden was in part an experiment in what is materially required to live well. But just as there are important material necessities for a life of wisdom, Thoreau thinks that excessive luxury is a barrier to good living. Simple clothes, shelter, and food are important because wisdom is nearly impossible in the lap of luxury. In this, he echoes the story of Jesus and the rich young man in the gospel passage I discussed in Chapter 3. From Thoreau's perspective, when Jesus told the man that he should sell everything, that advice was not for the sake of the man's eternal salvation. Thoreau's thoughts on eternity are not particularly clear. But Thoreau was sure that simple living was a key to wisdom in this life. Thoreau wrote that poverty was essential not simply to holiness, but also to knowledge. "None can be an impartial or wise observer of human life but from the vantage ground of what *we* should call voluntary poverty" (I, 19). Knowledge itself, and the practice of observation that Thoreau took to be so central to its pursuit, was impossible in the lap of luxury. Such luxuries are "positive hindrances to the elevation of mankind" (I, 19). A hindrance is an obstacle; it hides what lies behind it. Wisdom requires observation and the knowledge such observation imparts, and with respect to this what we call luxury is an impediment, and what we call poverty is an aid. Thus the emphasis on "we": *we* call it poverty, but it leads to true wealth.[14]

[14] Cavell observes that this is one of Thoreau's characteristic strategies for making the reader examine his own commitments.

"First, there is his insistence on the idea of what we call something, or what something is said by us to be. In the opening fifty pages of *Walden* there are a dozen instances of modifications like "so-called" or "what is called." The point of modification is to suggest that our words are our calls or claims upon the objects and contexts of our world; they show how we count phenomena, what counts for us. The point is to get us to withhold a word, to hold ourselves before it, so that we may assess our allegiance to it, to the criteria in terms of which we apply it. Our faithlessness to our language repeats our faithlessness to all our shared commitments." Cavell, *The Senses of Walden*, 64–65.

In this way, Thoreau suggested that voluntary poverty of the kind he was recommending could contribute to practices of attention that lead to knowledge. Thoreau called for Concordians to renounce "trouble and strain" not as a form of mere refusal, but *for the sake of* other practices that conduce to wisdom.[15] He recommended adopting voluntary poverty, a form of renunciation, but that poverty was not for itself alone. It enabled paying attention to the world around him.

The main practice of attention that Thoreau developed, and thus one of the central features of his political asceticism, was writing.

Writing to Learn Attention

Thoreau practiced voluntary poverty in his own life as an experiment in freedom. If you live on less, he found, you can find more time for other, better things, some of which are practices that enable resistance to injustice. In Chapter 2, I offered a list of some of the better things Thoreau pursued, having given up the "trouble and anxiety" of standard economic life in Concord. In their place, Thoreau pursued hospitality, housework and other labor, bathing, reading, writing, sitting, rowing, fishing, looking, walking, flute-playing, keeping appointments with trees, gossiping, visiting neighbors, and bean-hoeing. Among these, perhaps the most important, both to Thoreau himself and for my interpretation of his political asceticism, was writing, which in Thoreau's practice

[15] Gandhi's practice of nonviolence, which was in part inspired by Thoreau, was importantly not only the rejection of violence but more basically a constructive program. "The constructive programme entails founding a new society and strengthening the self-respect of one's own group during the struggle. New, alternative institutions are built up in parallel to the resistance against the institutions being supplanted." Stellan Vinthagen, *A Theory of Nonviolent Action: How Civil Resistance Works* (London: Zed Books, 2015), 32–34.

was sociable, oriented toward knowledge, and – for reasons I'll go on to explain in the last section of this chapter – thus political. Thoreau's writing practice was at the center of his political asceticism, and in the remainder of this chapter I will take it as another example of how practices that seem contemplative and individually oriented can be described as integrated into larger scales of action and thus oriented toward social and political life (examples in the first two chapters included manual labor and restraint with respect to clothes).

As Stanley Cavell notes, writing is rarely represented as an activity in *Walden*. "We seem to be shown this hero doing everything under the sun but, except very infrequently, writing."[16] But this may be in part *because* writing was so central to the Walden experiment. Writing was, I suggest, Thoreau's most important practice, and it can serve as a key example in understanding how the political ascetic practice he represents in *Walden* is supposed to function in the lives of those who take it up.

We know that writing was one of Thoreau's most important objectives when he moved to the woods. He was an ambitious writer, and he went there to finish one book and begin another. Writing was also, perhaps surprisingly, one of his most sociable practices. This may be surprising. The act of writing is often solitary, and to that extent seems intuitively related to interior, contemplative experience and removed from the realms of sociality and politics. This is especially true of the journal form Thoreau practiced most regularly at Walden, which I say more about elsewhere. However, as I argued in Chapter 1 and Chapter 2, Thoreau goes to Walden for social and political reasons, motivated, as I argued in Chapter 3, by a particular vision of Christian

[16] Cavell, *The Senses of Walden*, 5.

theology. Similarly, he writes for social and political reasons. He writes to transform himself and to move his audience, to persuade them that their lives could be different, and in both of these ways to foster forms of sociality and politics that are good. Thoreau's writing is a personal practice and an effort to represent the form of life that is political asceticism and encourage it in others.

In my account, writing can be sociable in at least four ways. First, even when the only relation involved in the practice of writing is between the author and the page, writing is a practice that contributes to broader forms of sociality by cultivating habits of attention in the author.[17] Writing as a practice does this to the extent that it forms writers into persons who attend to both themselves and others. When I write, according to this understanding, I put myself, as the (1) author, into relation with (2) a subject about which I write and (3) the writing that I create. In this way, writing enacts a trinity. (Recall Thoreau's chairs from Chapter 1: one for solitude, two for friendship, three for society.) This triangular shape undermines a common understanding of knowledge as a relation between a knowing subject and a known object. Conceived in this triangular way, writing requires particular forms of attention. In order to describe a thing, even if it is a thing inside myself, I first have to attend to it. And that attention, just the fact of aiming attention at an object and

[17] Caleb Smith's suspicion of postcritique's "disciplines of attention" within literary studies has motivated him to offer a genealogy of such disciplines, as a way of describing ethical motives he thinks the postcritics disavow. Caleb Smith, "Disciplines of Attention in a Secular Age," *Critical Inquiry* 45, 4 (June 1, 2019): 884–909. I remain committed to such disciplines of attention not because I think they disavow ethics or agency (it is not clear to me the postcritics are aiming to do this either), but because those practices seem to me a precondition for any relation (including one of knowledge) at all. They are thus not only ethically motivated, but also the beginning of all ethics.

then trying to capture in words something about what that practice of attention uncovered, is a way of reorienting the self and thus a preparation for true sociality.[18]

Thoreau wrote about something like the interior movement of attention I am trying to describe in a key paragraph in "Solitude." He wrote, "With thinking we may be beside ourselves in a sane sense" (V, 11). Writing creates opportunities for transformed relations in part by creating multiple roles, even within the same person. Thoreau points out that we have choices about what role we occupy when we do this kind of attending. "I may either be the driftwood in the stream, or Indra in the sky looking down on it" (V, 11). I can point my attention at the movements as they pass, immersed in immediacy, being the driftwood in the stream, or I can occupy a position that takes a greater distance on things, looking down on them from the sky. Both options are, in principle and all things being equal, perfectly reasonable choices. They are choices about how to envision the perspective from which and scale at which any particular situation ought to be described. When I am driftwood in the stream, I notice what goes by me, close at hand. When I am Indra in the sky, I see things from above and farther away. (This point ought to recall Thoreau's interest in scale and perspective from Chapter 1.)

[18] I do not mean to suggest that writing is required for good living, only that it was a practice Thoreau adopted for that purpose and one that is available for that purpose. There are many kinds of good human lives, and there are many reasons that writing might not be part of one. I have become especially interested lately in the strengths of human living that relies on other modes of communication besides written words. Anne Carson, *Eros the Bittersweet* (Princeton, NJ: Princeton University Press, 1986), 46–52. Nell Irvin Painter, "Representing Truth: Sojourner Truth's Knowing and Becoming Known," *The Journal of American History* 81, 2 (September 1994): 461–492. Tyson Yunkaporta, *Sand Talk: How Indigenous Thinking Can Save the World* (Melbourne, Victoria: Text Publishing, 2019), 164–181.

Thoreau describes this division as a kind of "doubleness." "I only know myself as a human entity; the scene, so to speak, of thoughts and affections; and am sensible of a certain doubleness by which I can stand as remote from myself as from another" (V, 11). In writing, I stand remote from myself for a moment as I occupy the position of the author.[19] Thoreau writes that this is the same kind of remoteness that I can have with respect to another person. And he acknowledges that this movement of human attention could have negative effects on social life. He writes, "This doubleness may easily make us poor neighbors and friends sometimes" (V, 11). Perhaps he thinks the author's remoteness can inhibit friendship because so often taking a removed view on our loved ones can alienate us from them.

But it may also be that writing's reorientation of the self beyond its narrow investments is the beginning of true sociality, over and against the common kind. Thoreau suggests something like this later in the same chapter when he writes, "society is commonly too cheap" (V, 13). In response to cheap society, Thoreau thought the writing life and other ascetic practices were oriented toward preparation for true society. They were the preparation that made any society at all

[19] Jorge Luis Borges offered a vivid picture of a competitive version of this doubleness of the author with the self in "Borges and I." But the story ends with the fact that it was never clear where the one began and the other ended. "I do not know which of us has written this page." Jorge Luis Borges, *Collected Fictions*, trans. Andrew Hurley (New York: Penguin Books, 1999), 324. Margaret Atwood has written about another, somewhat different kind of doubleness of the writer. "What is the relationship between the two entities we lump under one name, that of 'the writer'? The particular writer. By *two*, I mean the person who exists when no writing is going forward – the one who walks the dog, eats bran for regularity, takes the car to be washed, and so forth – and that other, more shadowy and altogether more equivocal personage who shares the same body, and who, when no one is looking, takes it over and uses it to commit the actual writing." Margaret Atwood, *Negotiating with the Dead: A Writer on Writing* (New York: Anchor, 2002), 35.

worthwhile. Thoreau thought that without these kinds of self-reflective practices, society lost its savor. "We meet at meals three times a day, and give each other a new taste of that old musty cheese that we are" (V, 13).[20] This kind of society can make people lonely even in a crowd.

But unlike the loneliness of crowds, when "we live thick and are in each other's way," the trinity of the author, the object, and the text in the writer's life teaches writers to attend to both themselves and others. An author writes what she thinks about something, growing closer to herself by coming to knowledge about her thoughts; but in the writing the thinking about her object becomes a third thing (the text) and thus a way of relating to what is outside herself. In this way, writing – even apart from anyone else's involvement – integrates parts of human experience that might otherwise be alienated from one another.

When the writing is about something at a further remove from the author herself, its social power only increases. Descriptive writing about something outside of the author, of the kind that Thoreau practiced while living in the woods and that only grew more important to him throughout the course of his life, is a particularly effective discipline of attention. It requires that the author press his self outward into the world, to see what else is there besides himself and to train his mind on other things besides the driftwood in the stream of his own mind. When Thoreau wrote with careful precision about the coming of the seasons, when he noticed the appearance of the flowers each year, he was doing it in part because he loved the flowers, but he was also doing it as a practice of

[20] In an earlier draft, Susannah Ticciati pointed out that "old musty cheese" is potentially a positive description. While I think the context points to the reading I assume in the text above, this is now one of my favorite of all the many multivalent moments in *Walden*.

attention that could make him the kind of person who could see beyond himself. The practice of this attention is a precondition for any flourishing relationship with another.[21] It transforms the writer (when they do it well) into someone who can see the world, a person who can make relation by way of attention. In Thoreau's case, the practice of attention to what was outside himself through writing opened him to an understanding of the social world he occupied, and to the political facts of that world.

Second, writing is social because it calls forth an imagined community. Nearly all (but not all) writing is directed at a reader.[22] When I sit, alone in a room with a pen and a piece of paper, my writing necessarily conjures an audience. When I write, I do it because I am motivated by the idea that people might read it, even if the audience is only myself in some future between five minutes and fifty years from now. I want to uncover what I think in order that I might remember what I once thought. And sometimes when I write, even when I expect that the writing is for myself, other people begin to

[21] Iris Murdoch argued that learning to see was the center of moral life. "We cease to be in order to attend to the existence of something else, a natural object, a person in need." Iris Murdoch, *The Sovereignty of Good* (New York: Routledge, 2001), 58.

[22] There is an important exception here, of writing that is intended as meditation or thinking for the author without the intention of its ever being read again, even by the author. One famous example of this practice comes from Julia Cameron, who encourages artists experiencing blocks to fill three letter-sized sheets with words each morning before doing anything else and then never to read them again. It's a practice she called "morning pages." Julia Cameron *The Artist's Way: 25th Anniversary Edition* (New York, NY: TarcherPerigee, 2016). The constraint that even the author never reads the pages again is particularly stringent, and that constraint is aimed at a particular purpose, which is to prohibit every editing voice that might interfere with the writing. Notice, though, that even in this seemingly hyper-solitary practice, "voice" is a feature of sociality. The practice of not allowing writing to be read is a way of avoiding one of writing's (negative) social features – it can call up demons.

listen in. They become auditors to my writing without my willing them there. They creep into the social setting of my writing. If they are friendly, it loosens the prose and makes me better able to express my thoughts. If they are hostile, my writing freezes under the anticipation of their objections. Whether or not the audience I have in mind ever actually sees my writing, their presence in the room means that the form itself is sociable, in that it is directed outward at an audience.

Third, writing is sociable when it actually meets an audience of readers, even if that audience is only one. In such cases, similarly to when a writer writes alone, a reader sits alone with a text in her hands, but in encountering the text, she populates a world – whether of narrative, physical description, or concepts and their relations. Readers use books to enter relationships with authors, characters, and ideas.

Fourth, in some special cases, readers gather together across space and time into a community of interpretation around a text. Not all writing does this, indeed most writing does not do anything close, but there are some pieces of writing that come to function as a central part of life within particular communities. Here, the most vivid cases are texts that function as scripture in religious traditions. Of course there are much less dramatic examples, as when a new novel captures the attention of many of my friends and we all talk about it together. I use the term scripture here to refer to the central function a text can come to serve for some sociologically particular community. I have in mind, for instance, the Constitution of the United States for US residents, John Milton's *Paradise Lost* for the generations of authors in English who came after him, and also, of course, texts commonly referred to as scriptures like the New and Old Testaments for Christians.

There are other ways of describing what makes a text belong to the strange generic category we call scripture.

Stanley Cavell writes that in *Walden*, Thoreau is aiming to write a scripture. "This writer is writing a sacred text."[23] Cavell suggests this feature of Thoreau's ambition commits Thoreau to the claim that *Walden* has been revealed; commits him to a form that encompasses creation, fall, judgment, and redemption; and commits him to creating a text that can be read on multiple levels.[24] Cavell does not point out how Thoreau's ambition to write scripture relates to Thoreau's investment in the sociality and politics of writing. Cavell's interests in religion are often more formal than practical. But my way of thinking about the sense in which *Walden* is a scripture is related to social and political traditions.

Walden functions as scripture by having established a tradition of readers around it. On this understanding, what makes a text a scripture is its actually calling together a community of readers, not in a disconnected spiritual way, but in a more concrete embodied way, which is to say, often in an institutional or ritual or otherwise practical way. A scripture is a text that establishes a tradition of readers and interpreters, a text that pulls readers together into the same spaces, that enables a community to grow up among them. In this sense, I take *Walden* to have achieved its ambition to become a scripture. It has established a tradition of interpretation and institutions in which that tradition lives.[25]

Thoreau's writing was thus social in the first way I described; it was a practice oriented toward bringing the self into relation. It was social in the second way; it was directed at a community of readers. It was social in the third way; it found a home among readers. And it is social in this fourth way; it in fact, in history, established a community of

[23] Cavell, 14. [24] Cavell, 15.
[25] One way to begin to think about the sociological reality of the institutions that *Walden* helped to build is Maynard, *Walden Pond*.

readers and institutions through which those readers enact their relation to the text and one another, often without reading it at all.

Some readers of *Thoreau's Religion* have wondered if the social life I described in Walden Woods in Chapter 1 stretches the significance of "society" so far as to render it meaningless. The society I described in Chapter 1 might seem to lack key features of social life that most people think of as integral to it, especially (1) institutions that persist through time and (2) certain important forms of mutuality and reciprocity. Similarly, the previous section on the sociality of writing might make a reader wonder. What kind of society is this? Maybe it seems to be mostly a rather interior one. Or, since much of the sociality I described in the previous section was abstracted from living persons, it seems disengaged from contemporary life. Thoreau's relationships with pine trees and chickadees and books and dead people and writing and readers may be social, but if those relationships lack reciprocity, then they might not be particularly good models of sociality for political life. For relationships and societies to flourish, this view would suggest, the parties to the relationships must have the capacity to hold one another accountable. The pine tree doesn't talk back, and that might mean that the model of Thoreau's society doesn't serve political life well.

But being held accountable in this way is only ever achieved by people who have the capacity to attend to others who are attempting to hold them to account. This was the point of Thoreau's positive practices in the woods that were aimed at coming to actually understand the voices of the chickadees and the trees and the frogs and the woodchopper and the generation who had occupied the woods before him. Such practices are not self-indulgent. They are the beginning of any relationship at all.

In *Writing Nature*, Sharon Cameron argues that Thoreau's daily, descriptive writing practice grew more and more important to him as his life went on. Thoreau's writing of his meditations on nature in the *Journal* convinced him that its form would be his greatest literary achievement. In the *Journal*, Cameron argues, Thoreau enacted a radically descriptive project. More and more through the course of his life, Thoreau refused to interpret "the observations recorded, as if the significance of the description of a tree were the description of that tree."[26] Cameron takes this as a sign that Thoreau's descriptions are efforts at establishing relation to that which is described. Cameron writes, "He records nature as if to remember it, and also suggests that what is crucial in nature is not in fact memorable, the reason to record it is not to recall it but to establish a relation to it, with record and relation synonymous with each other."[27] The act of descriptive writing is not oriented toward the recollection of the facts recorded, but recording those facts establishes relation between author and object.

Thoreau's writing practice insisted on establishing relation via attention and it was the central ethical practice of his life in Walden Woods. It was the exercise through which he sought to become the kind of person who could see things as they are, which is the beginning of relating to them rightly. Descriptive writing of the kind Cameron marks was, for Thoreau, an ethical practice that was the beginning of justice. Only persons formed to attend to what relationships are can then be capable of setting them right. Thoreau thought knowing what is was the beginning of ethics. His writing practice was oriented toward his own individual virtuous living. In addition, his seemingly contemplative practice of writing enabled him to

[26] Cameron, *Writing Nature*, 5. [27] Cameron, 148.

publish a book that contributed to a tradition of justice-seeking. Writing was a major part of Thoreau's political asceticism. It was ascetic because it was enabled by renunciation and other disciplined practices. It was political because it was social and justice-seeking.

Awakening for Politics

The tradition of justice-seeking that Thoreau helped to establish pushes back against a false binary I worry afflicts much public discourse about contemporary environmental politics, in which personal practices are criticized as inconsequential, and top-down politics is criticized as impossibly ambitious. In Thoreau's telling, personal, ascetic practices like writing or bean-hoeing are what enable people to transform themselves, and the self and the relationships they develop are the beginning of all politics.

One of Thoreau's main metaphors in *Walden* for the personal transformation that ascetic practice ought to instantiate was awakening. Awakening is, in Thoreau's account of it, a kind of being healed because renewed. It is a spiritual transformation and it is oriented toward the renunciation of domination. And the quintessential expression of the importance he places on it comes in a few pages at the center of "Where I Lived and What I Lived for" that begin thus:

> Every morning was a cheerful invitation to make my life of equal simplicity, and I may say innocence, with Nature herself. I have been as sincere a worshipper of Aurora as the Greeks. I got up early and bathed in the pond; that was a religious exercise, and one of the best things which I did.
>
> (II, 14)

This description of awakening as a religious exercise begins one of the longest meditations in *Walden* on waking up, and one of the central passages for understanding Thoreau's relationship to labor not only as self-reliance for its own sake but also for the renewal it allows of self and community. The passage describes what I take to be Thoreau's cardinal ethical mandate: "wake up."

> That man who does not believe that each day contains an earlier, more sacred, and auroral hour than he has yet profaned, has despaired of life, and is pursuing a descending and darkening way... It matters not what the clocks say or the attitudes and labors of men. Morning is when I am awake and there is a dawn in me. Moral reform is the effort to throw off sleep... To be awake is to be alive. I have never yet met a man who was quite awake. How could I have looked him in the face?
>
> (II, 14)

Thoreau takes it that this attitude to awakening – that we can always do it more, earlier, that it is never fully accomplished – is a religious pursuit.

To emphasize the point, Thoreau alludes to a story from Exodus 33:18–23 when God shows himself to Moses while Moses hides in the cleft of a rock. The Bible quotes God: "Thou canst not see my face: for there shall no man see me, and live." Because no one can see God's face and live, God protects Moses by only showing him his back. By way of the allusion, Thoreau suggests that the man who is fully awake is awesome like God: you cannot look on his face and live. Awakening is a kind of growth in spiritual power.

Elsewhere, Thoreau reiterates the necessity of continuous renewal. The epigraph of Stanley Cavell's *The Senses of Walden* invokes the use Thoreau makes of his daily bathing as a religious symbol when it quotes Luther:

> For all our life should be baptism, and the fulfilling of the sign, or sacrament, of baptism; we have been set free from all else and wholly given over to baptism alone, that is, to death and

> resurrection. This glorious liberty of ours, and this understanding of baptism have been carried captive in our day.[28]

Thoreau's morning bath is a daily reminder to wake up to his freedom, to "do it again, and again, and forever again." Here, as elsewhere in *The Senses of Walden*, Cavell emphasizes Thoreau as an interpreter of Christianity.

> We have heard it said, "We shall all stand before the judgment seat of Christ. . .every tongue shall confess to God. So then, every one shall give account of himself to God" (Romans 14:10–13). But *Walden* shows that we are there; every tongue has confessed what it can; we have heard everything there is to hear. There were prophets, but there is no Zion; knowing that, Jesus fulfilled them, but the kingdom of heaven is not entered into; knowing that, the Founding Fathers brought both testaments to this soil, and there is no America; knowing that, Jonathan Edwards helped bring forth a Great Awakening, and we are not awake.[29]

According to Cavell, Thoreau sees Christianity as a long story of disappointments and fulfillments, deaths and resurrections. In Thoreau's moment, that story calls each person to a true awakening.

Readings of *Walden* like Cavell's emphasize its focus on individual awakening. But this emphasis sometimes leads to neglect of the sense in which the awakening Thoreau called for was aimed at justice oriented by common goods. *Walden* called not only for individual awakening but also for liberating one another. The pages on awakening in *Walden* culminate in a key passage, one Jeffrey Stout has interpreted in the context of attempts at contemporary democratic reform. The text in *Walden* is about the railroad, which was being built through the woods when Thoreau lived there. In the passage, Thoreau crafts a metaphor from the structure of the railway.

[28] Cavell, *The Senses of Walden*. [29] Cavell, 29.

As the railway is built, the rails are laid over the wooden railroad ties. In the passage Thoreau refers to the railway ties in the British usage as "sleepers."

> We do not ride on the railroad; it rides upon us. Did you ever think what those sleepers are that underlie the railroad? Each one is a man, an Irishman, or a Yankee man ... I am glad to know that it takes a gang of men for every five miles to keep the sleepers down and level in their beds as it is, for this is a sign that they may sometime get up again.
>
> (II, 17)

The railroad is built on the backs of the men who labor on it, and in that sense is another form of labor injustice. Thoreau is also crafting a larger image for the Northern economy. In Stout's interpretation, the image is about "the dependence of the ruling elites on the deference of ordinary people."[30] The passage suggests that in the condition of domination, those who are dominated have powers they often have trouble recognizing. Even entirely prone, as the sleepers, ridden upon by the industrial economy, they have the power to withdraw their deference. This is why the gang of five men is required to keep them down.

Stout suggests *Walden* was asking its readers to get up. Thoreau was trying to help readers see their circumstances, to understand the ways in which they were both more prone and more free than they took themselves to be, and thus to encourage them to stop deferring to the powers that dominated them. Stout writes, "Thoreau is suggesting that there is ground for social hope in the nature of dependence. The system would have to change if the sleepers woke up and rose up together."[31] Such an act would require individual self-

[30] Jeffrey Stout, *Blessed Are the Organized: Grassroots Democracy in America* (Princeton, NJ: Princeton University Press, 2010), 278.

[31] Stout, 280.

transformation, as the sleepers practice refusing the deference to domination they have so deeply, so habitually learned. It would also require group collaboration to ensure they do not rise alone. Rising alone would be self-defeating for both the individual, whom Thoreau describes getting run over by the railcar if he acts alone, and the sleepers together, because there is no "together" if each one dies alone.

The passage on the sleepers suggests that the sleepers must rise together or be run over by the railroad. But it does not say that much about the collaboration that would be required to enable them to do so. My interpretation of Thoreau's life in Walden Woods suggests that the sociality of Thoreau's writing itself is part of his answer to that question about collaboration. In Chapter 1 I described a scene Thoreau recorded in his journal that I take as an icon of the sociality and politics he discovered there and through his writing tried to express in *Walden*. The scene happened one day when he and Alek Therien were in the woods and a chickadee landed on some firewood that Thoreau was holding. Thoreau wrote of the chickadee who landed among them, "it looked me familiarly in the face." I interpreted that scene as an interspecies moment of sociality in which the community of Walden Woods is clearly expressed.

I also began to suggest that Thoreau's writing of *Walden* functions in a way that is similar to the chickadee's mobbing calls. One thing a chickadee sometimes does when it calls is to notify other birds within hearing that there is a predator. Calls like this can encode a tremendous variety of information about the nature of a threat, such as its size and the direction from which it is approaching. They call out to let other birds know about the predator and to seek their help. If other birds hear, they flock to the caller's defense, and the group of birds that assemble is described as exhibiting mobbing behavior. The mob harasses the predator until the predator gives up and leaves, no longer posing a threat to the flock.

My interpretation of *Walden* suggests that Thoreau thought writing might be like the call of the chickadee, in that it could serve a similar function with respect to the threats he saw to human flourishing in Concord. In response to the punishing economic conditions he described in the first pages of the book, the "trouble and anxiety," that his townsmen suffered, he wanted to write. His desire to write could seem a strange response to oppressive economic conditions. How ascetic practices such as writing ought to help ameliorate unjust politics and economic conditions is not always clear. But Thoreau thought he might be like the chickadee and his writing might be like the chickadee's call: Can you hear me? Will you join me? This kind of collaboration, the call and response of the chickadee mob, is an image for how the sleepers might rise together. They cannot rise together without hearing a call.

My account of Thoreau suggests that the awakening of the sleepers would require that the sleepers renounce the advantages they receive from the system that dominates them. This is why practices of renunciation are important to him. But it would also require that their asceticism cultivates the forms of social, political, and spiritual life that will replace the system that dominates them.

Thoreau's insistence on the need for perpetual awakening is also an answer to the problems with environmental politics that I began to identify earlier. As contemporary citizens with environmental concern, we are wondering where to direct our finite energies toward the amelioration of a political situation that often seems intractable. And too often, our discussions of these matters fall into a binary I find troubling, one in which my choice is between small-scale community activities (that are ineffectual for massive problems such as climate change) and larger-scale political ambitions (that seem too far out of reach). But this bifurcated narrative is part of the political problem we face. "The rich and the lucky *benefit* from making large-scale democratic reform *appear* hopeless. Paradoxically, they also benefit from making large-scale change seem *easily* achievable, for example, by casting a vote every four years for a candidate who promises something called 'change.'"[32] A better future is neither secure nor out of reach. It depends on each of us aiming to get better ourselves and collaborate with others on the reform of our communities in the ways that our gifts and our situation allows.

Thoreau insisted that each of us is called to an incessant practice of awakening as freedom-seeking. But he situated those individual efforts within a broader context. He did not view them as separate. He was attentive to matters of position and scale in Walden Woods – whether about the self as the center as I discussed in Chapter 1 or about the doubleness of perspective made possible with the shift of attention from the stream to the sky that I discussed in the previous section. His integration of personal practice with his own activism and his thinking about larger-scale questions of political theory and practice ought to help us tell a different story about our politics. Personal practice is not a distraction from large-scale transformation. It is essential to it. We cannot have one without the other, because humans are social creatures, situated in contexts. Political asceticism consists in the practices that enable persons to cultivate their own transformation and contribute to the transformation of their communities.

Like the first chapter of *Walden*, the "Conclusion" argues that though Thoreau's neighbors' lives are lived with too

[32] Stout, 278.

much haste, they could be otherwise. "Why should we be in such desperate haste to succeed, and in such desperate enterprises?" it asks (XVIII, 10). There is an alternative to this life of trouble and anxiety, and it is the renewal of life, a form of spiritual awakening. The chapter suggests that one of the most important practices for spiritual awakening is the cultivation of poverty, the voluntary poverty of the beginning of the book.[33] "Cultivate poverty like a garden herb, like sage" (XVIII, 13). This is important because it will change our view of what goodness is.

> How long shall we sit in our porticoes practising idle and musty virtues, which any work would make impertinent. As if one were to begin the day with long-suffering, and hire a man to hoe his potatoes; and in the afternoon go forth to practise Christian meekness and charity with goodness aforethought!
>
> (XVIII, 16)

The sort of practices that Thoreau thinks are necessary in poverty, especially those required for food, shelter, and clothing (in an economy still largely focused on agriculture), should change what practitioners think is true Christian meekness and charity. Such practices change the very meaning of the words we use to describe them. "In proportion as he simplifies his life, the laws of the universe will appear less complex, and solitude will not be solitude, nor poverty poverty, nor weakness weakness" (XVIII, 5). They also conduce to a life like the one Thoreau had represented in the middle of book: a life of piety, wonder, praise, and delight.

[33] Buell has written about Thoreau as a central figure in a broader American tradition of voluntary simplicity. He does not emphasize the *reasons* Thoreau had for withdrawing from standard economic practices – specifically that they were unjust. Lawrence Buell, "Downwardly Mobile for Conscience's Sake: Voluntary Simplicity from Thoreau to Lily Bart," *American Literary History* 17, 4 (2005): 653–65.

Thoreau's Religion

Thoreau is usually taken to be so religiously eccentric as to be irreligious.[34] This is a mistake. Thoreau wrote once about himself that he was "a mystic—a transcendentalist—& a natural philosopher to boot."[35] There have been many studies of what it meant for Thoreau to be a Transcendentalist, and about what natural philosophy was and became in his practice. But our understanding of what kind of mystic he imagined himself to be is still nascent. Alan Hodder's excellent study *Thoreau's Ecstatic Witness* began this work, by insisting on the mystical features of Thoreau's life and work.[36] But like many studies of mystics, Hodder's account focuses quite narrowly on the ecstasies.[37]

[34] There are of course exceptions to this generalization in the secondary literature on Thoreau across disciplines. One is Terrance Wiley, who insists that "we must take seriously Thoreau's religion." In addition, Wiley's paragraphs on asceticism in Thoreau paved the way for my own interpretation. "Asceticism rests near the heart of Thoreau's ethics." Wiley, *Angelic Troublemakers*, chapter 1. Wiley suggests that asceticism is politically important because of how it forms the practitioner. We are agreed about that. But I suggest that Thoreau's asceticism is also politically engaged before the practitioner returns to society – he participates in the political life of his community by withdrawing from it and cultivating an alternative.

[35] Henry David Thoreau, *Journal*, Volume 5: *1852–1853*, ed. Patrick F. O'Connell (Princeton, N.J: Princeton University Press, 1997), 469.

[36] Hodder, *Thoreau's Ecstatic Witness*.

[37] "Religion was for him essentially a private concern, turning on moments of communion or, in a word he sometimes invokes in his journals, 'ecstasy,' to which he was apparently prone in the course of his daily rambles in the countryside around Concord." Alan D. Hodder, "The Religious Horizon," in *Henry David Thoreau in Context*, ed. James S. Finley (New York: Cambridge University Press, 2017), 79. Those who study Thoreau in the field of religion and ecology and who take him to be an early example of pagan or pantheist spirituality among modern nature religions also tend to focus on his beliefs and religious experiences over and against his disciplined practices. Bron Taylor's *Dark Green Religion*, for example, takes Thoreau as "an early expression of dark green religion, perhaps the earliest that can be clearly identified in American literature." But Taylor's interpretation of Thoreau's religion is focused almost exclusively on his religious beliefs. Taylor,

Mysticism studied apart from the ascetic life in which it is so often practiced can give a false impression of its practitioners. We have received images of them rapt in reveries. In fact, these images have stuck even to figures who were adamant religious reformers, specifically of an economic sort.[38] They usually spent a large portion of their days doing manual labor. The study of mysticism apart from the ascetic life has left the impression that Weber made famous, that ascetics are otherworldly, more focused on their spiritual lives than on the here and now.[39]

The problem with this story is that it imports contemporary assumptions about household economy that would have been completely foreign until the mid-twentieth century, when industrialization reached its peak in Western nations. Before the mechanistic household innovations upon which many contemporary societies have come to rely, there was no such thing as otherworldly in the sense we now have it. Those religious communities that did have money with which to hire out the labor required for their households would have gotten

Dark Green Religion, 50–58. There is one minor exception in the appendix, where Taylor collects the texts from Thoreau's writings that he takes to be important for the interpretation of Thoreau's religious views about nature. There Taylor comments briefly that, "Religion is about more than belief – it is about practice – and here Thoreau made an astute observation about the religious dimensions of some of his daily nature-related rites." Taylor, 237.

[38] I have in mind here especially Francis of Assisi and Teresa of Avila. Hamilton, "The Politics of Poverty"; Balthrop-Lewis, "Exemplarist Environmental Ethics: Thoreau's Political Asceticism against Solution Thinking"; Jodi Bilinkoff, *The Avila of Saint Teresa: Religious Reform in a Sixteenth-Century City*, 2nd ed. (Ithaca, NY: Cornell University Press, 2015).

[39] With respect to Max Weber, there is of course a vast literature. I am referring here to his descriptions of asceticism in *Economy and Society*, e.g., "From the point of view of the basic values of asceticism, the world as a whole continues to constitute a *massa perditionis*." Max Weber, *Economy and Society: An Outline of Interpretive Sociology* (Berkeley, CA: University of California Press, 1978), 543.

that money from the communities in which they lived. Indeed, Teresa's discalced communities were a response against what she and her fellow Carmelites viewed as the excesses of religious life in which the religious community took from surrounding lay families in order to support its own mystic reveries. Teresa was criticized and nearly forced out of the Church for saying that religious communities should be economically self-sufficient, that is, that they needed to do the labor their own lives required, rather than living on the charity of the lay community around them.

Like those medieval monastic reform movements, which were oriented by Jesus's radical economic message, Thoreau's asceticism was not merely mystical. Hodder has admirably shown the extent of Thoreau's religious life, where many interpreters have simply ignored his thinking about religion. But in focusing on the ecstasies to the neglect of the labor, he perpetuates what is a widespread problem in the study of religion, that we limit the religious lives of our subjects to texts and prayerful practice, but fail to describe the ways in which those texts and prayerful practices have bearing on day-to-day realities, or on economic and political life. Hodder writes,

> If a reading of Thoreau's journals convinces us of anything, it is that his "religiousness" had less to do with what he at any given moment believed and much more to do with what he perceived and felt in the fluctuating ebb and flow of this inward experience. Religion for him was an affair of the heart, an interior matter—intuitional and sensual, rather than propositional.[40]

Hodder is right, as far as he goes here. Thoreau was far less concerned with propositional religious life than he was with experience. But to say that his religious experience was

[40] Hodder, *Thoreau's Ecstatic Witness*, 36.

inward, that religion was an interior matter, participates in the quarantining of religion to the private and the personal, a realm that the relational Thoreau I am trying to uncover would not have recognized. Religion was never so tidy, and when we make it seem like it was, we are merely unearthing our own orthodoxies.

For Thoreau, "religion" was not only interior; it was a category with bearing on the political and economic realities of his time. "Religion" was a feature of human life that need not be associated with any particular tradition. It was the binding that tied people to whatever they were bound – in the best instances to society (in the good sense), to what was "sacred," to "virtue," to "divinity," and to "spirit," but also sometimes to fashion or vice, or just mundane life – in my favorite example to the cultivation of leaven for bread. "Leaven, which some deem the soul of bread, the *spiritus* which fills its cellular tissue, which is religiously preserved like the vestal fire ... this seed I regularly and faithfully procured from the village" (I, 85). Often, his favorite examples of right practice come from Roman religion.

> I would that our farmers when they cut down a forest felt some of that awe which the old Romans did when they came to thin, or let in the light to, a consecrated grove (*lucum conlucare*), that is, would believe that it is sacred to some god. The Roman made an expiatory offering, and prayed, Whatever god or goddess thou art to whom this grove is sacred, be propitious to me, my family, and children, etc.

Thoreau often recommends forms of religious practice drawn from particular traditions, as here. But for Thoreau "religion" is not associated strictly with Christianity or Hinduism or Roman religion in particular, not with "religions." "World religions" was an idea invented after him. Rather "religion" has three key senses.

1. In the good sense, he associates "religion" with moral categories, with virtuous living – reverence, blessing, devotion, holiness, sincerity, humility, faith, truth, simplicity, innocence, worship, piety – and with what is sacred.
2. In the ambivalent sense, he associates "religion" with habitual, committed patterns, be they good or bad.
3. And in the bad sense, Thoreau associates "religion" with attachment to those things that keep us from the good.

Thus, understanding Thoreau's appeal to religion rests fundamentally on our capacity to discern the normative judgments he is implying in each use of the term. He uses it in all of these ways, and he saw his own ascetic practice as a version of religion in the first sense.

With this polyvalent, normatively laden understanding of "religion" in mind, it is easier to understand how Thoreau considered himself a religious (in the good sense) practioner, despite his objections to religion (in the bad sense). Ethyl Seybold's 1951 *Thoreau: The Quest and the Classics* details Thoreau's deep knowledge of the classical authors that helped form Thoreau's view of philosophy. The "quest" of Seybold's title was, in her account, a religious vocation. She writes,

> Why should not a man's faith determine his work? Newspaper editors might think John Brown insane because he believed himself divinely appointed for his work, but, [quoting Thoreau] "They talk as if it were impossible that a man could be 'divinely appointed' in these days to do any work whatever; as if vows and religion were out of date as connected with any man's daily work..."

Here, Seybold quotes from "A Plea for Captain John Brown" and in doing so implies that Thoreau too had his own single-minded religious vocation. "He [Thoreau] was that rare phenomenon, a practitioner of his faith."[41]

[41] Ethel Seybold, *Thoreau: The Quest and the Classics*, Yale Studies in English 116 (New Haven, CT: Yale University Press, 1951), 6.

This fact, she thinks, may make us wonder about Thoreau's sanity. "One of the reasons we have been slow to admit the truth about Thoreau is that it seems to us the equivalent of calling him 'insane.'"[42] Seybold's point was that readers had tended to ignore the depth of Thoreau's religious practice and vocation, "as if vows and religion were out of date as connected with any man's daily work." She wanted to show the ways in which his life was the practice of his faith. Like John Brown, that faith was not merely private, or individual, though the practice of contemplation and the experience of ecstasy was important to him. Thoreau's religion was also tied to daily work and other practice, and through this daily practice, to broader social and political life.

Conclusion

"Political asceticism" became a key term for me because it enabled me to succinctly name something important that seemed to be missing from discussions of ascetic practice broadly and from two different common modes of appeal to Thoreau's life and work. On the one hand, there were interpreters who look to him as a spiritual exemplar for a kind of nature piety, or a model of what came to be called "nature writing," or an icon for environmentalism. These interpreters often seemed to neglect the radical economic critique that sprang from Thoreau's nature piety. On the other hand, there were interpreters who were attracted to Thoreau's political and economic critique. But they sometimes failed to articulate how Thoreau's convictions about politics and economics entailed a view of nature and the human within it as sacred. Both groups seemed to minimize the sense in which Thoreau

[42] Seybold, 7.

saw commitment to personal religious practice as vital to doing justice. When I read *Walden*, it seems to me that Thoreau's personal piety leads him to a practice that is both contemplative and actively aimed at doing justice. Political asceticism is the name I discovered for this practice.

At the same time, "political asceticism" as an idea seemed to be an effective way to intervene in some of the most interesting conversations currently ongoing in theology, religious ethics, and philosophy of religion about the significance and import of theological ideas and practices of renunciation, sacrifice, contemplation, mysticism and other associated terms. Thoreau's political asceticism adds a decidedly practical bent to conversations on those topics in those fields. Where many scholars have been interested recently in the forms of politics associated with these practices, it seemed to me that the particularities of Thoreau's economic life in Walden Woods could offer an interesting case study in just how ascetic practice can contribute to flourishing social life and political transformation.

Through the course of this work I have discovered scholars across the study of religion who find that thinking about political asceticism with respect to their own subjects helps them to articulate features of their subjects that usually get lost. I hope my work on Thoreau can contribute to and help to carry forward a much longer, larger conversation about the political and economic salience of religious practices that are too often described apart from the political and economic contexts to which they are responding.

I have also found that "political asceticism" has power as a key term within contemporary environmental politics. There, it can serve as a useful idea for people who are struggling to discern their own responsibilities in the context of climate change and other forms of environmental trouble. Many of the things individuals have power over – conceiving children, travel modes and patterns, managing household waste, sourcing food, and engaging as consumers and citizens with business and government – involve forms of individual renunciation, giving up some goods in pursuit of others. These are not easy matters, and you should never trust someone who pretends that they are. But you can take heart, I think, that even the most seemingly lonely practices – as, for instance, sitting alone in a room, writing, as I am now, or reading, as you are – contribute to the forms of society and politics that are to come. Your job is to discern which of your individual practices contributes best to your community and to the reform of the political bodies to which your community belongs.

This chapter has argued that Thoreau's life in Walden Woods was an example of political asceticism, by which I mean disciplined practice, often of renunciation, oriented toward better things, including enacting just social and political life. Thoreau worried that the ascetic practice of his townsmen, the strain of their economic lives, was bad for them. The economic models premised on debt and profit in which they were caught up were too harsh; those practices undermined the finest qualities of the townsmen's natures. Participating in those practices, the townsmen sacrificed better things for worse things. Thoreau knew about what they suffered because his sight had been "whetted by experience."

Thoreau had some ideas about how his townsmen (and he) might live better, by which he meant they could live tenderer economic lives oriented by true human goods. He wanted them to be able to work one day a week and take leisure for six rather than the other way around, as he described in his Harvard commencement address.[43] He wanted this both because it would be better for them and because he thought it would undermine the unjust economies by which they were

[43] Walls, *Thoreau*, 81.

being dominated. He went to Walden to see if it was possible. There, he practiced what I have called political asceticism. When he found that it *was* possible, he wrote *Walden* to persuade the townsmen that it was. Writing was a practice that political asceticism enabled; it helped make Thoreau into a person who could see relationships rightly; it persuaded him that the transformation of political life was one of his vocations; and it was the tool that he used to transform the politics of his time and our own.

5

Delight in True Goods

Philosophers are broken-down poets.

Thoreau, as quoted in Emerson's journal, September 1845[1]

At the end of Chapter 2, I suggested that Thoreau's rhetorical posture in *Walden* – especially the long, narrative, descriptive, middle of the book – was guided by his conviction that persuasion requires a seduction to the good. This may have been a conviction he acquired early, in his dissatisfaction with the philosophy of education in which he was tutored at Harvard and which he was encouraged to pursue in his short, ten-day career as a school teacher at Concord's Center Grammar School. He had good reason to think that the political and economic views he was advancing would fail to persuade if they were presented merely as a logical argument.[2] Thoreau did not think that human hearts turn on the basis of logical argumentation. He wrote *Walden* under the force of a different anthropology, one in which what turned human hearts toward anything was their enjoyment of the good in it. This chapter is about enjoyment of true goods, and why Thoreau's insight on this point is important for contemporary environmental action.

[1] Ralph Waldo Emerson, *Journals of Ralph Waldo Emerson, with Annotations*, vol. 7 (New York: Houghton Mifflin company, 1914), 99.

[2] He may also have noted the unhappy reception of Orestes Brownson's *Laboring Classes* and hoped to deliver a similar message in a more seductive package. I thank Laura Dassow Walls for conversation on this point.

In Chapter 4, I suggested that Thoreau's writing practice, the hours he spent writing those long, descriptive passages, was part of a moral practice of attention through which he cultivated his own capacity to relate rightly to a vast network of others – human, vegetable, mineral, past, and present. Before it was aimed at persuasion, Thoreau's writing was aimed at his own moral education. It was a kind of being tutored in appreciation for God's good world.

These insights about persuasion through seduction to the good and about the practice of attention required to see truly are among Thoreau's most powerful contributions to contemporary thinking about environmental ethics, as I discuss further in this chapter and the Conclusion. In this chapter, I focus on Thoreau's good humor and appreciation of true goods in part because asceticism often sounds so dour, and in part as a response to the difficulty of contemporary environmental politics. In current political settings, anger, frustration, and disappointment are all too often appropriate responses to the failures of Western nation states to take responsibility for environmental harm.[3] In this situation, it is of course important to name our disappointments and seek to rectify the injustices that cause our anger. It is also important to continue to practice – as Thoreau did in the woods – our capacity to recognize true goods and enjoy them.[4] This

[3] I do not mean to suggest in this chapter that negative affect should be avoided. I believe such affects are deeply important to contemporary politics. Interesting recent work on the importance of negative affect includes Joseph R. Winters, *Hope Draped in Black: Race, Melancholy, and the Agony of Progress* (Durham, NC: Duke University Press Books, 2016); Karen Bray, *Grave Attending: A Political Theology for the Unredeemed* (New York: Fordham University Press, 2019). The epilogue to *Thoreau's Religion*, "On Mourning," aims to acknowledge one way in which negative affect is essential to right relation to the world.

[4] E. B. White's beautiful essay on *Walden* suggests that these two impulses are at war in the Thoreau of *Walden*. "'Walden' is the report of a man torn by two powerful and opposing drives – the desire to enjoy the world (and not be derailed by a

chapter investigates Thoreau's good humor and enjoyment to see what might be in them for us.

Thoreau evidently knew enough about the history of Christian monasticism to make a few jokes about it in *Walden.*[5] These jokes pose an interesting question of interpretation, and one that no interpreter of *Walden* can avoid. How should we think about Thoreau's playful writing?[6] Thoreau's friend Ellery Channing wrote a biography of Thoreau; the epigraph to its first chapter read, "'Wit is the Soul's powder.' – Davenant."[7] Thoreau's sense of irony and humor run deep in his writing, and readers ought to wonder what to make of them. The specific case of those joking references to medieval Christianity is not only an important subject in the study of Thoreau's asceticism, but also an excellent test case for our reading of Thoreau's ironic spirit more broadly. Should we take those jokes as playful endorsements of the figures they poke fun at? Or are they dismissive jabs?

mosquito wing) and the urge to set the world straight." E. B. White, "Walden - 1954," in *Walden, Civil Disobedience, and Other Writings*, ed. William John Rossi, 3rd ed. (New York: Norton, 2008), 446. *Thoreau's Religion* aims to unify these drives by saying that Thoreau's enjoyment was not of "the world" but of truly good things. Thoreau thought that in order to enjoy such things rightly, you must at the same time be setting right the relationships in which they are caught up, which is to say, setting the world straight.

[5] I briefly mention these jokes in the Introduction (21–22). One example is when Thoreau writes of a neighbor, "he belonged to the ancient sect of Coenobites" (IX, 2). The description is also a pun. The man he describes turns out not to be a very good fisherman, thus see-no-bite.

[6] Richard Rorty said it was Plato's jokes that made him so interesting. "The permanent fascination of the man who dreamed up the whole idea of Western philosophy – Plato – is that we still do not know which sort of philosopher he was. Even if the *Seventh Letter* is set aside as spurious, the fact that after millenniums of commentary nobody knows which passages in the dialogues are jokes keeps the puzzle fresh." Richard Rorty, *Philosophy and the Mirror of Nature* (Princeton University Press, 1980), 369 n15.

[7] William Ellery Channing, *Thoreau: The Poet-Naturalist: With Memorial Verses* (Boston, MA: Roberts Brothers, 1873), 1.

Another early biography, that of Edward Emerson, suggested that readers often mistook Thoreau's jokes for earnestness, because readers had not met him in person and therefore didn't understand him. "Thoreau had the humour which often goes with humanity. It crops out slyly in all his writings, but sometimes is taken for dead earnest because the reader did not know the man."[8]

The extent of Thoreau's humor is a key question in the interpretation of Thoreau's ascetic practice because readers have not always seen Thoreau's simplicity as salutary. Many critics have viewed him as promoting a form of selfish American individualism, a pull-yourself-up-by-your-bootstraps Protestant Ethic, while also not really living up to it – his mother did his laundry, right? This view often coincides with an interpretation of Thoreau as lacking all humor. Robert Louis Stevenson was an early critic of Thoreau in this vein. He wrote in 1880 what would become a standard critique. Among Stevenson's complaints about Thoreau was that he didn't know how to enjoy life. Stevenson wrote, "his enjoyment was hardly smiling, or the smile was not broad enough to be convincing."[9] Stevenson himself came around (especially after learning the full extent of Thoreau's aid to enslaved people on the run). But Stevenson's view has been popular enough for long enough that a 2015 takedown of Thoreau in the *New Yorker* was incredulous that he has become an American hero. His abstinence was a particular affront to that author. Kathryn Schulz wrote, "I cannot idolize anyone who opposes coffee."[10] Of course, as Schulz neglected to mention, avoiding coffee was a popular practice among

[8] Emerson, *Henry Thoreau: As Remembered by a Young Friend*, 85.

[9] Robert Louis Stevenson, "Henry David Thoreau: His Character and Opinions," *The Cornhill Magazine* 41, 246 (June 1880): 665.

[10] Kathryn Schulz, "Pond Scum," *The New Yorker*, October 19, 2015, www.newyorker.com/magazine/2015/10/19/pond-scum (accessed August 21, 2020).

abolitionists, who worried that their own consumption would support slave labor. A reader wonders if Schulz can idolize anyone who avoids clothing produced in sweat shops. But for many critics, Thoreau's ethical rationale doesn't excuse his overzealous rejection of pleasure; they maintain that Thoreau was a dour naysayer who didn't know how to enjoy the good.

Thoreau does sometimes come off as dour in his thoroughgoing rejection of material goods that others enjoy. He wrote in *Walden*, "Most of the luxuries, and many of the so called comforts of life, are not only not indispensable, but positive hinderances to the elevation of mankind" (I, 19). Luxury, and even comfort, was not only unnecessary, and therefore avoidable, but it was also positively harmful. This came out most vividly in the chapter called "Higher Laws," which many readers have read as the apex of Thoreau's preachy rejection. There Thoreau addresses food gathering practices, especially fishing and hunting. He praises vegetarianism, and chastity as a virtue. He writes, "Put an extra condiment into your dish and it will poison you" (XI, 6).

This rejection of comfort and pleasure informed the basic message of *Walden*, which was – as Thoreau put it in its tersest form – simplify, simplify, simplify. This was the key to true philosophy for Thoreau. He sometimes seems to say you can't be good without giving up attachment to the very things you love.

This coincides with a popular view that asceticism consists of deprivation through which the ascetic grows in holiness, and most readers are not people inclined to think deprivation is good. So the suspicion becomes that Thoreau romanticized poverty, which *would be* deeply problematic. Romantic representations of poverty can excuse and even find good in the suffering of others, which is an injustice. In his renunciations, we may suspect Thoreau demonstrates a particular vice of the comfortable. He was never so poor that he had to be truly hungry, and then he recommended meager meals. Those among us who have actually been hungry might take offense.

But asceticism is not unwilled deprivation, which is so often harmful. Many ascetics, and I think Thoreau is among them, have been women and men who renounced money, sensual pleasures, or power not out of self-denial but because they already had more than they needed, and active renunciation enabled them to value rightly and relate justly to the things that remained. Thoreau insisted that the right kind of poverty was "voluntary" after all. As I began to suggest in Chapter 4, this voluntary poverty was not basically a rejection of good things, though it did require some renunciation. It was more basically oriented to the pleasure found *within* renunciation, delight that was made possible in his view *by* the asceticism he practiced.

But still, it seems difficult to hold together the deep earnestness of "Higher Laws" with the scatological humor and other jokes and wordplay that fill the pages of *Walden*.[11] How can we reconcile the one to the other? My sense is that Thoreau thought that writing ought to be both earnest and playful.[12] On the one hand, it was intended to promote a particular theological and ethical view: that simplicity yields appropriate gratitude for God's gifts of life and nature, and gratitude yields praise. This was its earnest message. On the other hand, through his playful style and refusal of dogmatism, Thoreau also acknowledged that praise without play is vacuous, just as work *or* play without praise is empty.

[11] On wordplay specifically, in the broader cultural context, see Michael West, *Transcendental Wordplay: America's Romantic Punsters and the Search for the Language of Nature* (Athens, GA: Ohio University Press, 2000).

[12] William Gleason places Thoreau at the beginning of a period in which the cultural significance of play rose in America and became "the culture's most vital work." William A. Gleason, *The Leisure Ethic: Work and Play in American Literature, 1840–1940* (Stanford, CA: Stanford University Press, 1999), vii.

Higher Laws

"Higher Laws" begins with a scene from everyday life, at least as such life played out in Walden Woods: Thoreau coming home through the woods in the dark. He had been fishing, and he was bringing the fish he had caught with him on a string and carrying his pole. Then, "I caught a glimpse of a woodchuck stealing across my path, and felt a strange thrill of savage delight, and was strongly tempted to seize and devour him raw; not that I was hungry then, except for that wildness which he represented" (XI, 1). The encounter with the woodchuck, who inspires a "savage delight" and "tempted" Thoreau to devour wildness, opens a chapter that treats fishing, hunting, eating, and sensuality broadly.[13]

But the chapter seems to pull in opposite directions. The "savage delight" that was inspired by the woodchuck is held against another pole. "I found in myself, and still find, an instinct toward a higher, or, as it is named, spiritual life, as do most men, and another toward a primitive rank and savage one, and I reverence them both." Thoreau aims to puzzle the reader, by reverencing opposites. The first half of the sentence sets up a comparison, and by using the words "higher" and "spiritual" over against "primitive," "rank," and "savage," aims to tempt the reader to prefer the first. But the sudden end of the sentence, "and I reverence them both," makes clear that

[13] Peter Coviello takes the "savage delight" of this passage as the opening of his fine essay on Thoreau's queer wild, focused especially on "Higher Laws." There, he interprets Thoreau's renunciation in terms amenable to mine: "What Thoreau fears in all is less the body as such than what capitalism would make of the body, how it will take hold of it and rewrite its economies, its dialectics of waste and efficiency, *away* from what Thoreau envisions are its best possibilities." Coviello means that much of Thoreau's emphasis in "Higher Laws" expresses "a yearning for a kind of embodied otherwise." Peter Coviello, "The Wild Not Less than the Good: Thoreau, Sex, Biopower," *GLQ: A Journal of Lesbian and Gay Studies* 23, 4 (October 1, 2017): 514–15.

such a judgment would be submission to temptation. The following sentence reiterates Thoreau's insistence that spiritual life does not have greater value than savage life: "I love the wild not less than the good" (XI, 1). In general, people think of Thoreau as enamored of wildness. He wrote, in the famous essay "Walking," "what I have been preparing to say is, that in wildness is the preservation of the world."[14] But his view in "Higher Laws" is not so straightforward. "Nature" is both the thing with which we should want to have acquaintance, and that which must be overcome.

Thoreau refuses to resolve the tension. On the one hand, the chapter glorifies what it calls savage life. "I like sometimes to take rank hold on life and spend my day more as the animals do" (XI, 1). And it suggests that hunting and fishing are some of the best ways of coming to know "Nature."

> Fishermen, hunters, woodchoppers, and others, spending their lives in the fields and woods, in a peculiar sense a part of Nature themselves, are often in a more favorable mood for observing her, in the intervals of their pursuits, than philosophers or poets even, who approach her with expectation. She is not afraid to exhibit herself to them.
>
> (XI, 1)

In this sense, those who spend their time in the woods for economic reasons are closer to Nature even than those who purposefully reverence her.

But on the other hand, the chapter recommends many forms of restraint *against* animal instinct, especially with respect to food practices. "I believe that every man who has ever been earnest to preserve his higher or poetic faculties in the best condition has been particularly inclined to abstain from animal food, and from much food of any kind" (XI, 5).

[14] Thoreau, Walden, *Civil Disobedience, and Other Writings*, 273.

Thoreau's motivation for vegetarianism seems to be that the killing of animals is "a miserable way" (XI, 6). Thoreau liked to fish, indeed had "a certain instinct for it," but "I have found repeatedly, of late years, that I cannot fish without falling a little in self-respect" (XI, 5). The human carnivorous habit is a reproach. "I have no doubt that it is part of the destiny of the human race, in its gradual improvement, to leave off eating animals, as surely as the savage tribes have left off eating each other when they came into contact with the more civilized" (XI, 6). The discourse on food began with some ambivalence. It ends with the conclusion that human improvement will necessarily yield vegetarianism (and with a pretty horrifying doctrine of human progress through civilization).

Refusing meat is just the beginning of Thoreau's discourse on the benefits of purity. The last five paragraphs of the chapter are especially condemnatory of the animal part of the human.

> We are conscious of an animal in us, which awakens in proportion as our higher nature slumbers. It is reptile and sensual, and perhaps cannot be wholly expelled; like the worms which, even in life and health, occupy our bodies. Possibly we may withdraw from it, but never change its nature. I fear that it may enjoy a certain health of its own; that we may be well, yet not pure.
>
> (XI, 11)

Unlike in the beginning of the chapter, when the wild and the good were equally reverenced, in this quotation, the animal nature is opposed to the higher nature and purity has become an ideal.

The stark terms in which Thoreau chastises the physical has led even sympathetic readers to view "Higher Laws" as the worst of Thoreau's alignment of physical and spiritual practice. Edward Abbey wrote of his own food practices:

> Scrambled eggs, bacon, green chiles for breakfast, with hot *salsa*, toasted tortillas, and leftover baked potatoes sliced and fried. A gallon or two of coffee, tea and – for me – the usual breakfast beer. Henry would not have approved of this gourmandising. To hell with him. I do not approve of his fastidious puritanism. For one who claims to crave nothing but reality, he frets too much about *purity*. Purity, purity, he preaches, in the most unctuous of his many sermons, a chapter of *Walden* called "Higher Laws."[15]

Abbey's accusation is that in "Higher Laws" Thoreau succumbed to "fastidious puritanism" that insisted above all on purity. Thoreau did write in praise of purity, and chastity for that matter – that Christian virtue whose meaning is now so little discussed. But Thoreau also suggested that Christian practice was generally insufficient to the achievement of purity.

> If you would avoid uncleanness, and all the sins, work earnestly, though it be at cleaning a stable. Nature is hard to be overcome, but she must be overcome. What avails it that you are Christian, if you are not purer than the heathen, if you deny yourself no more, if you are not more religious? I know of many systems of religion esteemed heathenish whose precepts fill the reader with shame, and provoke him to new endeavors, though it be to the performance of rites merely.
>
> (XI, 12)

Many interpreters are put off by the traditional language of chastity and purity, and view Thoreau as motivated by prudishness. Some readers of "Higher Laws" have noticed a line from an unpublished draft that points to Thoreau's personal experience with chastity. They take this as a reference to sexuality and as evidence that Thoreau himself struggled to remain sexually pure, in some sense. And they therefore

[15] Edward Abbey, "Down the River with Henry Thoreau," in *Down the River* (New York: Plume, 1991), 8.

conclude that he was referring in these pages to an effort to abstain from sexual activity.[16] Of course, we know little about the sexual lives of history. We know so little about the sexual lives of the present. Privacy is a human good. But I think it is important to take note of the fact that Thoreau excised that line in particular. It seems to me possible to interpret its excision as the effort on Thoreau's part to leave the content of chastity and purity more indeterminate than people usually read them.[17]

Of course, in "Higher Laws" Thoreau was very explicit about his view that humans would, with moral progress, leave off eating animals. But, as the chapter's beginning in the virtues of hunting and fishing indicates, this was a topic on which Thoreau was truly conflicted. If he were prescribing in "Higher Laws" some sort of rigid abstention from all pleasure, it would not match the rest of the text. Thoreau delights in sensual pleasures in much of the rest of the book, and he rarely expresses self-reproach. Some people find his lack of self-reproach off-putting, as if he were too big for his britches, but his general tendency to avoid self-accusation is of a piece with his insistence that the aim of the book is not to ode dejection but to brag lustily.

What should we make of the tension between, on the one hand, Thoreau's seeming condemnation of sensual pleasure in

[16] The excised line was "I do not know how it is with other men, but I find it very difficult to be chaste." Robert Sattelmeyer, "The Remaking of *Walden*," in Walden, *Civil Disobedience, and Other Writings*, ed. William John Rossi, 3rd ed. (New York: Norton, 2008), 498.

[17] There is a small, rich subfield on Thoreau and sexuality. For example, Henry Abelove, *Deep Gossip* (Minneapolis, MN: University Of Minnesota Press, 2005); Michael Warner, "Thoreau's Bottom," *Raritan* 11, 3 (1992): 53; Coviello, "The Wild Not Less than the Good: Thoreau, Sex, Biopower." For a contemporary account of the possible positive significance of renunciation in the example of celibacy see Benjamin Kahan, *Celibacies: American Modernism and Sexual Life* (Durham, NC: Duke University Press Books, 2013).

"Higher Laws" and on the other, his attachment to lusty bragging?

The "more" that true philosophy aims for in Thoreau's view, is a life lived pursuing wisdom. For Thoreau, this was a religious vocation to which he was called by his God. It included daily practice, indeed it entailed a sacral view of time and its seasons. It also called him to consider daily practices, like eating, dressing, housing, working, and writing as caught up in his religious life. In the most rigorous articulation of this practice, "Higher Laws," some passages strike people as overly austere. I interpret the "chastity" and "purity" Thoreau describes there as integral to the philosophy he articulates, but I insist that what chastity and purity will look like in any particular life is left purposefully indeterminate. Thoreau was not doctrinaire.

Making the Day Sacred

Thoreau thought about days as basic units of human life. *Walden* is loosely structured around the passing of a year in Walden Woods. I call this the book's annual structure. It begins with Thoreau's building his house in the spring of 1845. He moves to the pond in the beginning of July, and passes the summer, fall, and winter in his small house there. The penultimate chapter of the book, "Spring," is about the breaking up of the ice in the ponds and "the coming in of spring." At the end of that chapter Thoreau writes, "Thus my first year's life in the woods completed; and the second year was similar to it" (XVII, 26). This narrative of a year frames the entire book.

But this major structural device of the book is not rigid, just as the form of the book is not entirely narrative. Throughout the book the narrator speaks from different moments in time, from outside of the year the book purports to be about. What he describes is sometimes taken from Thoreau's life in 1845–46, but he also includes stories and ideas from a second year Thoreau spent in the little house in 1846–47 and Thoreau's visits to the pond and the woods between when he moved back to the village in 1847 and when *Walden* was published in 1854.

The tension between the annual structure and the inclusion of events across multiple years is not obscured by the text. In the place it is most obvious, Thoreau lists the spring dates on which Walden Pond was completely free of ice in 1846, 1847, 1851, 1852, 1853, and 1854, information he of course did not have in 1845–46 (XVII, 3). In another passage, the Thoreau of the 1854 publication comments on the text itself. He apologizes for the earlier author. "To speak critically, I never received more than one or two letters in my life – I wrote this some years ago – that were worth the postage" (II, 19). Within the dashes, the Thoreau of 1854 reflects back on the Thoreau who had never received good letters. Here, I imagine, he wanted to let the reader (perhaps a particular correspondent such as Harrison Blake) know that in the period between the initial writing of the comment and the publication of the book the quality of the letters he received had changed.[18] This is evidently something that happened outside the 1845–46 frame of the book. Thus, while the annual device is sometimes deployed straightforwardly, as though telling the story as it unfolded, at other times the author reflects back on the narrative, or intervenes in it from the present, and the annual device breaks open.

I am interested in the annual structure and the ways in which Thoreau often breaks it because the annual device is closely related to the theme of renewal, one of the major

[18] Thoreau's letters to Blake are collected in Thoreau, *Letters to a Spiritual Seeker*.

subjects of the book. The book ends in "Spring" for a reason. The images of the reawakening of life in spring – the breaking up of the ice, the return of birds, the greening of the grass – show the sense in which Thoreau thinks his readers can themselves experience spiritual renewal, which Thoreau intends to encourage with the book. "In a pleasant spring morning all men's sins are forgiven. Such a day is truce to vice. While such a sun holds out to burn, the vilest sinner may return" (XVII, 19). Thoreau's early essay, "A Winter Walk" suggested that a scripture had never been written that expressed the divinity of winter well enough. "We know of no scripture which records the pure benignity of the gods on a New England winter night."[19] But *Walden* ends in spring because it offers an image of pardon and renewal, the sort of reawakening to new life that Thoreau wants to encourage.

I am also interested in the annual structure because examination of it helps us open up Thoreau's understanding of time, which is related to his thinking about how we ought to pass our time, or his asceticism.

Both *Walden* and Thoreau's first book, *A Week on the Concord and Marrimack Rivers*, are organized by structures of time. In the first book each chapter is titled for a day of the week, beginning with "Saturday." Cycles of time's passing play an important role in Thoreau's thinking. *Walden* is organized around the seasons of a year, and Thoreau explained that part of the reason for the experiment at Walden was that he wanted to live close to the seasons. "While I enjoy the friendship of the seasons I trust that nothing can make life a burden to me" (V, 4). In *Walden*, Thoreau also suggests that just as we live the year through its seasons, with each offering its own pleasures, so we live the day through its hours. The day carries with it the

[19] Henry David Thoreau, "A Winter Walk," *The Dial*, October 1843, 226.

dynamics of the year, but on a smaller scale. "The day is the epitome of the year. The night is the winter, the morning and evening are the spring and fall, and the noon is the summer" (XVII, 2). Here, Thoreau takes the major organizing principle of the book and insists that it applies not only to life over the course of a year, but also to the unit of time we find closer to hand – the day.[20] He makes the spiritual dynamics of the whole year accessible every day. The book is organized around the passing of the year, but what it usually describes is the way Thoreau passed the days of that year. The day is the epitome of the year. It has seasons: "The morning, which is the most memorable season of the day, is the awakening hour." Here, he calls the *morning* a *season* of the day, conflating the two time frames. He continues,

> Then there is least somnolence in us; and for an hour, at least, some part of us awakes which slumbers all the rest of the day and night. Little is to be expected of that day, if it can be called a day, to which we are not awakened by our Genius, but by the mechanical nudgings of some servitor, are not awakened by our own newly acquired force and aspirations from within, accompanied by the undulations of celestial music, instead of factory bells, and a fragrance filling the air – to a higher life than we fell asleep from; and thus the darkness bear its fruit, and prove itself to be good, no less than the light. That man who does not believe that each day contains an earlier, more sacred, and auroral hour than he has yet profaned, has despaired of life, and is pursuing a descending and darkening way.
>
> (II, 15)

[20] Melissa Lane has written that while Rousseau and Thoreau are utopian thinkers (as many have argued) in that they are invested in "the good city" – *upolia* – in their later works they also share an emphasis on what she calls "the good day" or *uhemeria*. As I say here, Thoreau's interest in the day is also evident in the earlier work of *Walden*. Melissa Lane, "Thoreau and Rousseau: Nature as Utopia," in *A Political Companion to Henry David Thoreau*, ed. Jack Turner (Lexington, KY: The University Press of Kentucky, 2009), 342.

Thoreau invokes the mornings as moments when we are likely to be most capable of the sort of awakening he is aiming to promote.

In this vision of the day, each part has its place in the whole. Thoreau's insistence on the importance of the day and the marking of its parts – night, morning, evening, and noon – should encourage us to view him in a long tradition of thinking about time and its passage as spiritually significant. For instance, it calls to mind the practice of praying the hours, the cycle of daily prayers developed in the context of Christian monasticism.

Walden is richly descriptive, sometimes to the point of absurdity. There are whole paragraphs that describe what it is like to lie on your belly and look through the ice into Walden Pond. These passages draw attention to a central argument of the book, which is that if we will be wise, we must focus more closely on our everyday actions. In this, Thoreau takes what he knows of "Hindoo" practice to be exemplary.[21]

> Nothing was too trivial for the Hindoo lawgiver, however offensive it may be to modern taste. He teaches how to eat, drink, cohabit, void excrement and urine, and the like, elevating what is mean, and does not falsely excuse himself by calling these things trifles.
>
> Every man is the builder of a temple, called his body, to the god he worships, after a style purely his own, nor can he get off by hammering marble instead. We are all sculptors and painters, and our material is our own flesh and blood and bones.
>
> (XI, 13-14)

[21] What he knew of the religious traditions of India was not minor. His personal library of Asian texts was one of the largest in his era. The superlative comes from Nancy L. Rosenblum, "Introduction," in *Thoreau: Political Writings* (New York: Cambridge University Press, 1996), ix.

In Thoreau's view, every person builds a temple and worships some god there through his life. The choice we have available is to which god we will build our temple. Thus for Thoreau, the things that we do – even and perhaps especially those things which modern taste takes to be "mean" – determine what kind of people we are to become, what sort of art we make with our lives and bodies, and which god we will worship. *Walden* is a hyper close account of his own doings – from the budget for his house (as cheaply made as possible), to the data he gathered when surveying the pond. He thought this kind of accounting could put character (whether good or ill) on display.[22] As the pond can be measured in deep detail, our characters can be measured by our days. He wrote, "draw lines through the length and breadth of the aggregate of a man's particular daily behaviors and waves of life into his coves and inlets, and where they intersect will be the height or depth of his character" (XVI, 13). This goes some way to explaining why he makes the accounting of his days in such great detail. He hoped to survey his own character.[23]

Thoreau's Orientation to Delight

Though many moments in *Walden* suggest that Thoreau was motivated by a negative response to luxury, and a rejection of the goods of common life, dwelling on this feature of his

[22] It also left him subject to the critique that he was an "accountant of the spirit" as in Alan Harrington, *The Immortalist: An Approach to the Engineering of Man's Divinity* (New York: Random House, 1969), 52. Quoted in Abbey, "Down the River with Henry Thoreau," 31.

[23] Many others have hoped to survey his character too, and have found the measurement short. I'm not concerned with whether his character is good or bad, but what he takes the shape of a good day to be. I think it's interesting to notice, though, that many of the critiques of Thoreau were and are related to negative evaluations of his character. This seems to take for granted that he was right about how we come to know a person's character.

thought ignores passages that describe another, positive experience of renunciation. Thoreau can say in the same breath that too many condiments will poison you, and that living without luxury is pure pleasure. When we focus on the instances in which *he* rejects goods *we* enjoy, like coffee, we are likely to miss his basic orientation to delight.[24]

Delight features centrally in my work both because we face deeply dark days, and because it is through this capacity for delight that Thoreau recognizes simplicity's goodness. His asceticism makes his own life better, not just because it makes him good, but also because it enables him for pleasure.[25] Though Thoreau rejected coffee, he delighted in drinking water. After all, the water of Walden Pond was of such cool crystalline purity, why spoil it? He wrote about the water of the pond, "It was as good when a week old as the day it was dipped, and had no taste of the pump" (IX, 13).

From the third paragraph of *Walden*, Thoreau took pains to distinguish his practices of simplicity from the popular view of punishing asceticism, as I described in the beginning of

[24] I learned to recognize this in Thoreau partly thanks to conversation with Kris Culp and her chapter on "An Itinerary of Delight and Gratitude." Kristine A. Culp, *Vulnerability and Glory: A Theological Account* (Louisville, KY: Westminster John Knox Press, 2010), chapter 8. Conversation with David Craig about John Ruskin's "duty of delight" has also helped. David M. Craig, "The Duty of Delight," in *John Ruskin and the Ethics of Consumption* (Charlottesville, VA: University of Virginia Press, 2006). Dorothy Day took Ruskin's "duty of delight" as a continual motivation. "And now another disaster, the Heaney baby, 2 years old, drowned. The duty of delight – as Ruskin says. Today we have a picnic in the woods. The air is sweet with milkweed in bloom. The honeysuckle is past, the sweet clover goes on all summer." Dorothy Day, *The Duty of Delight: The Diaries of Dorothy Day*, ed. Robert Ellsberg (Milwaukee, WI: Marquette University Press, 2008), 163.

[25] Detroit activist adrienne maree brown, working in a Black feminist tradition, has written for activists about social justice as the most pleasurable human experience. adrienne maree brown, *Pleasure Activism: The Politics of Feeling Good* (Chico, CA: AK Press, 2019).

Chapter 4. He suggested that the *other* citizens of Concord practiced a painful form of penance, even more "incredible and astonishing" than those he had read about who practice bodily feats, like hanging upside down by their feet over fires. He drew this contrast because he knew that his abstemiousness might grate on his readers. He was himself troubled by the reforming spirit that surrounded him in the broader culture of the period. He wrote once in his journal, "I dont like people who are too good for this world."[26] And he worried that readers might get the wrong idea. Some of his friends apparently did. He wrote, "Some of my friends spoke as if I was coming to the woods on purpose to freeze myself" (XIII, 18).

Against this view – one he knew might tempt readers who were, he thought, already inclined to self-punishment – the text of *Walden* sparkles with accounts of the goods Thoreau enjoyed, the life that delighted him in the woods. His renunciations enabled him to live on less, and living on less provided its own blessings. He wrote,

> Sometimes, in a summer morning, having taken my accustomed bath, I sat in my sunny doorway from sunrise til noon, rapt in a revery, amidst the pines and hickories and sumachs, in undisturbed solitude and stillness, while the birds sang around or flitted noiseless through the house.
>
> (IV, 2)

On such occasions, he wrote, "I silently smiled at my incessant good fortune" (IV, 2).

Doing nothing, enjoying the sunshine after a bath, wasn't the only thing that delighted Thoreau about his life in the woods. Even a contemplative ascetic doesn't want to just sit

[26] Thoreau, *Journal*, Volume 1: *1837–1844*, 219.

all day. It's bad for the bottom, in any case. But everything about his life pleased him. He wrote, "My life itself was become my amusement and never ceased to be novel." This was true to such an extent that, as he wrote: "Housework was a pleasant pastime" (IV, 3).

Even in "Higher Laws," the chapter that seems most strictly to reject sensual pleasures, Thoreau insists that the success of the form of life he recommends can be tested by whether it provides joy.

> If the day and the night are such that you greet them with joy, and life emits a fragrance like flowers and sweet-scented herbs, is more elastic, more starry, more immortal, – that is your success. All nature is your congratulation, and you have cause momentarily to bless yourself.
>
> (XI, 7)

It may seem a contradiction, but Thoreau simplified for positive gain; he thought the simple life he led enabled him to value the goodness around him rightly, to have a proper emotional response to the world, to delight in true goods.[27]

The experience described in passages like these is, I think, interestingly different from wonder. Plato and Aristotle both

[27] In this, I hope my account of Thoreau responds constructively to Amy Hollywood's assessment that too much modern scholarship rests on an unstated assumption that damage and trauma are the only things that matter. She suggests that scholars are often deaf to joy. "For too long, the injunction to critique has rested on unquestioned – uncritiqued – melancholic foundations ... Those of us living in privilege – and those living, often barely, without it – are unable to look away, unable to act, unable, in the fullest sense of the word, to live. Yet the energy for efficacious action comes not solely through melancholy, but also through joy, through a love of the world that, in love, demands change. What Christianity shows ... is that this takes work, work on ourselves and work on the world, and unalienated labor in and through which we become who we are. Not suffering *or* joy, for we can't have the one without the other; we can't live well – we can't *live* – on sorrow and rage alone." Amy M. Hollywood, *Acute Melancholia and Other Essays: Mysticism, History, and the Study of Religion, Gender, Theory, and Religion* (New York: Columbia University Press, 2016), 63.

famously wrote that philosophy begins in wonder, and their attention to it has given way to its prominent place in the history of philosophy in the West since. Renewed attention in scholarly literature, especially within cultural studies, over the past twenty years has yielded a small subfield focused on the study of wonder.[28] Perhaps the most prominent among these has been Philip Fisher's *Wonder, the Rainbow, and the Aesthetics of Rare Experiences*. There, Fisher suggests that – with respect to aesthetic experience – modern thought has focused on the sublime over and against wonder. This, he argues, has been a mistake. "With the sublime we have for two hundred years built up a more and more intricate theory for a type of art that we do not actually have and would not care for if we did have it."[29] Instead, he insists, the modern and contemporary art that readers generally know best requires an aesthetics of wonder. Where the aesthetics of the sublime was an appeal to fear, architecture and painting after 1873 rejected that effort with their attempts at constant innovation and technical freshness, "as though some completely unprecedented thing were now going on at the spot where painting used to take place."[30]

Very often, understandings of wonder like Fisher's, focused as it is on "innovation" and "freshness," attend to the way in

[28] Recent work on wonder includes Philip Fisher, *Wonder, the Rainbow, and the Aesthetics of Rare Experiences* (Cambridge, MA: Harvard University Press, 1998); Mary-Jane Rubenstein, *Strange Wonder: The Closure of Metaphysics and the Opening of Awe* (New York: Columbia University Press, 2008); Lisa H. Sideris, "The Secular and Religious Sources of Rachel Carson's Sense of Wonder," in *Rachel Carson: Legacy and Challenge* (Albany, NY: State University of New York Press, 2008); Jeffrey L. Kosky, *Arts of Wonder: Enchanting Secularity – Walter De Maria, Diller Scofidio, James Turrell, Andy Goldsworthy* (Chicago, IL: University of Chicago Press, 2012); Sophia Vasalou, ed., *Practices of Wonder: Cross-Disciplinary Perspectives* (Cambridge, UK: James Clarke & Co, 2013); Sophia Vasalou, *Wonder: A Grammar* (Albany, NY: State University of New York Press, 2015).

[29] Fisher, *Wonder, the Rainbow, and the Aesthetics of Rare Experiences*, 3.

[30] Fisher, 5.

which phenomena – whether natural or made – sometimes strike us as puzzling or amazing, and the impetus such puzzlement provides to philosophical musings. In the archetypical example, also from ancient philosophy, the rainbow inspires me to wonder at it, and in coming to try to understand it I become a philosopher. Much recent work on wonder is invested in the way in which wonder has been a driver for the development of modern science.

Thoreau did have experiences that inspired wonder, and he devoted more and more time to scientific observation of the natural world as his life went on, but wonder is not the only emotional experience he has in the natural world. He is driven by his wanting to understand, a kind of curiosity, but there is more to it than that. Thoreau's delight is also an investment. It is not just a desire to understand. It is also a desire to be in relationship to, and live with, and care for.

Wonder classically refers to new experiences that usually cause puzzlement or awe. Delight is, rather, the recognition, sometimes sudden, of goodness – even where we least expect it, even in mundane repetitive practices, even in very dark days. Where wonder initiates intellected understanding of the wondered at phenomenon, delight initiates and sustains something rather different: enjoyment. Such enjoyment can come – we have textual evidence of this in numberless human lives – even in very trying circumstances. It is not assured to come in such circumstances, but it can. And this means that for people in difficult straits, for instance humans in a warming world, and people in a world that has been built around utilitarian values, delight is a fund for power we should remember. I hope this book can help you remember it.[31]

[31] Since the first draft of this work, I have been much inspired myself by the way that environmental activists in Australia are mobilizing enjoyment to help people reform their lives and communities for the better. Two Melbourne residents (one

I think of my own life. I am on my bicycle, coming home from work with my partner. Suddenly, I see something amazing – maybe it is bats flying low overhead in the dusk, maybe it is a ray of sun bursting out from behind grey clouds, maybe it is one of Melbourne's many rainbows. Whatever it is, I point and say to him, simply, "look!" And he looks, and then he turns and looks back at me, smiling. We enjoy the rainbow together. I think this "look!" – my calling out to him and waiting for his appreciative response – is an undertheorized gesture.[32]

The philosophers said philosophy begins in wonder, a kind of wanting to know. Thoreau can teach us a philosophy that begins in delight, a wanting to share. It begins with the delight I feel that makes me call out to you, "look!" My call makes you turn to see the thing, and then turn back to me to share the delight we have found together. When I see the rainbow and I say "look!" I am not merely puzzled, not even yet curious. When I see the rainbow I'm amazed, it's true, but there is also a social feeling in it – an investment in sharing the rainbow, a caring about the rainbow itself and a caring about sharing the rainbow with others. When I shout "look!" I see the potential the rainbow has for our life together, for shaping the world we live in together for the better. In that, my response to the rainbow is not the distancing of wonder, not merely curiosity. It pulls me into my relationship to the rainbow and to you because of what those relationships give me

of whom I met while he was leading a "Weed Walk," teaching us to eat plants commonly considered weeds) have written a contemporary handbook on enjoying things. Annie Raser-Rowland and Adam Grubb, *The Art of Frugal Hedonism: A Guide to Spending Less While Enjoying Everything More* (Victoria: Melliodora Publishing, 2016).

[32] Thinking about it productively might begin in conversation with Rebecca Kukla and Mark Lance, *"Yo!"And "Lo!" The Pragmatic Topography of the Space of Reasons* (Cambridge, MA: Harvard University Press, 2009).

when they are good: delight. In the gesture – "look!" – when I point, I am unable to stop my own appreciation. I just want to show you something good, something that I have seen and that if you see it too may change your life and our life together.

Delight and Moral Motivation

There has been developing interest over the last few decades among both humanists and social scientists of the extent to which affective moral emotions – like guilt, anger, admiration, and sympathy – are integral to human rationality and motivate human behavior.[33] Emotions are integral to rationality in that they enable knowledge. Think of the way that anger is often how we begin to understand that there has been an injustice done. And emotions motivate human behavior as much as if not more than intellected reasons for action. Think of the way that fear will motivate you to grab a child who is crossing the street, without your thinking explicitly that the street is dangerous.

This recent wave of interest in affect in philosophy and psychology coincides with a more ancient view.[34] Augustine,

[33] See, for examples from across disciplines: Jeff Goodwin, James M. Jasper, and Francesca Polletta, eds., *Passionate Politics: Emotions and Social Movements* (Chicago, IL: University of Chicago Press, 2001); Philip Fisher, *The Vehement Passions* (Princeton, NJ: Princeton University Press, 2002); June Price Tangney and Ronda L. Dearing, *Shame and Guilt* (New York: The Guilford Press, 2003). In moral philosophy, an ambitious recent statement of the role of admiration in moral living is in Linda Trinkaus Zagzebski, *Exemplarist Moral Theory* (New York: Oxford University Press, 2017).

[34] Martha Nussbaum is one contemporary expositor of the connection between ancient philosophy of the passions and the issues in contemporary philosophy and psychology of emotions. See especially Martha C. Nussbaum, *Upheavals of Thought: The Intelligence of Emotions* (Cambridge: Cambridge University Press, 2001).

the fifth-century Christian bishop of Hippo, is famous for attention to human psychology.[35] He developed – as one important biographer put it - a "psychology of 'delight.'"[36] His view was that humans are lovers, which is to say that we cannot help but love. The most basic motivation of the human will – the thing that moves anyone to do anything – is delight, that is, enjoyment of what is loved. The key to living well, on this view, was ordering our loves according to the relative goodness of the beloved. This turned out to be unceasingly difficult, because humans notoriously love the wrong things and have to tutor our delight, so that it is in true goods, rather than false ones. But the basic insight was that delight in the beloved was what moved anyone to act at all.

In a 2009 essay in the journal *Ethics & The Environment* Carol Booth argued that environmental ethics needs a "motivational turn."[37] Booth pointed out that even those who express concern about environmental problems are unlikely to take pro-environmental action. What environmental ethics needs now, she argued, is to pay more attention to what actually motivates people to enact our moral concern. Booth was not alone. Widespread frustration with the seeming inefficacy of the field of environmental ethics has many of us wondering whether what we do – that is, read and write – does any actual good for the issues we care most about, for the flourishing of the places, and creatures, and plants, and

[35] Eric Gregory, *Politics and the Order of Love: An Augustinian Ethic of Democratic Citizenship* (Chicago, IL: University of Chicago Press, 2008); James Wetzel, *Augustine and the Limits of Virtue* (Cambridge: Cambridge University Press, 1992); Peter Brown, *Augustine of Hippo: A Biography* (Berkeley, CA: University of California Press, 2000).

[36] Brown, *Augustine of Hippo*, 148. Quoted in Gregory, *Politics and the Order of Love*, 241.

[37] Carol Booth, "A Motivational Turn for Environmental Ethics," *Ethics & the Environment* 14, 1 (2009): 53–78.

human communities many of us aim to nurture. I know not a small number of once enthusiastic environmental activists and philosophers who have retreated from activism and writing about environmental issues because of anger, frustration, and disappointment with the intransigence of contemporary environmental politics. A motivational turn, Booth suggested, would refocus the work of environmental ethicists on what features of life move people to action and keep them committed to it.

In the last decade or so, much of the work on motivation and environment has focused on guilt. Some social scientists have discussed how moral emotions – especially guilt – might motivate citizens to give up environmentally detrimental ways of life.[38] In environmental ethics, some have focused on the importance of guilt in motivating pro-environmental behavior, and some contemporary work on climate guilt and shame suggests that negative moral emotions can be an impediment to pro-environmental behavior and therefore need to be tended.[39] But to the extent that these scholars have focused on negative moral emotions, they have underplayed a major feature of right human relationship to nature, which in its finest form includes not only guilt and shame at the wrongs we have committed but also, and more basically, positive emotional relationships with the world around us. We only feel guilt when we feel there has been a wrong, and we feel there has been a wrong when we see a good betrayed.

[38] For an example, see Jonas H. Rees, Sabine Klug, and Sebastian Bamberg, "Guilty Conscience: Motivating Pro-environmental Behavior by Inducing Negative Moral Emotions," *Climatic Change*, October 14, 2014, 1–14.

[39] See especially the work of Sarah Fredericks, for example, Sarah E. Fredericks, "Online Confessions of Eco-Guilt," *Journal for the Study of Religion, Nature, and Culture* 8, 1 (2014): 64–84.

Given this situation, I think it should do us some good to recall that delight rather than shame or guilt motivated Thoreau, one of the canonized saints of the environmental movement. In a period when one of the major tension lines in popular environmental discourse is about what we can hope for with respect to the future of our life on earth, I think that conscientiously cultivating delight in present goods is one of our most basic obligations. It does not refer to the ultimate result of our environmental efforts but teaches us to take pleasure in more near-term effects and to value rightly the goods among which we live.

The Woodchopper's Mirth, Thoreau's Laughter

One of those goods, and one that was central to Thoreau's life, was good humor. Thoreau made a friend while living in the woods, the "woodchopper" I discussed in Chapters 1 and 3 and briefly in Chapter 4. The woodchopper is most compelling and attractive to Thoreau in his good humor and unalloyed mirth. This was a feature of the woodchopper's personality that Thoreau emphasized.

> He interested me because he was so quiet and solitary and so happy withal; a well of good humor and contentment which overflowed at his eyes. His mirth was without alloy. Sometimes I saw him at his work in the woods, felling trees, and he would greet me with a laugh of inexpressible satisfaction, and a salutation in Canadian French, though he spoke English as well. When I approached him he would suspend his work, and with half-suppressed mirth lie along the trunk of a pine which he had felled, and, peeling off the inner bark, roll it up into a ball and chew it while he laughed and talked. Such an exuberance of animal spirits had he that he sometimes tumbled down and rolled on the ground with laughter at any thing which made him think and tickled him.
>
> (VI, 10)

Here, Thoreau writes that his interest was inspired by the woodchopper's quiet, solitary happiness. Like the spring where Thoreau got drinking water in the summer when Walden Pond was too warm, the woodchopper was a "well" which "overflowed." The overflowing brought his happiness into Thoreau's life. The image of the woodchopper lying "along the trunk of a pine which he had felled" is, for me, one of the most haunting of *Walden*. Here, a man who spends his life in the woods chopping wood, has the freedom to "suspend his work" when Thoreau comes along. This was a marked contrast to the form of relentless, driven labor Thoreau described in "Economy." The woodchopper was so good at taking this leisure that he knew how to lie comfortably on a tree and enjoy it. Thoreau describes his laughter twice. When Thoreau comes upon him in the woods, the woodchopper offered in greeting "a laugh of inexpressible satisfaction." And then after the image of the woodchopper lying on the tree trunk, Thoreau says sometimes the woodchopper "tumbled down and rolled on the ground with laughter."

The portrait of the woodchopper shows Thoreau appreciating laughter, but did he ever write about himself laughing? It is hard to imagine someone so insistent on renunciation was able to laugh. But Thoreau does laugh in *Walden* and even play. The fourth chapter called "Sounds," follows the one called "Reading." In "Sounds" Thoreau suggests that, however much he praised reading in the previous chapter, it is only one part of living well.

> But while we are confined to books, though the most select and classic, and read only particular written languages, which are themselves but dialects and provincial, we are in danger of forgetting the language which all things and events speak without metaphor, which alone is copious and standard.
>
> (IV, 1)

The chapter pivots from the first three chapters' focus on economic and educational practice to show what it's like to live in a place and be awake to it. Here, Thoreau practices listening, both to the railroad and to the creatures that live in the woods. "No method nor discipline can supersede the necessity of being forever on the alert" (IV, 1). This is the first time we see Thoreau considering contemplative practices, which is what most scholars of religion focus on when writing about Thoreau.

The title of the chapter is "Sounds," and it is certainly the case that part of what Thoreau means by being forever on the alert is cultivating attentiveness to sounds. But he suggests that "the language which all things and events speak" also includes seeing. Thoreau poses a question to the reader: "Will you be a reader, a student merely, or a seer?" That sight is mentioned here, in a chapter about sound, seems to indicate that it's not either the listening or the seeing that Thoreau means to recommend, but something broader: some attending, waiting. "No method nor discipline can supersede the necessity of being forever on the alert." This way of putting it, however, makes it sound a little desperate to our ears, as though Thoreau is recommending a sort of anxious waiting. That is not it at all.

The "being on alert" that Thoreau recommends is different from a frenetic expectation. Though Thoreau thought that labor was important, he writes that sometimes the present moment was too precious to sacrifice it to work. Here, I quote a larger portion of the passage about the bath I quoted earlier.

> There were times when I could not afford to sacrifice the bloom of the present moment to any work, whether of the head or hands. I love a broad margin to my life. Sometimes, in a summer morning, having taken my accustomed bath, I sat in my sunny doorway from sunrise till noon, rapt in revery, amidst the pines and hickories and sumachs, in undisturbed solitude and stillness,

> while the birds sang around or flitted noiseless through the house, until by the sun falling in at my west window, or the noise of some traveller's wagon on the distant highway, I was reminded of the lapse of time. I grew in those seasons like corn in the night, and they were far better than any work of the hands would have been. They were not subtracted from my life, but so much over and above my usual allowance.
>
> (IV, 2)

As in the rest of *Walden*, the paragraph is full of words that allude to economic accounting: "afford," "margin," "subtracted," and "allowance" all suggest that Thoreau is playing with currently prevailing economic models.[40] The allusions begin with one that is obvious, perhaps to call the reader's attention to the metaphor at play. Thoreau says "I could not afford to sacrifice..." But where the phrase would at first lead the reader to think he could not afford to sacrifice time for reading when he was busy hoeing beans (this is the topic at hand), he writes, instead, that he cannot afford to sacrifice "the bloom of the present moment." (Recall from Chapter 4 the bloom of fruits that is "the finest qualities of our nature" and requires tender treatment.) "Bloom" refers to the delicate surface on many fruits that protects them while they are growing – the whiteness you might see on grapes is one example. That sort of bloom is easily brushed off, and, when it is, the fruit becomes much more susceptible to spoilage. To preserve fruit once it has been picked, it is best to preserve the bloom. But fruits must be handled delicately to preserve that bloom. "Margin" refers both to the edges of the page of a book – and therefore to the time Thoreau spent on things besides

[40] Stanley Cavell wrote that Thoreau's charts about the costs of food and building materials are "parodies of America's methods of evaluation." Cavell, *Senses of Walden*, 30. For a broader look at Thoreau's writing in the context of American economic discourse of the time, see Leonard N. Neufeldt, *The Economist: Henry Thoreau and Enterprise* (New York: Oxford University Press, 1989).

writing – and also to the margin of profit over loss in a business. "Subtraction" is one of the arithmetic functions required for keeping accounts. And "allowance" often refers to the amount of money a person is given to spend in a particular period.

But the passage makes clear that Thoreau is not *actually* accounting, as some critics have suggested. Instead, he is making fun of the way in which many people think about time, and also articulating what he hopes will be a more attractive vision of life: sitting in the doorway, not noticing the lapse of time, or worrying that it is being spent badly. Because, as he says later, time is not for spending, time is precisely something other than spending. The wordplay of this passage represents one important form of Thoreau's humor. To write like this, I think, you have to find it sort of funny.

Thoreau also represents his good humor in passages in *Walden* where he is happy. One follows the previously quoted part of "Sounds."

> For the most part, I minded not how the hours went. The day advanced as if to light some work of mine; it was morning, and lo, now it is evening, and nothing memorable is accomplished. Instead of singing like the birds, I silently smiled at my incessant good fortune. As the sparrow had its trill, sitting in the hickory before my door, so had I my chuckle or suppressed warble which he might hear out of my nest.
>
> (IV, 2)

Here, Thoreau likens himself to the birds, but he does so by comparing his "chuckle" to the sparrow's trill, implying both that Thoreau sometimes chuckles to himself while alone in his house, and that the sparrow's trill is an expression of good humor.

Others in *Walden* also laugh, and the one who laughs the most is the loon. The loon appears, laughing, frequently. In "Solitude," when Thoreau is explaining why he is not lonely, he compares himself to the loon. "I am no more lonely than the loon in the pond that laughs so loud" (V, 15). And then in "Brute Neighbors," the loon makes its biggest appearance, in a long description that includes a game Thoreau plays, chasing him. In the fall the loon comes to the pond, "making the woods ring with his wild laughter before I had risen" (XII, 16).

Thoreau also laughs with Ellery Channing, whose visits he describes with warmth in the end of "Former Inhabitants; Winter Visitors."

> The one who came from farthest to my lodge, through deepest snows and most dismal tempests, was a poet. A farmer, a hunter, a soldier, a reporter, even a philosopher, may be daunted; but nothing can deter a poet, for he is actuated by pure love. Who can predict his comings and goings? His business calls him out at all hours, even when doctors sleep. We made that small house ring with boisterous mirth and resound with the murmur of much sober talk, making amends then to Walden vale for the long silences. Broadway was still and deserted in comparison. At suitable intervals there were regular salutes of laughter, which might have been referred indifferently to the last-uttered or the forthcoming jest. We made many a "bran new" theory of life over a thin dish of gruel, which combined the advantages of conviviality with the clear-headedness which philosophy requires.
>
> (XIV, 20)

Here, Thoreau makes plain his preference for poets over even philosophers, and he says that the difference between them is motivation: the poet "is actuated by pure love." Such a one is Ellery Channing, who came to Thoreau's house, even in winter, from farther than any other. And once he arrived, he and Thoreau "made that small house ring with boisterous mirth." This was their contribution to the region's soundscape. Thoreau writes that the sounds made amends "to Walden vale for the long silences." He even says that their boisterousness made Broadway look "still and deserted in comparison." Their laughter was generous and abstract too: "At suitable intervals there were regular salutes of laughter, which might have been referred indifferently to the last-uttered or the forth-coming jest." The laughter between them was so generous that it sometimes referred to a joke not yet made. They laughed with the joy of being together, waiting for the joke that was yet to come.

Eschatology

The laughter of anticipation between friends is a kind of forward-reaching social moment, one that extends a hope for the future between them. The end of the chapter in which Channing comes and they laugh together features one of two important moments in which Thoreau projects an off-beat eschatology that demonstrates the sense in which his writing achieved the combination of earnestness and humor. The first moment describes how Thoreau was everywhere waiting for "the Visitor who never comes."

> There too, as every where, I sometimes expected the Visitor who never comes. The Vishnu Purana says, "The house-holder is to remain at eventide in his court-yard as long as it takes to milk a cow, or longer if he pleases, to await the arrival of a guest." I often performed this duty of hospitality, waited long enough to milk a whole herd of cows, but did not see the man approaching from town.
>
> (XIV, 24)

The paragraph describes a practice oriented toward hospitality: standing outside, waiting to welcome a guest. This echoes other practices Thoreau emphasized in his life that required the attentiveness he recommended. But it also offers a playful perspective on the passage it quotes when he writes that he "waited long enough to milk a whole herd of cows." The line plays with the way in which time is expressed in the text, and it calls up a funny image: Thoreau in front of his tiny house milking a whole herd of cows.

The second playfully eschatological moment appears in "House-Warming," when fall comes to Thoreau in his house, and he begins to warm it with a fire in the hearth he had built. This marks a transition in his relationship to the house: "I now first began to inhabit my house, I may say, when I began to use it for warmth as well as shelter" (XIII, 6). "Inhabit"is a key term in *Walden*. "Inhabitants" is the term Thoreau uses most often for the creatures who live or have lived in Walden Woods. Inhabiting a place seems to indicate for him the style of life that he endorses.[41] It also refers to the ancient sense in which virtue must be habitual. Inhabitation is a virtuous relationship with a place. Thoreau's dependence on the house for warmth is the marker of inhabitation of it, which suggests that Thoreau thinks there is no virtue without dependence.

Rather than being a limitation, for Thoreau the house's small size suggests that in it he has all the satisfactions that would, in a larger house, be distributed among its residents. "All the attractions of the house were concentrated in one room; it was kitchen, chamber, parlor, and keeping-room; and whatever satisfaction parent or child, master or servant, derive from living in a house, I enjoyed it all" (XIII, 6). A small house might seem to be lacking, compared to a house with many rooms. Where is Thoreau's parlor, if he only has one room? And where will he host his guests? Thoreau thinks instead that a one-room house concentrates the enjoyment it

[41] On the matter of "inhabitants" see also the first paragraph of the posthumous 1862 essay "Walking." "I wish to speak a word for Nature, for absolute freedom and wildness, as contrasted with a freedom and culture merely civil, – to regard man as an inhabitant, or a part and parcel of Nature, rather than a member of society." Thoreau, Walden, *Civil Disobedience, and Other Writings*, 260.

may offer. And Thoreau's role as parent and child and master and servant allows him, the inhabitant of this one-room house, to enjoy it more. He gets to have all of the experiences each of those others would have; his satisfactions are concentrated.

The one-room house also offers the occasion for Thoreau's eschatological play, when he describes a dream he has of another, different, house – also of only one room, but bigger. The description of the spacious one-room house begins, appropriately, in one extensive sentence.

> I sometimes dream of a larger and more populous house, standing in a golden age, of enduring materials, and without gingerbread work, which shall still consist of only one room, a vast, rude, substantial, primitive hall, without ceiling or plastering, with bare rafters and purlins supporting a sort of lower heaven over one's head, – useful to keep off rain and snow; where the king and queen posts stand out to receive your homage, when you have done reverence to the prostrate Saturn of an older dynasty on stepping over the sill; a cavernous house, wherein you must reach up a torch upon a pole to see the roof; where some may live in the fire-place, some in the recess of a window, and some on settles, some at one end of the hall, some at another, and some aloft on rafters with the spiders, if they choose; a house which you have got into when you have opened the outside door, and the ceremony is over; where the weary traveller may wash, and eat, and converse, and sleep, without further journey; such a shelter as you would be glad to reach in a tempestuous night, containing all the essentials of a house, and nothing for housekeeping; where you can see all the treasures of the house at one view, and every thing hangs upon its peg that a man should use; at once kitchen, pantry, parlor, chamber, store-house, and garret; where you can see so necessary a thing as a barrel or a ladder, so convenient a thing as a cupboard, and hear the pot boil, and pay your respects to the fire that cooks your dinner and the oven that bakes your bread, and the necessary furniture and utensils are the chief ornaments; where the washing is not put out, nor the fire,

> nor the mistress, and perhaps you are sometimes requested to move from off the trap-door, when the cook would descend into the cellar, and so learn whether the ground is solid or hollow beneath you without stamping.
>
> (XIII, 7)

The house of Thoreau's dream could not be more different from the one by Walden Pond. It is large and populous. This seems a strange contrast to the house that Thoreau built for himself, single occupancy, by the shores of the pond. He had the opportunity to share a larger and more populous house at Brook Farm, and he didn't take it, precisely because there would be too many people around. He joked about how they were like boarding houses in his journals, and wrote that in heaven he would like to bake his own bread.[42] But I think this passage about the "larger and more populous house" indicates that Thoreau hoped for a different future for himself, that he considered something about living alone not perfect in an eschatological sense. He thought, as Emerson's "Literary Ethics" had suggested, that solitude was for something. It was for being redeemed into a more sociable world.

Another way to think about this passage about the larger and more populous house is as a lovely, long-winded joke about the eschaton, the kind of joke you might play out with your friend, in the middle of winter, when he laughed before you even told the punchline. Thoreau's eschatology was part of his off-beat, good humor. He wrote jokes like this about the

[42] "As for these communities – I think I had rather keep batchelor's hall in hell than go to board in heaven. – Dost think thy virtue with be boarded with you? It will never live on the interest of your money, depend on it. The boarder has no home. In heaven I hope to bake my own bread and clean my own linen – The tomb is the only boarding house in which a hundred are served at once – in the catacomb we may dwell together and prop one another without loss." Thoreau, *Journal*, Volume 1: *1837–1844*, 277–78.

eschaton to suggest the possibility that – whatever the present political horrors – there could be a future in which human society might be a shelter where any traveler would be welcome in out of the "tempestuous night."

Conclusion

Thoreau was famously earnest. This was the man who wrote, "The mass of men lead lives of quiet desperation" (I, 9). He was also, at the same time, deeply playful. The rest of the paragraph in which that famous sentence appears suggests that it is precisely their lack of play that reveals the men's desperation.

> The mass of men lead lives of quiet desperation. What is called resignation is confirmed desperation. From the desperate city you go into the desperate country, and have to console yourself with the bravery of minks and muskrats. A stereotyped but unconscious despair is concealed even under what are called the games and amusements of mankind. There is no play in them, for this comes after work. But it is characteristic of wisdom not to do desperate things.
>
> (I, 9)

Even the games and amusements men pursue are expressions of unconscious despair. What does it mean, "There is no play in them, for this comes after work"? Does it mean that there is no play in them, because in order to play you have to have worked, and they have not worked? Or does it mean that the games come after work, but play should be all day? Recall the woodchopper who, in the midst of his work was free to lay down on a tree and laugh. In any case, the logic of the passage seems to suggest that what wisdom requires is play without desperation. And the way to achieve this, in Thoreau's view, was to live a life of such simplicity that there was room in it for play. As a writer, Thoreau insisted that there are some things so serious you have to say them playfully.[43]

At the time of his son Waldo's death, Emerson wrote about Thoreau in a catalogue of the people who had cared for Waldo, on January 30, 1842:

> Then Henry Thoreau had been one of the family for the last year, and charmed Waldo by the variety of toys, – whistles, boats, popguns, – and all kinds of instruments which he could make and mend; and possessed his love and respect by the gentle firmness with which he always treated him.[44]

According to those who knew Thoreau, he also told jokes in person. One story tells that as he was dying, Thoreau's aunt asked him if he had made peace with God. Thoreau is supposed to have responded, "I did not know we had ever quarreled."[45] It was a funny way to say that his life had been aimed at giving praise to God and doing justice.

This chapter has aimed to respond to common worries about asceticism: that it rejects pleasure and is humorless. This is in part because contemporary environmental discourse does risk succumbing to this classic critique of ascetic practice. Militant vegans are admirable in their commitment, but they

[43] I am reminded of Myles Horton, who wrote:

> I used to [be critical and disagree] whenever Martin Luther King, Jr., argued with me about nonviolence. He'd say, "Myles, you don't go all the way with nonviolence, you've got reservations." I'd say, "Yes, I've got reservations." For all practical purposes, I supported the nonviolence of the civil rights movement. It would have been counterproductive, in my opinion, to use violence; but philosophically, I reserved the right to say that at times I might be for violence in a revolutionary situation. *He used to kid me* and say, "Well, we're going to get you to love everybody one of these days," and I'd say, "When they get worth loving, I'll love them."

Horton, *The Long Haul*, 195–96. Emphasis added.

[44] Ralph Waldo Emerson, *Journals of Ralph Waldo Emerson, with Annotations*, vol. 6 (New York: Houghton Mifflin company, 1914), 152–53.

[45] Emerson, *Henry Thoreau: As Remembered by a Young Friend*, 118.

do not always help people see how veganism can transform our lives for the better. Thoreau's writing and his political asceticism more broadly were oriented toward humor and pleasure for both principled and strategic reasons. The principled reason to emphasize delight was that enjoyment of what is truly good is a basic human obligation, both to God and to the good that is enjoyed. The strategic reason to emphasize delight was that human motivation runs on it. For any of us to learn to practice an asceticism that will help us achieve the kind of awakening Thoreau recommended, to transform ourselves and our world, he thought we would have to learn to take delight in true goods.

Conclusion: The Promise of a Delighted Environmental Ethic

Thoreau's Ideas

This book is primarily an interpretation of *Walden*. Focusing on *Walden* as I have, however, ignores some of the most interesting scholarship on Thoreau of the past few decades. Sharon Cameron and William Howarth have both argued for the centrality of Thoreau's *Journal* in any assessment of his life and work as a whole.[1] For both, the *Journal* is Thoreau's great work, both by external literary criteria and in his own view. This argument rests on the way in which the ongoingness of the *Journal* suits Thoreau's sense that thinking itself is ongoing, that it can never rest, that it always happens in place, as I suggested in the Introduction. In this, Thoreau's first book, *A Week on the Concord and Merrimack Rivers*, was formative. A river provides an image of the way in which a thing can stay the same and keep moving, like a person who has different thoughts and experiences over time but remains the same in some important sense. For Thoreau, the first book did not come easily or simply.

Despite difficulty, Thoreau got from Goethe the heart to believe that he could write a great book. This would not have

[1] Cameron, *Writing Nature*; Howarth, *The Book of Concord*. This movement has also led contemporary scholars to a deeper understanding of Thoreau's growing interest in naturalist observation. Robert Kuhn McGregor, *A Wider View of the Universe: Henry Thoreau's Study of Nature*, Revised edition (Jefferson, NC: McFarland, 2017).

been obvious. Though it was something he wanted very badly, it took a long time to come to fruition in his life. Early in the process, it seems to have been Goethe who persuaded him that whatever his own strengths and (more pressingly) weaknesses, it would be possible for him to write a book. In the early years of his journal keeping, Thoreau wrote under subject headings. On December 8, 1837, while reading *The Italian Journey*, under the heading "Goethe," he wrote, "He is generally satisfied with giving an exact description of objects as they appear to him." Goethe's aim seemed to be "faithfully to describe what he sees, and that too, for the most part, in the order in which he saw it." This, Thoreau admired. I think he found it inspiring. In a new, one-sentence paragraph, Thoreau took heart in the idea that a book could be built on the faithful description of what the writer saw. "It would thus be possible for inferior minds to produce invaluable books."[2] The strategy Goethe taught was to write what you see, to look closely enough that you can put into words the world around you. This strategy also had the virtue of leaving whatever ideas came out of the writing in their native habitat, and thus legible to readers without distortion.

A Week was published in 1849, the year Thoreau turned 32. He paid for its production himself, and he seems to have taken its poor critical reception as a sign that it was not the invaluable book he had set out to write. He felt that success was slow, and might never come. This was true not only of his writing, but also of his life in society. On July 19, 1851, he wrote, "Here I am 34 years old, and yet my life is almost wholly unexpanded. How much is in the germ! There is such an interval between my ideal and the actual in many instances that I may say I am unborn. There is the instinct for society – but no society. Life is

[2] Thoreau, *Journal*, Volume 1: *1837–1844*, 16.

not long enough for one success."[3] Even as he was writing the book that would become *Walden*, Thoreau suggested that his life itself was like a seed that had not yet sprouted. There was more promise in it than fruition. His ideals were always surpassing his actual achievements. And it felt that this would be true for the whole of his life, thus, no success.

This perfectionism, the pursuit of an ideal that remains yet to come, shaped Thoreau's view on how writing ought to express thought. One of the key features of Thoreau's writing is that it represents his own attempt to come to understand, rather than to lay out an argument. This is related to the importance of the form of the *Journal*. For him, writing was not primarily *for* expressing a position that would be immutable in time. Writing was for investigation, which in many cases meant a description of his own experience of unknowing.

Thus, trying to write about his writing should not, I have come to believe, involve an attempt to articulate what he thought in some timeless sense, to express what his positions were. His writing insists on a more narratival form. This is a problem with the reception by Furtak and others in philosophy who are trying to draw him into professional conversations in their fields, which are often conducted as though ideas could be taken out of history.[4] Rather, to write about Thoreau must always necessarily be a form of storytelling; that is, it must take place in time, and with attention to his own context, and to ours.

This understanding of interpretation entails a view about what ideas themselves are. Thoreau and his friends were caught up in a spirit of the time, one that took from German

[3] Thoreau, *Journal*, Volume 3: *1848–1851*, 313.

[4] Rick Anthony Furtak, Jonathan Ellsworth, and James D. Reid, eds., *Thoreau's Importance for Philosophy* (Bronx, NY: Fordham University Press, 2012).

philosophy, often through Goethe and the British Romantics, the sense that ideas were not abstract, decontextualized things without being, but were instead, as much else is, living things who took shape in a community and coevolved with that community.

This book has tried to tell a story about the world in which Thoreau's ideas took shape, and to say something about the shape that they took. This story runs against prevalent understandings of Thoreau as asocial, apolitical, and areligious. In the first two chapters, I focused on Concord as the setting in which Thoreau's thinking took shape. Chapter 1 aimed to show the social world that *Walden* illuminated, the alternative community in the woods that Thoreau joined when he moved there among humans, trees, animals, and former inhabitants. Chapter 2 uncovered the political relevance of Thoreau's practices of renunciation by situating them in the developing industrial economy of the period. In Chapter 3, I argued that Thoreau's critique of philanthropy was theologically motivated. In Chapter 4, I aimed to synthesize the interpretive arguments of the first three chapters by describing the alternative religious response Thoreau suggested and experimented with: political asceticism. Chapter 5 argued that Thoreau's severe earnestness and good humor surprisingly go together, because there are some very serious things you can only think to say out of joy. Delight in true goods is the most serious thing in the world.

In writing about him, then, I have tried to tell a story about him, the things he did, the world he lived in, and the things that world made him think. Of course, there is also us, and the world where we live.[5] The rest of this Conclusion addresses that context.

[5] Our world has deeply shaped our understandings of Thoreau, as the environmental historian Kent Curtis showed in a survey of the uses to which Thoreau has been put in contemporary environmental history. Curtis, "The Virtue of Thoreau," 33–38. For a treatment of Thoreau's reception from his lifetime up to the 1990s, see Gary

Our World

Lynn White's classic article, "The Historical Roots of our Ecological Crisis," has had an enormous impact on the way the academic study of religion and ecology as a whole has developed.[6] White wrote five years after Rachel Carson's *Silent Spring* had touched off a new phase of environmental politics. Carson had written in the early 1960s about the dangers of the indiscriminate use of pesticides, including their effects as carcinogens. Her writing had found a huge audience. And then she had died of breast cancer in 1964. The citizens who had been her audience became the first mass movement of environmentalists. Ecological concerns were suddenly important to a much broader swath of the American public. As one history of the environmental movement described the massive shift of the early 1960s, "environmentalism moved from being the concern of the affluent and elderly of the boardroom on the one hand or the backwoods hunters and fishers on the other, to being the stuff of everyday life – and politics – for millions."[7]

White wrote in a context in which it had suddenly become newly apparent to many citizens that human technologies can have massive unintended harmful ecological consequences. While all living creatures affect their environments, White's view was that "the impact of our race upon the environment

Scharnhorst, *Henry David Thoreau: A Case Study in Canonization* (Columbia, SC: Camden House, 1994). Lawrence Buell's essay on the same topic is Lawrence Buell, "How Thoreau Enters the American Canon," in *New Essays on* Walden, ed. Robert F. Sayre (Cambridge: Cambridge University Press, 1992), 23–52.

[6] Lynn White, Jr., "The Historical Roots of Our Ecologic Crisis," *Science*, New Series, 155, 3767 (March 10, 1967): 1203–7; Willis Jenkins, "After Lynn White: Religious Ethics and Environmental Problems," *Journal of Religious Ethics* 37, 2 (June 1, 2009): 283–309.

[7] Kirkpatrick Sale, *The Green Revolution: The American Environmental Movement, 1962–1992* (New York: Hill and Wang, 1993), 14.

has so increased in force that it has changed in essence."[8] And White was concerned that the "many calls to action" of the period seemed "too partial, palliative, negative." It was no good to go back and try to fix every ecological problem individually. The whole thing had to be rethought at a deeper level. White proposed that what was required was a rethinking of "fundamentals," "our axioms," "the presuppositions that underlie modern technology and science."[9] But whereas in the beginning of the article he attributed human exploitative power over nature to "the Baconian creed" (dated to about 1850 in his account), he ended up arguing that the dominative view of nature ought to be dated to medieval Europe and attributed to Christian theology. The Christian teaching of human transcendence of and mastery over nature was a major cause of unjustified human exploitation of the natural world. White thus argued that a new understanding of Christian teaching about nature was a prerequisite to righting human-nature relationships.

White's view has shaped Christian reflection on the environment since, as many Christian theologians and ethicists have worked to offer the more wholesome understanding of human life integrated into nature that White called for. This has been important, productive work, in that it has offered the churches and all people of goodwill better, more integrated ways of talking and thinking and praying and living in the world.

But notice a feature of White's view that has often gone unexamined but has frequently been repeated. Recall the shape of White's argument: there was a *problem*, an ecological crisis, "our ecologic crisis" he called it. It consisted of those environmental impacts whose force he thought had shifted so much that they were now different in kind:

[8] White, "The Historical Roots of Our Ecologic Crisis," 1204. [9] White, 1204.

hydrogen bombs, fossil fuel combustion, population explosion, urban growth without planning, and the massive sewage and garbage that go with them – all these were the problems that constituted the crisis. In White's view, all these problems were *caused* most basically by a religious worldview, one he said developed in medieval Christendom. Thus, he asserted, they would not be resolved by "applying to our problems more science and more technology."[10] What was required was a new, nondominative doctrine of nature. The problematic principle in play was that humans are created by God to dominate nature. The principle that would solve the problem was "an alternative Christian view of nature and man's relation to it."[11] Thus, White proposed a theoretical solution (a new doctrine of nature) to a series of practical problems (risks of atomic war, atmospheric changes, and otherwise inhospitable human environments).

Whatever our various opinions on the merits of this argument – and the profusion of theoretical questions about anthropocentrism and value that came after it – the thing I want to draw your attention to is its shape. The ecologic crisis as he described it, though made of many parts, was rendered in the end as attributable to a singular, abstract problem: the dominative view of nature. From there, it seemed natural to seek a rather abstract solution, through a renovation of the Christian worldview and a nondominative doctrine of nature.

White was not the first to take the view he did of the basic situation, and he has certainly not been the last to offer a renovated worldview as a solution to the practical problems of our warming and otherwise threatened world. But even where White's particular rendering of the problem and its solution are not at issue, this shape of thinking has been widespread in environmental ethics of the last fifty years and

[10] White, 1206. [11] White, 1207.

has taken many diverse forms. Environmental ethicists have often taken the view that their writing should contribute to the amelioration of environmental problems. Otherwise, what would we even be doing? This is a vision of environmental ethics in which its task is to contribute to the resolution of environmental problems, often through the renovation of worldviews. Call it the White thesis, as Willis Jenkins has, or more pejoratively, "solution thinking."

Obviously, it is natural enough to want to resolve practical problems, especially to want to reform our communities to make them more just and more livable in what will necessarily be a painful ecological future. My own ethnographic work, which I described in the Preface, attended to the environmental harms one community is undergoing. I would like their ecological problems to ease, and I try to enable whatever political efforts seem to me most likely to produce that end. But I also know that my academic work so far has next to no bearing on the practical problems that community faces. Their problems are being settled by the courts and the Army Corps of Engineers, not in my writing. What is my work doing, I wonder, if it is not contributing to the resolution of practical problems?

On my view, White's assumption that a new way of thinking about nature would contribute to solving the practical problems he identified was lovely, and true in some important ways. I am drawn to the thesis White hinted at in the beginning of the article when he blamed the "Baconian creed" for exploitative attitudes. This thesis would suggest that exploitative attitudes to nature were cultivated in the West during controversies among scientists of the eighteenth-century Royal Society about the meaning of matter.[12] But I also find

[12] Akeel Bilgrami, "The Wider Significance of Naturalism: A Genealogical Essay," in *Naturalism and Normativity*, ed. Mario De Caro and David MacArthur (New York: Columbia University Press, 2010).

the view that a new doctrine of nature would redeem ecological problems massively naïve about the scope and nature of such problems. Even if we were all converted tomorrow to a nondominative worldview, all the practical problems we have about how to reshape our cultures and economies would remain.

Moral Theory and Problem Solving

In addition, there is something suspicious about the basic instinct that ethics should respond primarily to problems. To see this, take a broader view of a bigger landscape, moving from the conversation in religion and ecology and environmental ethics to a hasty sketch of a broader context in the wider field of ethics and moral philosophy. I am clearly not the first person who studies ethics to think that the problem/solution shape of thinking, what I called above "solution thinking," is insufficient as a mode of inquiry for the study of ethics. Objections to the role of thinly described moral quandaries in ethical inquiry has been a feature of the discipline from, say, the mid-twentieth-century dissenters in secular moral philosophy who pushed against an understanding of ethics as primarily concerned with rational principles for making difficult moral decisions.[13] This movement made way for the resurgence of what has frequently been called virtue ethics among both secular philosophers, who have often taken ancient philosophy as a corrective to the problems they saw in twentieth-century moral philosophy, and Christian ethicists, who have usually taken Christian reflection on the virtues as a corrective.

[13] Examples include G. E. M. Anscombe, "Modern Moral Philosophy," *Philosophy* 33, 124 (January 1, 1958): 1–19; Murdoch, *The Sovereignty of Good.*

To take one example from midcentury secular moral philosophy, think of Edmund Pincoffs's 1971 article, "Quandary Ethics." It began like this: "There is a consensus concerning the subject-matter of ethics so general that it would be tedious to document it. It is that the business of ethics is with 'problems', i.e. situations in which it is difficult to know what one should do."[14] Doing ethics with these sorts of problems, or quandaries, as the central subject implied that "the ultimate relevance of ethics is to the resolution of the problematic situations into which we fall."[15] "Quandary Ethics," as he called it, usually treats these practical cases – in the typical example an "anonymous collision situation" – on analogy to legal practice; which is to say that "what is relevant [to the case] must have nothing to do with *me*, but only with the situation: a situation in which anyone could find himself. What is right for me must be right for anyone."[16] In trying to offer ethical assistance to those of us who aim to live more ethical lives, Quandary Ethics insisted on describing the quandaries into which an agent might fall in the most general terms. This shortchanged the ethical task in advance, on Pincoffs's view, by removing from consideration the very features of experience that make life ethically difficult. Pincoffs's language about an "anonymous collision situation" was a terrifically dry joke about how lifeless trolley problems are.[17]

[14] Edmund Pincoffs, "Quandary Ethics," *Mind*, 80, 320 (October 1971): 552.

[15] Pincoffs, 556. [16] Pincoffs, 558.

[17] Trolley problems are a standard feature of much moral philosophy, where they function as simplified examples of moral dilemmas for the purpose of theorizing. Typically, they describe a situation in which someone standing at a switch has to decide where to send an out of control train bound to collide with other people. In what I can only view as a strange coincidence, Philippa Foot introduced the trolley problem in an article about abortion during the same year as White's famous article, 1967. Though the coincidence also makes a person wonder. Philippa Foot,

Quandary Ethics had a serious flaw, in Pincoffs's view: it aimed to discern what is right for anyone in the same circumstances to do. But agents do not carry out actions as general anyones in generic situations. "The question what is right for anyone in the same circumstances therefore provides the agent with but the beginnings of an answer to the question what he should do."[18] Whereas ethical inquiry aims to offer guidance to agents trying to live well, Quandary Ethics abstracted so much from agents and the ethical situations they face that it disallowed consideration of the very standards and ideals a moral agent uses to carry out moral deliberation. It is never the case that an act is carried out by an abstracted version of a human. "We are not then morally featureless." Pincoffs wrote:

> We are not disembodied, historyless, featureless creatures. We are beings who have developed to a point, have even cultivated ourselves. The problems which we face must qualify as problems for us, be our problems: it makes a difference who we are. We cannot describe the problem by describing an anonymous collision situation. Aristotle did not give open lectures; St. Paul did not write open letters. When they used the word "we", they spoke from within a community of expectations and ideals: a community within which character was cultivated.[19]

Every individual agent has special features, features that are relevant to his moral deliberation. Indeed "It is precisely these special features which are likely to give form to the perplexities which arise. They arise for us, not in a void."[20]

In this way, Pincoffs brought attention to the issue of character and context in ethical inquiry, and the title of his paper, "Quandary Ethics," became a slur within Christian

"The Problem of Abortion and the Doctrine of the Double Effect," in *Virtues and Vices and Other Essays in Moral Philosophy* (Oxford: Clarendon, 2002).

[18] Pincoffs, "Quandary Ethics," 564. [19] Pincoffs, 570. [20] Pincoffs, 570.

ethics. No one wants to be a quandarist, and the work that this movement yielded on the importance of formation and character in ethical life has been tremendously fruitful. It was part of a movement that yielded a renaissance within virtue thinking, both within religious and secular ethics. It has also, among other cultural influences, encouraged some ethicists to write about ideas in the first person, on the understanding – one they shared with Thoreau – that there is no view from nowhere.[21]

Problems in Environmental Ethics

Among those who work specifically on environmental ethics, there has lately been a wave of rethinking with respect to the White paradigm I described earlier, perhaps thanks in some part to that movement against thinly described problems in moral philosophy earlier in the twentieth century. A slate of recent scholars has tried to find ways out of thinking about new worldviews as solutions to environmental problems. Lisa Sideris has argued insistently and controversially that new cosmologies focused on the mythopoetical possibilities of science – such as those advanced under the descriptions New Story, Universe Story, or Epic of Evolution – are at best unnecessary to and at worst self-defeating of their aim to motivate environmental commitment.[22]

Willis Jenkins described and sought to avoid what he called "the cosmological temptation" in *The Future of Ethics*.

[21] "In most books, the *I*, or the first person, is omitted; in this it will be retained ... We commonly do not remember that it is, after all, always the first person that is speaking" (I, 2).

[22] A special issue of the *Journal for the Study of Religion* focuses on the controversy. Lisa H. Sideris, "Science as Sacred Myth? Ecospirituality in the Anthropocene Age," *Journal for the Study of Religion, Nature & Culture* 9, 2 (June 2015): 136–53.

According to Jenkins, scholars who submit to this temptation usually, like White, "propose a new moral worldview within which to make sense of the problems of sustainability and social justice."[23] This is a temptation to be avoided for Jenkins because "while often compelling, cosmological critiques pose a practical tradeoff: they make our inherited moral world seem incapable of facing difficult problems."[24] This is an illusion, of course, because our moral world is mostly inherited. We do not invent practicable new moralities out of thin air; we adapt them from our inheritances. Thus "cosmological critiques defeat the ethical task before it begins."[25] Sideris and Jenkins have different reasons for wanting to avoid the new cosmologies, but they agree that doing environmental ethics well will require forms that do not present any particular myth or doctrine as a singular solution to environmental woes. Call them purposeful pluralists. In my view, they announce a major trend in environmental ethics.

But Jenkins's alternative to "the cosmological temptation" is interesting with respect to what problems are and what their role is in environmental thought. He aimed to eschew the common framework I have called the White paradigm, the one I characterized as seeking solutions to problems, but Jenkins did it not by avoiding the shape of problem/solution, but precisely by beginning with concrete problems. The preface to his book explains why.

> Students had pressed me to say what difference ecotheologies make for confronting particular problems, and colleagues in

[23] Willis Jenkins, *The Future of Ethics: Sustainability, Social Justice, and Religious Creativity* (Washington, DC: Georgetown University Press, 2013), 4.

[24] Jenkins, 8. Here, Jenkins echoes movements toward "strengths-based approaches" among communities that have long been studied as sites of damage. See, for example, Eve Tuck, "Suspending Damage: A Letter to Communities," *Harvard Educational Review* 79, 3 (September 1, 2009): 409–28.

[25] Jenkins, *The Future of Ethics*, 8.

> other disciplines wanted to know how I think theology matters to processes of cultural change. So I set out to describe how grammars of belief could generate satisfactory responses to representative problems of human power like: climate change, human poverty, biodiversity loss, and chemical exposures.[26]

He started the book thinking that ecotheologies could serve as "satisfactory responses" to problems. But what he found in actually writing the book was that describing the problems was a challenge in and of itself, and it did not in fact lead naturally to the "satisfactory responses" to those problems he had set out to offer. Ecotheology wasn't a solution to anything; beginning with detailed descriptions of actual problems transformed the way he thought about the whole field, and the role he thought religious ethics could play in it. He wrote:

> Ethics cannot start by responding to problems, but must participate in the interpretation and construction of problems, which requires attending to climate science, models of poverty, and the economics of discounting. Ethics cannot be a disciplinary operation performed by specialists after some problem is posed; it must be a capacity of practical reasoning cultivated within interdisciplinary research struggling to interpret and frame emerging problems.[27]

Jenkins began the project hoping for satisfactory responses to environmental problems, but engaging deeply with the problems themselves changed his views of what environmental problems *are*, who is competent to describe them, and how they and the act of their description are related to ethics.

Thus, Jenkins undertook thick descriptions of environmental problems and found that in doing so he reframed the question – not "how can we solve the environmental crisis?" But "what will ethics in the face of unprecedented problems

[26] Jenkins, vii. [27] Jenkins, 9.

look like?" His answer pushed back against the White paradigm as I have described it. He wrote, "Religious ethics, I argue, should focus less on constructing and applying religious worldviews and more on inviting, tutoring, and pressuring moral communities to make better use of their inheritances."[28] This was a specifically pluralist vision. Whether human communities can find ways of adapting and living through the inevitably difficult environmental future, religious ethicists should participate in helping all moral communities adapt their diverse moral inheritances to Earth's drastically changed situation.

Rethinking White's Problem

Like Jenkins and the other scholars resisting new cosmologies as solutions to environmental failure, I think the prevalence of the White paradigm has been unfortunate, in that it has put an unnecessary constraint on our imaginations about what environmental ethics is, and has committed us to claims that seem straightforwardly false about the good people do by changing their minds about their doctrine of nature. As Jenkins has argued, it has been commonplace for religious ethicists to argue that "unprecedented challenges require religious and ethical thinkers to narrate a new story or retrieve a forgotten moral vision in order to reorient humanity's moral consciousness."[29] But who really hopes that we can reorient humanity's moral consciousness wholesale? And many environmental problems (like those faced by my community in Florida) require more complicated, in-depth attention than the White paradigm suggested.

[28] Jenkins, vii. [29] Jenkins, 4.

Stories are important, and moral vision helps us orient ourselves. However, communities facing environmental trouble had better not need to *share* a singular moral vision in order to address the problems they face. The fact of pluralism will persist in any community, even a largely homogenous one. Sociologist Justin Farrell published an ethnography of Yellowstone in which he argues that environmental conflict persists in the Greater Yellowstone Ecosystem, even with an abundance of scientific, economic, legal and technical evidence. This intransigent, often toxic conflict persists, on Farrell's view, because it reflects "an underlying struggle over deeply held 'faith' commitments, feelings, and desires that define what people find sacred, good, and meaningful in life at a most basic level."[30] *That* struggle is not going to come to an end until history itself does, and seeking unity of moral vision under such conditions is not only futile; it refuses the diversity inherent in necessarily differentiated human personhood. The strength of the purposefully pluralist direction that environmental ethics is taking among scholars of religion is that it insists on finding a way forward in the midst of this vast diversity.

But while scholars like Sideris and Jenkins are offering productive new visions for religion and ecology, it would be premature to dismiss White. When you go back to White's article and read it with Jenkins's proposal in mind – the proposal that ethics "should focus less on constructing and applying religious worldviews and more on inviting, tutoring, and pressuring moral communities to make better use of their inheritances" – you can see White himself doing something like what Jenkins describes. After all, White did not propose a new cosmology. He appealed to Francis of Assisi, a canonized

[30] Justin Farrell, *The Battle for Yellowstone: Morality and the Sacred Roots of Environmental Conflict* (Princeton, NJ: Princeton University Press, 2015), 3.

saint, as "the greatest spiritual revolutionary in Western history." He suggested that Francis should be "a patron saint for ecologists."[31] And when you look back on what has happened since White – perhaps especially Jorge Mario Bergoglio taking Francis as his papal name, and the warm reception the encyclical *Laudato Si'* has received among all who share concern for the environment, including non-religious environmentalists who recognize the importance of religious environmentalism for environmental politics – White looks like he may have been somewhat successful at pressuring both Christians and Western environmentalists to make better use of the inheritance they had in Francis. In any case, he seems to have had an idea that has gained a lot of traction.

Still, while I notice that White was doing something like what Jenkins describes in "inviting, tutoring, and pressuring moral communities to make better use of their inheritances," I persist in thinking White might have done something more useful with the inheritance Christians and Western environmentalists have in Francis, something that has a lot to do with the "political asceticism" I have aimed to describe in this book. White described Francis as a "spiritual revolutionary," whose view of nature as a co-equal part of creation would have brought about a different history if it had been the doctrine of nature adopted in the West.[32] In doing so, White contributed to a long reception history in which Francis's poverty has been depoliticized.[33] In White's account, Francis was revolutionary because he had a different doctrine of

[31] White, "The Historical Roots of Our Ecologic Crisis," 1207. [32] White, 1207.

[33] And in which "Protestant writers came to terms with [Catholic saints] as heroic individuals acting in spite of, or even against, the church." Patricia Appelbaum, "St. Francis in the Nineteenth Century," *Church History* 78, 4 (December 2009): 793. Appelbaum was citing Jenny Franchot, *Roads to Rome: The Antebellum Protestant Encounter with Catholicism* (Berkeley, CA: University of California Press, 1994), 203, 256.

nature from those around him. As Brian Hamilton's work on Francis and the other medieval poverty movements shows, this popular image often subtracts the sharp political critique that was central to those movements. Francis did not merely have a different view of nature; he pushed back against the accumulation of wealth that was driving economic inequality in the period. Hamilton resituates the poverty movements in their political contexts, and shows how they were also social and political movements of protest over the accumulation of wealth ongoing in medieval Europe. Francis was not merely, as White's treatment and so many others suggest, exemplary with respect to his doctrine of nature. Rather, as Hamilton writes, "In turning to the apostolic life as he did, Francis embroiled himself in a long-standing struggle over the structures of power that defined medieval Europe."[34]

The current environmental movement, when it is successful, is less and less about doctrines of nature and more and more about achieving the democratic political power required to push back against the accumulation of capital and power by exploitative industries. To the extent that White made Francis seem as though his goodness existed only in his character or his principles, White undermined one of Francis's essential lessons for our age, which is that good character sometimes means living your life so that it will transform the politics of your period, so that it will undermine the structures of domination to which your life would otherwise contribute.

Connecting Character to Structural Change

Ethical theory of the last sixty years has had a complicated relationship to problems. On the one hand, it is clear that

[34] Hamilton, "The Politics of Poverty," 40.

moral problems often drive ethical inquiry. Trolley problems provide a hook for students by giving them straightforward examples of moral difficulty. But on the other hand, many ethicists, both in environmental ethics and more broadly, have been dissatisfied with ethical theories that prioritize ethical problems and the attempt to resolve them with ethical principles over attention to moral character and social context. I have described two important movements in ethics in the last sixty years or so: the suspicion of thinly described problems or quandaries that would rely on an abstract set of principles for their solution (whether deontologist or consequentialist), and the resultant turn to character and thick description of problems rather than thin moral quandaries or abstract problems (whose shorthand has become "virtue ethics"). There is also a contemporary movement toward virtue ethics in some corners of environmental ethics.[35]

In some cases, however, scholars have responded to the movement for virtue ethics by noticing a shortcoming of its emphasis on character: it does not always make clear how a person of good character, a virtuous person, actually addresses difficult, institutional, large-scale political and social problems.[36] Scholars with this concern recommend a

[35] Ronald L. Sandler, *Character and Environment: A Virtue-Oriented Approach to Environmental Ethics* (New York: Columbia University Press, 2007); Rosalind Hursthouse, "Evironmental Virtue Ethics," in *Working Virtue*, ed. Rebecca L. Walker and Philip J. Ivanhoe (Oxford: Oxford University Press, 2007), 155–72; Matt Zwolinski and David Schmidtz, "Environmental Virtue Ethics," in *The Cambridge Companion to Virtue Ethics*, ed. Daniel C. Russell (Cambridge: Cambridge University Press, 2013), 221–39; Philip Cafaro, "Environmental Virtue Ethics Special Issue: Introduction," *Journal of Agricultural and Environmental Ethics* 23, 1–2 (2010): 3–7; Philip Cafaro, "Environmental Virtue Ethics," in *The Routledge Companion to Virtue Ethics*, ed. Lorraine Besser-Jones and Michael Slote (New York: Routledge, 2015), 427–44.

[36] Readers can look for discussion of virtue ethics and its attention to or neglect of politics in a series of articles focused on method in comparative religious ethics. Elizabeth M. Bucar and Aaron Stalnaker, "On Comparative Religious Ethics as a

form of inquiry that is concerned not only with individual character and the virtues but also with the evaluation and transformation of the social forms and institutions in which those individuals take part. The concern about a focus on character and virtue comes from the important intuition that thick descriptions of good people do not actually do much on their own to address the most intransigent social and political problems moral agents face. One of the most recurrent questions in this field has been how to connect the small scale, where the focus is on character and community, to the big scale, where the problems of systemic injustice rage. This scalar problem was never new, and it has only been intensified by the wicked problems of the anthropocene.[37]

Connecting character to structural change is difficult because being a good person in a complicated world is difficult. And some ethicists are making a turn in ethical theory to examine what we can learn from examples of moral success. Linda Zagzebski's *Exemplarist Moral Theory* is the most ambitious program statement yet for this form of ethical inquiry.[38] She suggests that attention to specific examples of admirable persons may be the foundation for a successful moral theory. She provides a strong role for narrative. In this

Field of Study," *Journal of Religious Ethics* 42, 2 (2014): 358–84; John Kelsay, "Response to Bucar and Stalnaker," *Journal of Religious Ethics* 42, 3 (2014): 564–70; Jung Lee, "Comparative Religious Ethics Among the Ruins," *Journal of Religious Ethics* 42, 3 (2014): 571–84.

[37] "Wicked problem" is a technical term taken from academic literature on public policy, where it refers to problems whose social complexity means they do not yield solutions. It appeared first in Horst W. J. Rittel and Melvin M. Webber, "Dilemmas in a General Theory of Planning," *Policy Sciences* 4, 2 (June 1, 1973): 155–69. The phrase has proliferated in literature about climate change in the intervening years. See Jenkins on the ethics of wicked problems. Jenkins, *The Future of Ethics*, chapter 4.

[38] Linda Trinkaus Zagzebski, *Exemplarist Moral Theory* (New York, NY: Oxford University Press, 2017).

context, hagiography – which is to say writing the stories of those we admire – begins to look a lot like a mode of ethics.

But if hagiography is important in ethics, the narratives we tell about exemplary persons and the things we admire when we admire their stories will have a large role in how we live our lives. That is why it matters that Hamilton is retelling Francis's story to emphasize the resistance Francis provided to the structures of domination in medieval Europe. The centrality of admirable examples to the moral life also provides a rationale for reexamining other admired figures – as I have examined Thoreau in this book – to see if we cannot, as Jenkins suggested, invite, tutor, and pressure our moral communities to make better use of their inheritances.

Rereading Thoreau: Political Asceticism in the Context of Contemporary Politics

I interpret Thoreau's *Walden* as taking the community he found in Walden Woods as *his* moral example, and as inspiration for a form of economy that no one had yet imagined – an economy that would submit neither to the domination of slavery nor to the exploitation of industrial capitalism. This interpretation of Thoreau can shift what Thoreau is an example of for those who admire him in the environmental movement. Not all will agree that he should serve as a moral exemplar, but, for those who do, I think we ought to admire something rather different in him than we might have learned in school. Yes, he embraced individualism – marching to the beat of a different drummer – and yes, his independent living is inspiring to those of us hoping to live lighter on the Earth. But the thing I admire about him is that he saw the deep connections between justice among humans and justice for all beings. He had a nondominative doctrine of nature, it is true, and what it yielded in his life was a radical politics for labor justice that contributed to the enfranchisement of many oppressed people throughout the twentieth century. *That* is something to admire.

In this, my interpretation of Thoreau joins those who want to emphasize asceticism's positive role in the formation of individuals. It also suggests that scholars might find political aims at the heart of much ascetic practice, if we will give more in-depth attention to the social, cultural, and economic worlds that surround it. And it suggests ways of bringing important historical materials to bear on an environmental ethics that takes account of the three-part movement I described earlier – a way that resists orienting itself by the desire to solve technical problems ethicists are not competent to address, that accounts for the centrality of character in the moral life, and that realizes that the cultivation of virtue apart from politics is not sufficient to address the most intransigent moral problems we face. Good character sometimes means living your life so that it will transform politics. What was admirable in Francis and Thoreau was both their nondominative doctrine of nature, and the politics that doctrine yielded, a politics that resisted economic injustice.

In my account, political asceticism is religious practice oriented toward transforming social, political, economic, and spiritual life. My interest in political asceticism responds to what I view as a widespread problem with the way people, including some scholars, understand the category of religion. The past few decades in religious studies have seen scholars insist that the study of religion has focused for too long on the study of religious belief over against religious practice. But even where interpreters are not overly focused on belief to the exclusion of practice, often they conceive "religious practice" as somehow isolated from the social, political, and economic worlds in which it is enmeshed (and sometimes even from the theological traditions in which practices are situated). Too much scholarship on religion, and especially on ascetic practice, isolates one of these realms from the others, or conceives of religion as essentially private.

In the case of scholarship on asceticism, much of it focuses exclusively on practices of contemplation and individual mystical experience, or what is sometimes called "spirituality." The problem is not that scholars are interested in practices of contemplation and mystical experience. I am also interested in those features of religious life and of asceticism. The problem is when that focus on so-called spirituality leads to neglect of the social, political, and economic features of religious practices. Spirituality in my understanding can be closely tied to social, political, and economic life. If it is actually life with the spirit, it ought not be politically quietist.

The tendency to obscure the broader significance of individual practice is not only a problem within a scholarly context, however. One feature of much contemporary public discourse about climate change and other environmental problems is the way it encourages citizens to naïve moralism about the individual personal practices that are supposed to contribute to better environmental outcomes, for example bicycling and recycling. When I was a teacher of first-grade students in the Bay Area of California in the late 2000s, my students had clearly been taught this kind of moralism. They took recycling as a sign of their personal goodness. Some particularly anxious students would be upset with their peers if they did not follow the process for recycling that they had been taught was the solution to environmental problems.

In response to this kind of individual moralism, other commentators respond that what environmental problems require is not personal reformation, of the kind my first-graders were trying to help one another pursue, but rather "political" action. These commentators insist on this because there is a sense in which it is true: the most problematic features of present economies cannot be reformed without the reform of business and government. Recycling will not be sufficient (especially as it becomes clearer and clearer that it is not a sustainable way of processing waste). The reformation necessary requires collaborative action on a massive scale against the stranglehold of capital and power on public goods.[39]

Where I live, in Melbourne, Australia, these two perspectives on environmental reform – on the one hand personal or small-scale communal activity, and on the other larger-scale political reform – are often made explicit within activist communities. In fact, as I finished the manuscript of this book in October 2019 there was an ongoing series of public conversations being advertised under the title: "Politics vs. Community Activism: Which Has the Most Influence in Helping Reduce the Crises?" People designing these community programs and people attending them were asking what I take to be very important questions about how to direct their finite energy. But it strikes me that the zero-sum form of a debate question is a problem with respect to a supposed contrast between nation state politics and smaller-scale activism. Putting the question in the form of a debate suggests that one or the other of the alternatives posed is better, and that at the end of the contest everyone in the room should choose to devote all of their energy to the side that wins the question. In response to what I take to be this very common false binary, Thoreau's political asceticism offers an understanding of personal practice that is integrated into larger forms of sociality and politics. How we each live is connected to what politics will become.

[39] As Michael Northcott has argued, practices aimed at reducing individual emissions are insufficient to the economic reform required to stop the burning of coal. Northcott, *A Political Theology of Climate Change*, 50–84.

This understanding of personal practice as contributing to political life requires what is for some people a counterintuitive understanding of the key term, politics. Sometimes people who insist on the necessity of a "political" response to environmental problems implicitly assume a concept of politics that excludes small-scale action. In this way, they imply that so-called individual activities, like buying carbon offsets, cultivating native plants, or contributing to a neighborhood garden organization, do not contribute to the reformation of ecological life for the better. I fear that when we insist on the necessity of "politics" – where we mean a vision of politics that is vigorous, unstinting, and aimed at nation states – we often fail to see the political and ethical import of disciplined personal practice, small-scale community activities, and even local government. When this happens, we may demotivate people from wielding the political powers that they in fact do have. It often feels like the powers each of us has are too small to face vast environmental problems. But politics as I conceive it is not only about the government of the nation state.

Politics is just people doing what they can, in the realms over which they have actual power, to make arrangements for living together better. Each of us has power over a different set of circumstances. Many of us have greater powers than we acknowledge. Many of us should be trying to build power for ourselves and our communities to effect social and environmental change. But because we are all different and hold different roles in different communities, each of us will thus also have a different set of considerations in view when the question arrives: What political effort shall I undertake? Answering this question should throw us back to discernment about what communities we belong to, what talents we have, and what power we have the capacity to build. "Just keep trying" is an anticlimactic conclusion to a long book, but it is the truest thing I know how to say. In order to do it, we will need to remember what delights us.

The Place I Love

When I was a child, at home on a bay in the Gulf of Mexico, my mom and I would go fishing with my cousins for specimens to keep for a day or two in our salt-water aquarium before setting them free again. We have a short seine net – a rectangular net with brown square mesh – floats on the top and weights on the bottom. Each end has a pole attached. In shallow sea grass, wearing our bathing suits in the warm water of the bay, she would hold one pole and I the other. I would stand in the shallows, at the edge of the grass, while she ventured out into deeper water. As she walked, the water inched up her waist until she stood nearly neck deep. She turned, and she looked at me, and we would start to walk parallel to the shore, she a little ahead of me, so that fish scared by our steps and swimming out to the deep would be caught nonetheless in our net. The grass got caught in our toes. When the net was full, I would plant my pole and she would swing in toward the shore so we were both facing the beach, the net between us bulging with the baby animals that call this estuary bay home. We would pull the net up to the shore, lift it, and, surrounded by a little crowd of cousins, set it on the sand to see what we had caught.

The children, my cousins, would gather around after we had pulled in the net to see baby grouper, fat and black; little puffer fish, prickling like pineapples; sea grass-shaped needlefish, wriggling; mounds and mounds of shiners – the bait-fish that are silvery with yellowish stripes; and every now and then, for the luckiest searchers, a tiny seahorse, clinging to the grass that got pulled in. That was the most precious of all finds. For a brief moment when I saw a seahorse, hidden among the seaweed in the net, I swear it felt like the kingdom had indeed come. We would collect what we wanted for the aquarium in a bucket, and throw the rest back, to swim free in their ocean home. It was an exhilarating introduction to the variety of life that exists in this, God's great, wide world.

The ecosystem my mother showed us when we fished was not only delightful to us as children. It is also the basis of the livelihoods for an entire fishing culture. Seventy percent of the commercial species caught in the Gulf spend some juvenile period in the sea grass beds she showed us we should love. But that fishery has been struggling for decades through environmental change. Since the summer of 2010, when the oil rig Deepwater Horizon exploded and fell into the sea, killing eleven workers and setting off the largest marine oil spill in the history of the petroleum industry, I have conducted intermittent fieldwork in a seafood town near where I grew up, in a place just beyond where the oil from the Macondo well washed ashore. During the summer of 2014, as the local oyster industry faced collapse or transformation – we still don't quite know which – I worked at a coffee shop, attended local government meetings, got to know seafood workers, marine biologists and environmentalists, and had individual conversations with as many of these people as I could about their thinking about the various environmental changes that face the region now, and are coming in the future.

One of these conversations presented what I have come to view as a major challenge to the kind of humanistic ethnographic research for ethics I went there to pursue. On August 11, 2014, in a discussion about how I might focus the topic of my research, a local environmental activist complained about a relational dynamic he thought was slowing down political efforts to resolve a water conflict. He said, "Part of the problem is because of this relationship dynamic going on amongst us [by which he meant the environmental organization he runs], the seafood workers, and the state. If you could put your finger on what that is we might be able to make some progress." In fact, the dynamic he described was what I was most interested in: finding out how people who share some aims, like "saving the bay" as they might say, but hardly any ways of thinking about the values that animate those aims end up talking to one another and making decisions on the issues they care most about. But his suggestion for my research, that I help them address problems they were having, showed his wanting my research to make things better in a concrete way, as the social scientists who so often study their community and what they call its "resilience" usually promise they can.[40]

Despite my own investment in the place and the success of his efforts, I couldn't make such a promise. I had to say, "I don't think I have a solution to that problem." From my perspective, the relational dynamic he described was part of the ubiquitous difficulties of politics, difficulties that in this case weren't puzzles to be solved, via social science, but muddles they had to work through as well as they could.

[40] Some examples focused on the Gulf Coast generally, which is often seen as a laboratory of resilience because of the cyclical nature of hurricane destruction: Bret J. Blackmon et al., "Adapting to Life after Hurricane Katrina and the Deepwater Horizon Oil Spill: An Examination of Psychological Resilience and Depression on the Mississippi Gulf Coast," *Social Work in Public Health* 32, 1 (January 2, 2017): 65–76; Craig E. Colten and Alexandra Giancarlo, "Losing Resilience on the Gulf Coast: Hurricanes and Social Memory," *Environment: Science and Policy for Sustainable Development* 53, 4 (June 24, 2011): 6–19; T. C. Hansel and Tonya Hansel, "Gulf Coast Resilience Coalition: An Evolved Collaborative Built on Shared Disaster Experiences, Response, and Future Preparedness," *Disaster Medicine & Public Health Preparedness* 9, 6 (December 1, 2015): 657–65; John R. Logan, Sukriti Issar, and Zengwang Xu, "Trapped in Place? Segmented Resilience to Hurricanes in the Gulf Coast, 1970–2005," *Demography* 53, 5 (October 1, 2016): 1511–34; Paula A. Madrid, "Resilience Challenged: Thoughts on Children's Mental Health in the Gulf Coast 5 Years after Katrina," *Pediatrics* 128, Suppl 1 (August 1, 2011): S26–27.

Muddles that *they* were the people most qualified to work through. He, however, took my saying I didn't have a solution to his problem as an expression of despair, as though if I didn't have a solution to a practical problem my research was futile. Having assumed this, our conversation continued with his commiserating and trying to encourage me. I didn't know how to tell him that it wasn't despair. I just figured I wasn't the most competent person in that situation to address the problem he was describing.

I tell you this story from that moment in my life – when I was wondering how I might use ethnography to think through some issues in environmental ethics – to explain one way I have experienced the search for solutions to environmental problems as constraining for my work. I am looking for productive ways around this constraint because I maintain faith that religious ethics has much to contribute to a suffering world, even if we cannot solve its problems.

When one of my most important interlocutors for that ethnographic project took my sense of what my research was *about* as a sign of despair, I began to think there was some preliminary work I needed to do before I could write the ethnography I had set out to write. Maybe I needed to learn to describe a form of thinking that can show people like him what I mean to do, why I am interested in their efforts and their communities without thinking I can offer them solutions, and how I hope to contribute to the flourishing of our shared life without directing my research at solving the most pressing problems they themselves see.

Thoreau had his own worries about people with the instinct to solve. Philanthropy was, in his view, a field full of those who wanted to solve problems. Remember the one who ate green apples in Chapter 3 and then set about reforming – the world? The solution-oriented reformers that Thoreau encountered troubled him. Change works more slowly than we would like in many cases, and the instinct to solve can make us impatient. But Thoreau's work shows that there are many things our work in religious ethics can continue to profitably do, even if we give up grand solutions: We can redescribe problems, can see old problems as only the symptom of a deeper problem, can imagine new, more democratic solutions, and – perhaps most pressingly for a warming world – can see what we once thought were problems, like living within limits and the acts of renunciation such living requires, as blessings instead. Such renunciation can sometimes help us delight in true good.

I hope that though my interpretive work about Thoreau is not focused on the practical environmental problems of the community I focused on in that ethnographic work, it nonetheless follows Jenkins's recommendation that religious ethics should focus less on constructing and applying religious worldviews and more on "inviting, tutoring, and pressuring moral communities to make better use of their inheritances." Thoreau is an heir of ancient religious asceticism, and an important father figure for environmental thought and democracy in an industrial age. He is thus a major figure for diverse contemporary ethical communities.

Thoreau's political asceticism is not a straightforward model for our own politics.[41] Neither is it nostalgia for a golden age of Romanticism. Thoreau sought to envision a way out of the economies that were on offer – the developing industrial wage labor of the North, the collapsing slave labor of the South, and the financial capitalism in which the farmers of Concord were caught up. We still struggle to find a

[41] Josh Kotin argues that almost all interpreters take *Walden* as a model, but he adamantly disagrees that it ought to be read as one. Kotin, *Utopias of One*.

communal, economic life that can embody our highest ideals, and I do not pretend to have invented it here.[42]

But environmental ethics needn't only be about how to solve a practical problem with abstract ideas. Philosophy is also a way of life. And living well is pushing as you can from where you are for the future of the world we share, it is loving some place and some people well enough – my mother taught me and my cousins to love sea grass beds and the communities that rely upon them – that you can mourn well the harms they undergo, work like hell to protect them, and in the meanwhile delight like a child in this beautiful world. Such delight – as ours when we fished – sustains the work we must do to protect the goods that remain.

[42] I take hope, however, in creative people who are trying to work it out. See, for example, John Michael Colón et al., "Community, Democracy, and Mutual Aid," 2017, https://thenextsystem.org/community-democracy-mutual-aid (accessed August 20, 2020). Also see Thomas M. Hanna, *Our Common Wealth: The Return of Public Ownership in the United States* (Manchester: Manchester University Press, 2018). Jedidiah Purdy has also written recently on the idea of commonwealth. Jedediah Purdy, *This Land Is Our Land: The Struggle for a New Commonwealth* (Princeton, NJ: Princeton University Press, 2019).

Epilogue: On Mourning

I began to think seriously about environmental ethics in the aftermath of the explosion of the oil rig Deepwater Horizon in 2010. The disaster inspired my first fieldwork trip to Franklin County, Florida. As the oil gushed from the uncapped well for months, I – like everyone else who cares about the Gulf coast – felt a surge of sadness and anxiety: What if everything we loved was gone? I became obsessed, in the early days of the oil gush, with reading the news. As "solution" after "solution" for closing the so-called leak failed, as the estimates of the rate of flow climbed ever upward, from leak, to gush, to rip-roaring unstoppable tide, my heart fell. I couldn't sleep. I cried. I watched the animated map of the surface oil on the *New York Times* website grow and grow. I stared at satellite images of the slick, imagining just how close everything there was to ruin. And I talked to people who were on the coast, waiting for the oil to arrive. They were not panicked; they were heartbroken. It is impossible to be panicked when there is nothing you can do. They were working overtime at their various jobs but none of their efforts could alter the course of the oil. They tried to make the most of what they thought might be their last days with that beautiful place. They said they felt like they were waiting for a friend to die. They prayed, desperately, and they had a new sense of what their community meant, because it was under threat.

While my partner and I were there that summer for the fieldwork I was doing, talking to people about their grief, we swam one night in the bay where my parents lived. It was a new moon, and the bioluminescent creatures that live in the water sparkled as fish darted away from our feet. I had not swum there on a new moon in years, and I remembered as the streaks of glowing blue-white flashed away, out of sight, just how full of life the ocean is. David exclaimed, "there are so many things living here!" And the living things that are the most amazing of all, I think, are the ones that illuminate the world thriving under the surface. Those nearly microscopic creatures sparkle and shake; they seem to have a shape, but they are so small I cannot make it out; from a distance, there are so many that they seem just a glow. When I swim my feet and hands light up, as though the sea is sparkling back at the stars.

The main thing I talked to people about that summer was their grief that the life they had relied on was changing in ways they did not yet know. A psychologist came to study them and found they were anxious and depressed.[1] At the time, it felt like something I needed to tell people about: Here is what it feels like when your way of life is passing away. But now... This feeling is likely familiar to you, even if you don't talk about climate change much (most people don't[2]), even if you are not grieving in the intensified form that comes with catastrophic loss. We are all facing changes to the world we live in and rely on, and the intervening years have also brought much more attention to the psychological effects of environmental change.[3]

[1] Lynn M. Grattan et al., "The Early Psychological Impacts of the Deepwater Horizon Oil Spill on Florida and Alabama Communities," *Environmental Health Perspectives* 119, 6 (June 2011): 838–43.

[2] "Climate Change in the American Mind: March, 2016," *Yale Program on Climate Change Communication* (blog), http://climatecommunication.yale.edu/publications/climate-change-american-mind-march-2016/ (Accessed August 22, 2020).

[3] Pathbreaking work on this included: Glenn Albrecht, "'Solastalgia': A New Concept in Health and Identity," *PAN: Philosophy Activism Nature*, 3 (2005):

Along with the anxiety and depression psychologists study, there is something else. We are mourning the lives and worlds we are losing. This kind of mourning is good work too. Mourning the things we love and lose is a form of justice. It renders what is due.

While I was working on this manuscript, those people on the Gulf Coast were recovering from Hurricane Michael, which hit the Panhandle on October 10, 2018. It was the first storm to hit that region at a Category 5. After it hit, my mom said when she drove the coast highway she couldn't tell what had changed and what had stayed the same, because it was all so different. A young man I met during my fieldwork, who helps run his family's seafood business, was featured in the *New York Times*. There, he said the business likely sustained losses from $400,000 to $500,000.[4] One man I know, 70 years old, lived in Lanark. When he leaves me voice messages they always end with a slightly wry, "God Bless America!" I've heard half his house went in the bay and half went in the woods. The funding package passed by the US Congress in February 2019 to keep the government open withdrew federal hurricane relief funding from those impacted by Michael, in preference for border security.

Thoreau's Religion does not offer people on the Panhandle recovering (despite their government) from Michael and the storms that inevitably followed panaceas for climate change and other environmental harm. It does not mitigate the unpredictable future they (and we) face. But the book does try to

41–55; Glenn Albrecht et al., "Solastalgia: The Distress Caused by Environmental Change," *Australasian Psychiatry: Bulletin of Royal Australian and New Zealand College of Psychiatrists* 15 Suppl 1 (2007): S95–98.

[4] Patricia Mazzei, "For a Struggling Oyster Town, Hurricane Michael May Be One Misery Too Many," *The New York Times*, October 13, 2018, sec. U.S., www.nytimes.com/2018/10/12/us/fishing-communities-damage-hurricane.html (accessed August 23, 2020).

entice you to remember that some of the best things we have, we only have in common; and that when we enjoy those things together, enjoyment can offer some of the finest satisfactions humans know.

As we mourn, we will have to make choices about how to live in difficult times. Will our losses make us mean? Or can we put the common good at the center of our shared life, enjoy the necessary renunciations, delight in the simple gifts that remain, and create the politics required to sustain justice?

Bibliography

Abbey, Edward. "Down the River with Henry Thoreau." In *Down the River*, 13–48. New York: Plume, 1991.

Abelove, Henry. *Deep Gossip*. Minneapolis, MN: University Of Minnesota Press, 2005.

Abram, David. *The Spell of the Sensuous: Perception and Language in a More-than-Human World*. New York: Pantheon, 1996.

Agamben, Giorgio. *Profanations*. Translated by Jeff Fort. New York: Zone Books, 2007.

Albanese, Catherine. Review of *Thoreau: Mystic, Prophet, Ecologist*, by William J. Wolf. *Church History* 44, 1 (1975): 133–34.

Albrecht, Glenn. "'Solastalgia': A New Concept in Health and Identity." *PAN: Philosophy Activism Nature*, 3 (2005): 41–55.

Albrecht, Glenn, Gina-Maree Sartore, Linda Connor, Nick Higginbotham, Sonia Freeman, Brian Kelly, Helen Stain, Anne Tonna, and Georgia Pollard. "Solastalgia: The Distress Caused by Environmental Change." *Australasian Psychiatry: Bulletin of Royal Australian and New Zealand College of Psychiatrists* 15, Suppl 1 (2007): S95–98.

Anderson, Elizabeth. "Liberty, Equality, and Private Government." In *The Tanner Lectures in Human Values*. Princeton, NJ: Princeton University Press, 2015. https://tannerlectures.utah.edu/Anderson%20manuscript.pdf (accessed August 20, 2020).

Anscombe, G. E. M. "Modern Moral Philosophy." *Philosophy* 33, 124 (January 1, 1958): 1–19.

Anson, April. "The Patron Saint of Tiny Houses." In *Henry David Thoreau in Context*, edited by James Finley. Cambridge: Cambridge University Press, 2017.

Appelbaum, Patricia. "St. Francis in the Nineteenth Century." *Church History* 78, 4 (December 2009): 792–813.

Arendt, Hannah. *Crises of the Republic: Lying in Politics; Civil Disobedience; On Violence; Thoughts on Politics, and Revolution*. New York: Harcourt Brace & Company, 1969.

Atwood, Margaret. *Negotiating with the Dead: A Writer on Writing*. New York: Anchor, 2002.

Bibliography

Bales, Stephen Lyn. *Natural Histories: Stories from the Tennessee Valley*. Knoxville, TN: University of Tennessee Press, 2007.

Balthrop-Lewis, Alda. "Active and Contemplative Lives in a Changing Climate: The Emersonian Roots of Thoreau's Political Asceticism." *Journal of the American Academy of Religion* 87, 2 (May 30, 2019): 311–32.

"Exemplarist Environmental Ethics: Thoreau's Political Asceticism against Solution Thinking." *The Journal of Religious Ethics* 47, 3 (September 2019): 525–50.

"Thoreau's Woodchopper, Wordsworth's Leech-Gatherer, and the Representation of 'Humble and Rustic Life.'" In *Theology and Ecology across the Disciplines: On Care for Our Common Home*, edited by Celia Deane-Drummond and Rebecca Artinian-Kaiser. London: Bloomsbury, 2018.

Bawaka Country, Sarah Wright, Sandie Suchet-Pearson, Kate Lloyd, Laklak Burarrwanga, Ritjilili Ganambarr, Merrkiyawuy Ganambarr-Stubbs, Banbapuy Ganambarr, Djawundil Maymuru, and Jill Sweeney. "Co-Becoming Bawaka: Towards a Relational Understanding of Place/Space." *Progress in Human Geography* 40, 4 (August 1, 2016): 455–75

Bell, Shannon Elizabeth. *Our Roots Run Deep as Ironweed: Appalachian Women and the Fight for Environmental Justice*. Urbana, IL: University of Illinois Press, 2013.

Bender, Courtney. *The New Metaphysicals: Spirituality and the American Religious Imagination*. Chicago, IL: University of Chicago Press, 2010.

Bennett, Jane. *Thoreau's Nature: Ethics, Politics, and the Wild*. Thousand Oaks, CA: Sage Publications, 1994.

Bilgrami, Akeel. "The Wider Significance of Naturalism: A Genealogical Essay." In *Naturalism and Normativity*, edited by Mario De Caro and David MacArthur. New York: Columbia University Press, 2010.

Bilinkoff, Jodi. *The Avila of Saint Teresa: Religious Reform in a Sixteenth-Century City*. 2nd ed. Ithaca, NY: Cornell University Press, 2015.

Blackmon, Bret J., Joohee Lee, David M. Cochran Jr., Bandana Kar, Timothy A. Rehner, and Alvin M. Baker Jr. "Adapting to Life after Hurricane Katrina and the Deepwater Horizon Oil Spill: An Examination of Psychological Resilience and Depression on the Mississippi Gulf Coast." *Social Work in Public Health* 32, 1 (January 2, 2017): 65–76.

Blanding, Thomas. "Historic Walden Woods." *The Concord Saunterer* 20, 1/2 (1988): 2–74.

Blum, Elizabeth D. *Love Canal Revisited: Race, Class, and Gender in Environmental Activism.* Lawrence, KS: University Press of Kansas, 2008.

Booth, Carol. "A Motivational Turn for Environmental Ethics." *Ethics & the Environment* 14, 1 (2009): 53–78.

Borges, Jorge Luis. *Collected Fictions.* Translated by Andrew Hurley. New York: Penguin Books, 1999.

Branch, Michael P. *Reading the Roots: American Nature Writing before Walden.* Athens, GA: University of Georgia Press, 2004.

Bray, Karen. *Grave Attending: A Political Theology for the Unredeemed.* New York: Fordham University Press, 2019.

brown, adrienne maree. *Pleasure Activism: The Politics of Feeling Good.* Chico, CA: AK Press, 2019.

Brown, Peter. *Augustine of Hippo: A Biography.* Berkeley, CA: University of California Press, 2000.

Brownson, Orestes Augustus. *The Laboring Classes: An Article from the Boston Quarterly Review.* Boston, MA: B. H. Greene, 1840.

Bucar, Elizabeth M., and Aaron Stalnaker. "On Comparative Religious Ethics as a Field of Study." *Journal of Religious Ethics* 42, 2 (2014): 358–84.

Buell, Lawrence. "Disaffiliation as Engagement." In *Thoreau at 200: Essays and Reassessments*, edited by Kristen Case and K. P. Van Anglen. New York: Cambridge University Press, 2016.

"Downwardly Mobile for Conscience's Sake: Voluntary Simplicity from Thoreau to Lily Bart," *American Literary History* 17, 4 (2005): 653–65.

The Environmental Imagination: Thoreau, Nature Writing, and the Formation of American Culture. Cambridge, MA: Belknap Press, 1996.

"How Thoreau Enters the American Canon." In *New Essays on* Walden, edited by Robert F. Sayre, 23–52. Cambridge: Cambridge University Press, 1992.

Bullard, Robert D. *Dumping in Dixie: Race, Class, and Environmental Quality.* Boulder, CO: Westview Press, 1990.

Bush, Sargent, Jr. "The End and Means in Walden: Thoreau's Use of the Catechism." *ESQ: A Journal of the American Renaissance* 31, 1 (1985): 1–10.

Cafaro, Philip. "Environmental Virtue Ethics Special Issue: Introduction." *Journal of Agricultural and Environmental Ethics* 23, 1–2 (2010): 3–7.

"Environmental Virtue Ethics." In *The Routledge Companion to Virtue Ethics*, edited by Lorraine Besser-Jones and Michael Slote, 427–44. New York: Routledge, 2015.

Cameron, Julia. *The Artist's Way: 25th Anniversary Edition.* New York, NY: TarcherPerigee, 2016.

Cameron, Sharon. *Writing Nature: Henry Thoreau's Journal*. New York: Oxford University Press, 1985.

Carson, Anne. *Eros the Bittersweet*. Princeton, NJ: Princeton University Press, 1986.

Cavell, Stanley. *The Senses of Walden*. New York: Viking Press, 1972.

Cities of Words: Pedagogical Letters on a Register of the Moral Life. Cambridge, MA: Belknap Press, 2005.

Conditions Handsome and Unhandsome: The Constitution of Emersonian Perfectionism: The Carus Lectures, 1988. Chicago, IL: University of Chicago Press, 1991.

Chakrabarty, Dipesh. *Provincializing Europe: Postcolonial Thought and Historical Difference*. Princeton, NJ: Princeton University Press, 2000.

Chaloupka, William. "Thoreau's Apolitical Legacy for American Environmentalism." In *A Political Companion to Henry David Thoreau*, edited by Jack Turner. Lexington, KY: The University Press of Kentucky, 2009.

Channing, William Ellery. *Thoreau: The Poet-Naturalist: With Memorial Verses*. Boston, MA: Roberts Brothers, 1873.

Chernus, Ira. *American Nonviolence: The History of an Idea*. Maryknoll, NY: Orbis Books, 2004.

Clavin, Matthew J. *Aiming for Pensacola: Fugitive Slaves on the Atlantic and Southern Frontiers*. Cambridge, MA: Harvard University Press, 2015.

Collins, Stephanie. *The Core of Care Ethics*. New York: Palgrave Macmillan, 2015.

Colón, John Michael, Mason Herson-Hord, Katie S. Horvath, Dayton Martindale, and Matthew Porges. "Community, Democracy, and Mutual Aid," 2017. https://thenextsystem.org/community-democracy-mutual-aid (accessed August 20, 2020).

Colten, Craig E., and Alexandra Giancarlo. "Losing Resilience on the Gulf Coast: Hurricanes and Social Memory." *Environment: Science and Policy for Sustainable Development* 53, 4 (June 24, 2011): 6–19.

Coviello, Peter. "The Wild Not Less than the Good: Thoreau, Sex, Biopower." *GLQ: A Journal of Lesbian and Gay Studies* 23, 4 (October 1, 2017): 509–32.

Craig, David M. "The Duty of Delight." In *John Ruskin and the Ethics of Consumption*. Charlottesville, VA: University of Virginia Press, 2006.

Cramer, Jeffrey S. *Solid Seasons: The Friendship of Henry David Thoreau and Ralph Waldo Emerson*. Berkeley, CA: Counterpoint, 2019.

Culp, Kristine A. *Vulnerability and Glory: A Theological Account*. Louisville, KY: Westminster John Knox Press, 2010.

Cummings, John. "Negro Population in the United States 1790–1915." *US Census Bureau*, 1918. www.census.gov/library/publications/1918/dec/negro-population-1790-1915.html (accessed August 20, 2020).

Cunliffe, Marcus. *Chattel Slavery and Wage Slavery: The Anglo-American Context, 1830–1860*. Athens, GA: University of Georgia Press, 1979.
Curtis, Kent. "The Virtue of Thoreau: Biography, Geography, and History in Walden Woods." *Environmental History* 15, 1 (2010): 31–53.
Dann, Kevin. *Expect Great Things: The Life and Search of Henry David Thoreau*. New York: TarcherPerigee, 2017.
Day, Dorothy. *The Duty of Delight: The Diaries of Dorothy Day*, edited by Robert Ellsberg. Milwaukee, WI: Marquette University Press, 2008.
Delano, Sterling F. *Brook Farm: The Dark Side of Utopia*. Cambridge, MA: Belknap Press, 2004.
Descartes, René. *Descartes: Selected Philosophical Writings*. Translated by John Cottingham, Robert Stoothoff, and Dugald Murdoch. Cambridge: Cambridge University Press, 1988.
Despret, Vinciane, and Michel Meuret. "Cosmoecological Sheep and the Arts of Living on a Damaged Planet." *Environmental Humanities* 8, 1 (May 1, 2016): 24–36.
Dillard, Annie. *An American Childhood*. New York: Harper & Row, 1987.
Dimock, Wai Chee. *Through Other Continents: American Literature across Deep Time*. Princeton, NJ: Princeton University Press, 2008.
Dixon, Melvin. *Ride Out the Wilderness: Geography and Identity in Afro-American Literature*. Urbana, IL: University of Illinois Press, 1987.
Dowling, David O. *Emerson's Protégés: Mentoring and Marketing Transcendentalism's Future*. New Haven, CT: Yale University Press, 2014.
Dryden, John. *The Works of John Dryden*, edited by Walter Scott. Vol. 6. 18 vols. London: James Ballantyne and Co. Edinburgh, n.d.
Dublin, Thomas. *Women at Work: The Transformation of Work and Community in Lowell, Massachusetts, 1826–1860*. New York: Columbia University Press, 1979.
Emerson, Edward Waldo. *The Centennial of the Social Circle in Concord: March 21, 1882*. Riverside Press, 1882.
Henry Thoreau: As Remembered by a Young Friend. Boston, MA: Houghton Mifflin, 1917.
"Interview with Ann Bigelow (Transcribed from the Manuscript Notes of His 1892 Interview)." Concord Free Public Library. http://con5635.verio.com/scollect/antislavery/68.html (accessed August 20, 2020).
Emerson, Ralph Waldo. *Journals of Ralph Waldo Emerson, with Annotations*. Vol. 5. New York: Houghton Mifflin company, 1914.
Journals of Ralph Waldo Emerson, with Annotations. Vol. 6. New York: Houghton Mifflin company, 1914.
Journals of Ralph Waldo Emerson, with Annotations. Vol. 7. New York: Houghton Mifflin company, 1914.
Ralph Waldo Emerson: Essays & Poems, edited by Joel Porte, Harold Bloom, and Paul Kane. New York: Library of America, 1996.

Farrell, Justin. *The Battle for Yellowstone: Morality and the Sacred Roots of Environmental Conflict*. Princeton, NJ: Princeton University Press, 2015.

Finley, James S. "'Justice in the Land': Ecological Protest in Henry David Thoreau's Antislavery Essays." *The Concord Saunterer* 21 (2013): 1–35.

"A Free Soiler in His Own Broad Sense: Henry David Thoreau and the Free Soil Movement." In *Thoreau at 200: Essays and Reassessments*, edited by Kristen Case and K. P. Van Anglen, 31–44. New York: Cambridge University Press, 2016.

"Pilgrimages and Working Forests: Envisioning the Commons in 'The Maine Woods.'" *Rediscovering the Maine Woods: Thoreau's Legacy in an Unsettled Land*, edited by John Kucich, 141–167. Amherst, MA: University of Massachusetts Press, 2019.

Fischer, Michael R. "*Walden* and Contemporary Literary Theory." In *New Essays on* Walden, edited by Robert F. Sayre, 95–113. Cambridge: Cambridge University Press, 1992.

Fisher, Philip. *The Vehement Passions*. Princeton, NJ: Princeton University Press, 2002.

Wonder, the Rainbow, and the Aesthetics of Rare Experiences. Cambridge, MA: Harvard University Press, 1998.

Fleck, Richard F. *Henry Thoreau and John Muir Among the Native Americans*. Portland, OR: WestWinds Press, 2015.

Foner, Eric. *Free Soil, Free Labor, Free Men: The Ideology of the Republican Party before the Civil War*. New York: Oxford University Press, 1995.

Foot, Philippa. "The Problem of Abortion and the Doctrine of the Double Effect." In *Virtues and Vices and Other Essays in Moral Philosophy*. Oxford: Clarendon, 2002.

Franchot, Jenny. *Roads to Rome: The Antebellum Protestant Encounter with Catholicism*. Berkeley, CA: University of California Press, 1994.

Francis. *Laudato Si'* [Encyclical Letter on Care for Our Common Home]. http://w2.vatican.va/content/francesco/en/encyclicals/documents/papa-francesco_20150524_enciclica-laudato-si.html (accessed August 20, 2020).

Francis, Richard. *Fruitlands : The Alcott Family and Their Search for Utopia*. New Haven, CT: Yale University Press, 2010.

Transcendental Utopias: Individual and Community at Brook Farm, Fruitlands, and Walden. Ithaca, NY: Cornell University Press, 1997.

Fredericks, Sarah E. "Online Confessions of Eco-Guilt." *Journal for the Study of Religion, Nature, and Culture* 8, 1 (2014): 64–84.

Freeberg, Todd M. "Social Complexity Can Drive Vocal Complexity: Group Size Influences Vocal Information in Carolina Chickadees." *Psychological Science* 17, 7 (2006): 557–61.

Friedrich, Paul. "The Impact of Thoreau's Political Activism." In *Thoreau's Importance for Philosophy*, edited by Rick Anthony Furtak, Jonathan Ellsworth, and James D. Reid, 218–22. Bronx, NY: Fordham University Press, 2012.

Furtak, Rick Anthony, Jonathan Ellsworth, and James D. Reid, eds. *Thoreau's Importance for Philosophy*. Bronx, NY: Fordham University Press, 2012.

Gatta, John. "'Rare and Delectable Places': Thoreau's Imagination of Sacred Space at Walden." In *There Before Us: Religion, Literature & Culture from Emerson to Wendell Berry*, edited by Roger Lundin, 23–48. Wm. B. Eerdmans Publishing Co., 2007.

Giblett, Rodney James. *Postmodern Wetlands: Culture, History, Ecology*. Edinburgh: Edinburgh University Press, 1996.

Gilligan, Carol. *In a Different Voice: Psychological Theory and Women's Development*. Cambridge, MA: Harvard University Press, 1982.

Glaude, Eddie S. *African American Religion: A Very Short Introduction*. New York: Oxford University Press, 2014.

Gleason, William A. *The Leisure Ethic: Work and Play in American Literature, 1840–1940*. Stanford, CA: Stanford University Press, 1999.

Glickman, Lawrence B. *Buying Power: A History of Consumer Activism in America*. Chicago, IL: University of Chicago Press, 2009.

Goodwin, Jeff, James M. Jasper, and Francesca Polletta, eds. *Passionate Politics: Emotions and Social Movements*. Chicago, IL: University of Chicago Press, 2001.

Gottlieb, Robert. *Forcing the Spring: The Transformation of the American Environmental Movement*. Washington, DC: Island Press, 2005.

Gourevitch, Alex. *From Slavery to the Cooperative Commonwealth: Labor and Republican Liberty in the Nineteenth Century*. Cambridge: Cambridge University Press, 2014.

Graeber, David. *Bullshit Jobs: A Theory*. New York: Simon & Schuster, 2018.

Grattan, Lynn M., Sparkle Roberts, William T. Mahan, Patrick K. McLaughlin, W. Steven Otwell, and J. Glenn Morris. "The Early Psychological Impacts of the Deepwater Horizon Oil Spill on Florida and Alabama Communities." *Environmental Health Perspectives* 119, 6 (June 2011): 838–43.

Greenberg, Jonathan D. "Occupy Wall Street's Debt to Melville." *The Atlantic*, April 30, 2012. www.theatlantic.com/politics/archive/2012/04/occupy-wall-streets-debt-to-melville/256482/ (accessed August 20, 2020).

Gregory, Eric. *Politics and the Order of Love: An Augustinian Ethic of Democratic Citizenship*. Chicago, IL: University of Chicago Press, 2008.

Gura, Philip F. *American Transcendentalism: A History*. New York: Hill and Wang, 2008.

Hamilton, Brian David. "The Politics of Poverty: A Contribution to a Franciscan Political Theology." *Journal of the Society of Christian Ethics* 35, 1 (2015): 29–44.

Hanna, Thomas M. *Our Common Wealth: The Return of Public Ownership in the United States*. Manchester: Manchester University Press, 2018.

Hansel, T. C., and Tonya Hansel. "Gulf Coast Resilience Coalition: An Evolved Collaborative Built on Shared Disaster Experiences, Response, and Future Preparedness." *Disaster Medicine & Public Health Preparedness* 9, 6 (December 1, 2015): 657–65.

Harrington, Alan. *The Immortalist: An Approach to the Engineering of Man's Divinity*. New York: Random House, 1969.

Harrison, Robert Pogue. *Forests: The Shadow of Civilization*. Chicago, IL: University of Chicago Press, 1992.

Hasketh, Ian. "Technologies of the Scientific Self: John Tyndall and His Journal." *Isis* 110, 3 (September 1, 2019): 460–82.

Hendrick, George. "The Influence of Thoreau's 'Civil Disobedience' on Gandhi's Satyagraha." *The New England Quarterly* 29, 4 (December 1, 1956): 462–71.

Herdt, Jennifer A. "Excellence-Prior Eudaimonism." *Journal of Religious Ethics* 47, 1 (2019): 68–93.

Hill, Christopher. *The World Turned Upside down: Radical Ideas during the English Revolution*. London: Temple Smith, 1972.

Hodder, Alan D. "The Religious Horizon." In *Henry David Thoreau in Context*, edited by James S. Finley, 78–88. New York: Cambridge University Press, 2017.

Thoreau's Ecstatic Witness. New Haven, CT: Yale University Press, 2001.

Hollywood, Amy M. *Acute Melancholia and Other Essays: Mysticism, History, and the Study of Religion. Gender, Theory, and Religion.* New York: Columbia University Press, 2016.

Horton, Myles. *The Long Haul: An Autobiography*. New York: Teachers College Press, 1997.

Howarth, William L. *The Book of Concord: Thoreau's Life as a Writer*. New York: Viking Press, 1982.

Hu, Hsiao-Lan. *This-Worldly Nibbana: A Buddhist-Feminist Social Ethic for Peacemaking in the Global Community*. Albany, NY: SUNY Press, 2012.

Hubbard, John. *The American Reader: Containing a Selection of Narration, Harangues, Addresses, Orations, Dialogues, Odes, Hymns, Poems, &c.* Bellows Falls: Bill Blake & Co., 1820.

Huffman, Carl. "Pythagoras," *The Stanford Encyclopedia of Philosophy* (Summer 2014 Edition), edited by Edward N. Zalta, https://plato.stanford.edu/archives/sum2014/entries/pythagoras/ (accessed August 20, 2020).

Hui, Andrew. *The Poetics of Ruins in Renaissance Literature*. New York: Fordham University Press, 2016.

Hursthouse, Rosalind. "Evironmental Virtue Ethics." In *Working Virtue*, edited by Rebecca L. Walker and Philip J. Ivanhoe, 155–72. Oxford: Oxford University Press, 2007.

Japp, Alexander H. *Thoreau: His Life and Aims*. Boston: Osgood, 1877.

Jenco, Leigh Kathryn. "Thoreau's Critique of Democracy." *The Review of Politics* 65, 3 (2003): 355–81.

Jenkins, Willis. *The Future of Ethics: Sustainability, Social Justice, and Religious Creativity*. Washington, DC: Georgetown University Press, 2013.

"After Lynn White: Religious Ethics and Environmental Problems." *Journal of Religious Ethics* 37, 2 (June 1, 2009): 283–309.

Jones, Martha S. *Birthright Citizens: A History of Race and Rights in Antebellum America*. Cambridge: Cambridge University Press, 2018.

Jorgensen, David W. "Approaches to Orthodoxy and Heresy in the Study of Early Christianity." *Religion Compass* 11, 7–8 (July 1, 2017).

Kahan, Benjamin. *Celibacies: American Modernism and Sexual Life*. Durham, NC: Duke University Press Books, 2013.

Kateb, George. *The Inner Ocean: Individualism and Democratic Culture*. Ithaca, N.Y: Cornell University Press, 1994.

Patriotism and Other Mistakes. New Haven, CT: Yale University Press, 2006.

Keats, John. *Selected Letters. Oxford World's Classics*. Oxford: Oxford University Press, 2002.

Kelly, Kathleen Coyne. "Medievalism." In *Henry David Thoreau in Context*, edited by James S. Finley, 67–77. New York: Cambridge University Press, 2017.

Kelsay, John. "Response to Bucar and Stalnaker." *Journal of Religious Ethics* 42, 3 (2014): 564–70.

King, Jr., Martin Luther. *Strength to Love*. Philadelphia, PA: Fortress Press, 1980.

"The Time for Freedom Has Come," New York Times Magazine (10 September 1961): p. 25ff.

Klein, Lauren. "What Bartleby Can Teach Us About Occupy Wall Street." ARCADE. Accessed October 1, 2018. https://arcade.stanford.edu/blogs/what-bartleby-can-teach-us-about-occupy-wall-street (accessed August 20, 2020).

Kosky, Jeffrey L. *Arts of Wonder: Enchanting Secularity – Walter De Maria, Diller Scofidio, James Turrell, Andy Goldsworthy*. Chicago, IL: University of Chicago Press, 2012.

Kotin, Josh. *Utopias of One*. Princeton, NJ: Princeton University Press, 2017.

Kukla, Rebecca, and Mark Lance. *"Yo!" And "Lo!": The Pragmatic Topography of the Space of Reasons*. Cambridge, MA: Harvard University Press, 2009.

Kuklick, Bruce. *A History of Philosophy in America, 1720–2000*. New York: Oxford University Press, 2001.

Lane, Charles. "A Day with the Shakers." *The Dial*. October 1843.

Lane, Melissa. "Thoreau and Rousseau: Nature as Utopia." In *A Political Companion to Henry David Thoreau*, edited by Jack Turner, 341–71. Lexington, KY: The University Press of Kentucky, 2009.

Lasch, Christopher. *The True and Only Heaven: Progress and Its Critics*. New York: W. W. Norton & Company, 1991.

Latour, Bruno. *Reassembling the Social: An Introduction to Actor-Network-Theory*. New York: Oxford University Press, 2005.

Lee, Jung. "Comparative Religious Ethics Among the Ruins." *Journal of Religious Ethics* 42, 3 (2014): 571–84.

Lemire, Elise. *Black Walden: Slavery and Its Aftermath in Concord, Massachusetts*. Philadelphia, PA: University of Pennsylvania Press, 2009.

"Review of *To Set This World Right: The Antislavery Movement in Thoreau's Concord*, by Sandra Harbert Petrulionis." *The New England Quarterly* 80, 2 (2007): 338–40.

Ljungquist, Kent P. "Lectures and the Lyceum Movement." In *The Oxford Handbook of Transcendentalism*, edited by Joel Myerson, Sandra Harbert Petrulionis, and Laura Dassow Walls, 330–37. New York: Oxford University Press, 2010.

Logan, John R., Sukriti Issar, and Zengwang Xu. "Trapped in Place? Segmented Resilience to Hurricanes in the Gulf Coast, 1970–2005." *Demography* 53, 5 (October 1, 2016): 1511–34.

Lott, Eric. *Love & Theft: Blackface Minstrelsy and the American Working Class*. 2nd ed. New York: Oxford University Press, 2013.

Lysaker, John T., and William Rossi, edited by *Emerson and Thoreau: Figures of Friendship*. Bloomington, IN: Indiana University Press, 2010.

MacCulloch, Diarmaid. *Christianity: The First Three Thousand Years*. New York: Penguin Books, 2009.

McCaughey, Robert A. "The Usable Past: A Study of the Harvard College Rebellion of 1834." *William and Mary Law Review* 11, 3 (April 1, 1970): 587–610.

McRae, Elizabeth Gillespie. *Mothers of Massive Resistance: White Women and the Politics of White Supremacy*. New York: Oxford University Press, 2018.

McGregor, Robert Kuhn. *A Wider View of the Universe: Henry Thoreau's Study of Nature*. Revised ed. Jefferson, NC: McFarland, 2017.

McKenzie, Jonathan. *The Political Thought of Henry David Thoreau: Privatism and the Practice of Philosophy*. Lexington, KY: University Press of Kentucky, 2016.

Madrid, Paula A. "Resilience Challenged: Thoughts on Children's Mental Health in the Gulf Coast 5 Years after Katrina." *Pediatrics* 128 Suppl 1 (August 1, 2011): S26–27.

Malesic, Jonathan. "Henry David Thoreau's Anti-work Spirituality and a New Theological Ethic of Work." *Journal of Religious Ethics* 45, 2 (June 1, 2017): 309–29.

Mariotti, Shannon L. *Thoreau's Democratic Withdrawal: Alienation, Participation, and Modernity*. Studies in American Thought and Culture. Madison, WI: University of Wisconsin Press, 2010.

Maris-Wolf, Ted. "Hidden in Plain Sight: Maroon Life and Labor in Virginia's Dismal Swamp." *Slavery & Abolition* 34, 3 (September 1, 2013): 446–64.

Martyris, Nina. "A Patron Saint for Occupy Wall Street." *The New Republic*, October 15, 2011. https://newrepublic.com/article/96276/nina-martyris-ows-and-bartleby-the-scrivener (accessed August 20, 2020).

Marx, Leo. "The Two Thoreaus," October 26, 1978. www.nybooks.com/articles/1978/10/26/the-two-thoreaus/ (accessed August 20, 2020).

Maul, Christian. "'A Sort of Hybrid Product': Thoreau's Individualism between Liberalism and Communitarianism." In *Thoreauvian Modernities: Transatlantic Conversations on an American Icon*, edited by François Specq, Laura Dassow Walls, and Michel Granger, 157–70. Athens, GA: University of Georgia Press, 2013.

Maynard, W. Barksdale. *Walden Pond: A History*. Oxford: Oxford University Press, 2005.

Mazzei, Patricia. "For a Struggling Oyster Town, Hurricane Michael May Be One Misery Too Many." *The New York Times*, October 13, 2018, sec. U.S. www.nytimes.com/2018/10/12/us/fishing-communities-damage-hurricane.html (accessed August 20, 2020).

Melish, Joanne Pope. *Disowning Slavery: Gradual Emancipation and "Race" in New England, 1780–1860*. Ithaca, NY: Cornell University Press, 2000.

Mercedes, Anna. *Power For: Feminism and Christ's Self Giving*. London: Bloomsbury, 2011.

Midgley, Mary. *Beast and Man: The Roots of Human Nature*. Revised ed. London and New York: Routledge, 1995.

Miller, David. *Dark Eden: The Swamp in Nineteenth-Century American Culture*. Cambridge: Cambridge University Press, 2010.

Millett, Nathaniel. *The Maroons of Prospect Bluff and Their Quest for Freedom in the Atlantic World*. Gainesville, FL: University Press of Florida, 2013.

Montrie, Chad. *A People's History of Environmentalism in the United States*. London: Continuum, 2011.

Murdoch, Iris. *The Sovereignty of Good*. New York: Routledge, 2001.

Myers, Jeffrey. *Converging Stories: Race, Ecology, and Environmental Justice in American Literature*. Athens, GA: University of Georgia Press, 2005.

Nash, Jennifer C. *Black Feminism Reimagined: After Intersectionality*. Durham, NC: Duke University Press, 2019.

Neely, Michelle C. "Radical Minimalism: *Walden* in the Capitalocene." *Concord Saunterer* 26 (2018): 144–50.
"Embodied Politics: Antebellum Vegetarianism and the Dietary Economy of *Walden*." *American Literature* 85, 1 (March 1, 2013): 33–60.
Neufeldt, Leonard N. *The Economist: Henry Thoreau and Enterprise*. New York: Oxford University Press, 1989.
Newheiser, David. *Hope in a Secular Age: Deconstruction, Negative Theology, and the Future of Faith*. Cambridge: Cambridge University Press, 2019.
Newman, Lance. *Our Common Dwelling: Henry Thoreau, Transcendentalism, and the Class Politics of Nature*. New York: Palgrave Macmillan, 2005.
Nikiforuk, Andrew. *The Energy of Slaves*. Vancouver, BC: Greystone Books, 2014.
Northcott, Michael S. *A Political Theology of Climate Change*. Grand Rapids, MI: Wm. B. Eerdmans Publishing Co., 2013.
Norton, Bryan G. "Thoreau's Insect Analogies: Or Why Environmentalists Hate Mainstream Economists." *Environmental Ethics* 13, 3 (1991): 235–51.
Nunziato, Joshua. *Augustine and the Economy of Sacrifice: Ancient and Modern Perspectives*. Cambridge: Cambridge University Press, 2019.
Nussbaum, Martha C. *Upheavals of Thought: The Intelligence of Emotions*. Cambridge: Cambridge University Press, 2001.
Oliver, Egbert S. "A Second Look at 'Bartleby.'" *College English* 6, 8 (1945): 431–39.
Orsi, Robert A. *History and Presence*. Cambridge, MA: Harvard University Press, 2016.
Oshatz, Molly. *Slavery and Sin: The Fight against Slavery and the Rise of Liberal Protestantism*. New York: Oxford University Press, 2011.
Outka, Paul. *Race and Nature from Transcendentalism to the Harlem Renaissance*. New York: Palgrave Macmillan, 2008.
Painter, Nell Irvin. *The History of White People*. New York: Norton, 2010.
"Representing Truth: Sojourner Truth's Knowing and Becoming Known." *The Journal of American History* 81, 2 (September 1994): 461–492.
Pellow, David Naguib. *What Is Critical Environmental Justice?* Cambridge, UK: Polity Press, 2017.
Perry, Lewis. *Civil Disobedience: An American Tradition*. New Haven, CT: Yale University Press, 2013.
Petrarca, Francesco. *The Triumphs of Petrarch*. London: Longman, Hurst, Rees, and Orme, 1807.
Petrulionis, Sandra Harbert. *To Set This World Right: The Antislavery Movement in Thoreau's Concord*. Ithaca, NY: Cornell University Press, 2006.

Petrulionis, Sandra Harbert, and Laura Dassow Walls, eds. *More Day to Dawn: Thoreau's Walden for the Twenty-First Century*. Amherst, MA: University of Massachusetts Press, 2007.

Pieper, Josef. *Guide to Thomas Aquinas*. San Francisco, CA: Ignatius Press, 1991.

Scholasticism: Personalities and Problems of Medieval Philosophy. Translated by Richard and Clara Winston. New York: McGraw-Hill, 1964.

Pincoffs, Edmund. "Quandary Ethics." *Mind*, 80, 320 (October 1971): 552–71.

Plumwood, Val. *Feminism and the Mastery of Nature*. London: Routledge, 1993.

Posmentier, Sonya. *Cultivation and Catastrophe: The Lyric Ecology of Modern Black Literature*. Baltimore, MD: John Hopkins University Press, 2020.

Posnock, Ross. *Renunciation: Acts of Abandonment by Writers, Philosophers, and Artists*. Cambridge, MA: Harvard University Press, 2016.

Powell, Timothy B. *Ruthless Democracy: A Multicultural Interpretation of the American Renaissance*. Princeton, NJ: Princeton University Press, 2000.

Pughe, Thomas. "Brute Neighbors: The Modernity of a Metaphor." In *Thoreauvian Modernities: Transatlantic Conversations on an American Icon*, edited by François Specq, Laura Dassow Walls, and Michel Granger, 249–64. Athens, GA: University of Georgia Press, 2013.

Pulido, Laura. *Environmentalism and Economic Justice: Two Chicano Struggles in the Southwest*. Tucson, AZ: University of Arizona Press, 1996.

Purdy, Jedediah. "The Long Environmental Justice Movement." *Ecology Law Quarterly* 44, 4 (2017): 809–64.

This Land Is Our Land: The Struggle for a New Commonwealth. Princeton, NJ: Princeton University Press, 2019.

After Nature: A Politics for the Anthropocene. Cambridge, MA: Harvard University Press, 2015.

Raboteau, Albert J. *Slave Religion: The "Invisible Institution" in the Antebellum South*. New York: Oxford University Press, 1978.

Raser-Rowland, Annie, and Adam Grubb. *The Art of Frugal Hedonism: A Guide to Spending Less While Enjoying Everything More*. Victoria: Melliodora Publishing, 2016.

Rawls, John. *A Theory of Justice*. Cambridge, MA: Belknap Press, 1971.

Rees, Jonas H., Sabine Klug, and Sebastian Bamberg. "Guilty Conscience: Motivating Pro-Environmental Behavior by Inducing Negative Moral Emotions." *Climatic Change*, October 14, 2014, 1–14.

Reinert, Hugo. "About a Stone Some: Notes on Geologic Conviviality." *Environmental Humanities* 8, 1 (May 1, 2016): 95–117.

Reynolds, David S. *Beneath the American Renaissance: The Subversive Imagination in the Age of Emerson and Melville*. New York: Oxford University Press, 2011.

Reynolds, Larry J. *Righteous Violence: Revolution, Slavery, and the American Renaissance*. Athens, GA: University of Georgia Press, 2011.

Richardson, Robert D. *Henry Thoreau: A Life of the Mind*. Berkeley, CA: University of California Press, 1988.

Rifkin, Mark. *Settler Common Sense Queerness and Everyday Colonialism in the American Renaissance*. Minneapolis, MN: University of Minnesota Press, 2014.

Rittel, Horst W. J., and Melvin M. Webber. “Dilemmas in a General Theory of Planning.” *Policy Sciences* 4, 2 (June 1, 1973): 155–69.

Roberts, Neil. *Freedom as Marronage*. Chicago, IL: University of Chicago Press, 2015.

Rogin, Michael. *Subversive Genealogy: The Politics and Art of Herman Melville*. Berkely, CA: University of California Press, 1985.

Rorty, Richard. *Philosophy and the Mirror of Nature*. Princeton, NJ: Princeton University Press, 1980.

Rose, Suzanne Dvorak. “Tracking the Moccasin Print: A Descriptive Index to Henry David Thoreau’s Indian Notebooks and a Study of the Relationship of the Indian Notebooks to Mythmaking in ‘Walden.’” PhD, Oklahoma, The University of Oklahoma, 1994.

Rosenblum, Nancy L. *Another Liberalism: Romanticism and the Reconstruction of Liberal Thought*. Cambridge, MA: Harvard University Press, 1987.

“Introduction.” In *Thoreau: Political Writings*. New York: Cambridge University Press, 1996.

Rubenstein, Mary-Jane. *Strange Wonder: The Closure of Metaphysics and the Opening of Awe*. New York: Columbia University Press, 2008.

Ruffin, Kimberly N. *Black on Earth: African American Ecoliterary Traditions*. Athens, GA: University of Georgia Press, 2010.

Sale, Kirkpatrick. *The Green Revolution: The American Environmental Movement, 1962–1992*. New York: Hill and Wang, 1993.

“Salem Lyceum.” *Salem Observer*. November 25, 1848.

Sanborn, Franklin Benjamin. *Henry D. Thoreau*. Boston, MA: Houghton, Mifflin, 1882.

Sandler, Ronald L. *Character and Environment: A Virtue-Oriented Approach to Environmental Ethics*. New York: Columbia University Press, 2007.

Sattelmeyer, Robert. “The Remaking of *Walden*.” In *Writing the American Classics*, edited by James Barbour and Tom Quirk, 53–78. Chapel Hill, NC: University of North Carolina Press, 1990.

“The Remaking of Walden.” In Walden, *Civil Disobedience, and Other Writings*, edited by William John Rossi, 3rd ed. New York: Norton, 2008.

Thoreau's Reading: A Study in Intellectual History with Bibliographical Catalogue. Princeton, NJ: Princeton University Press, 2014.

Sayers, Daniel O. *A Desolate Place for a Defiant People: The Archaeology of Maroons, Indigenous Americans, and Enslaved Laborers in the Great Dismal Swamp*. Gainesville, FL: Society for Historical Archaeology, 2014.

Sayre, Robert F. *Thoreau and the American Indians*. Princeton, NJ: Princeton University Press, 1977.

Scharnhorst, Gary. *Henry David Thoreau: A Case Study in Canonization*. Columbia, SC: Camden House, 1994.

Schmidt, Leigh. *Restless Souls: The Making of American Spirituality*. San Francisco, CA: HarperOne, 2005.

Schulz, Kathryn. "Pond Scum." *The New Yorker*, October 19, 2015. www.newyorker.com/magazine/2015/10/19/pond-scum (accessed August 20, 2020).

Serres, Michel. *The Natural Contract*. Translated by Elizabeth MacArthur and William Paulson. Ann Arbor, MI: University of Michigan Press, 1995.

Seybold, Ethel. *Thoreau: The Quest and the Classics*. *Yale Studies in English*, v. 116. New Haven, CT: Yale University Press, 1951.

Shanley, J. Lyndon. *The Making of* Walden, *with the Text of the First Version*. Chicago, IL: University of Chicago Press, 1957.

Shulman, George M. *American Prophecy: Race and Redemption in American Political Culture*. Minneapolis, MN: University of Minnesota Press, 2008.

Radicalism and Reverence: The Political Thought of Gerrard Winstanley. Berkeley, CA: University of California Press, 1989.

Sideris, Lisa H. "Science as Sacred Myth? Ecospirituality in the Anthropocene Age." *Journal for the Study of Religion, Nature & Culture* 9, 2 (June 2015): 136–53.

"The Secular and Religious Sources of Rachel Carson's Sense of Wonder." In *Rachel Carson: Legacy and Challenge*. Albany, NY: State University of New York Press, 2008.

Sinha, Manisha. *The Slave's Cause: A History of Abolition*. New Haven, CT: Yale University Press, 2017.

Sklar, Kathryn Kish, and James Brewer Stewart. *Women's Rights and Transatlantic Antislavery in the Era of Emancipation*. New Haven, CT: Yale University Press, 2017.

Smith, Caleb. "Disciplines of Attention in a Secular Age." *Critical Inquiry* 45, 4 (June 1, 2019): 884–909.

Smith, Harmon. *My Friend, My Friend: The Story of Thoreau's Relationship with Emerson*. Amherst, MA: University of Massachusetts Press, 1999.

Smith, Mitzi. "'Unbossed and Unbought': Zilpha Elaw and Old Elizabeth and a Political Discourse of Origins." *Black Theology* 9, 3 (June 22, 2011): 287–311.

Smith, Ted A. *Weird John Brown: Divine Violence and the Limits of Ethics*. Stanford, CA: Stanford University Press, 2014.
Solnit, Rebecca. "Mysteries of Thoreau, Unsolved." *Orion*, June 2013, 18–23.
Specq, François, Laura Dassow Walls, and Michel Granger, eds. *Thoreauvian Modernities: Transatlantic Conversations on an American Icon*. Athens, GA: University of Georgia Press, 2013.
Spence, Mark David. *Dispossessing the Wilderness: Indian Removal and the Making of the National Parks*. New York: Oxford University Press, 2000.
Stevenson, Ana. *The Woman as Slave in Nineteenth-Century American Social Movements*. Cham, Switzerland: Palgrave Macmillan, 2019.
Stevenson, Robert Louis. "Henry David Thoreau: His Character and Opinions." *The Cornhill Magazine* 41, 246 (June 1880): 665–82.
Stout, Jeffrey. *Ethics after Babel*. Boston, MA: Beacon Press, 1988.
Blessed Are the Organized: Grassroots Democracy in America. Princeton, NJ: Princeton University Press, 2010.
Democracy and Tradition. Princeton, NJ: Princeton University Press, 2004.
Tangney, June Price, and Ronda L. Dearing. *Shame and Guilt*. New York: The Guilford Press, 2003.
Tanner, Kathryn. *Christianity and the New Spirit of Capitalism*. New Haven, CT: Yale University Press, 2019.
Tauber, Alfred I. *Henry David Thoreau and the Moral Agency of Knowing*. Berkeley, CA: University of California Press, 2001.
Taylor, Bob Pepperman. *America's Bachelor Uncle: Henry Thoreau and the American Polity*. American Political Thought. Lawrence: University Press of Kansas, 1996.
Taylor, Bron. *Dark Green Religion: Nature Spirituality and the Planetary Future*. Berkeley, CA: University of California Press, 2009.
Taylor, Dorceta E. "American Environmentalism: The Role of Race, Class and Gender in Shaping Activism, 1820–1995." *Race, Gender & Class* 5 1 (1997): 16–62.
The Rise of the American Conservation Movement: Power, Privilege, and Environmental Protection. Durham, NC: Duke University Press Books, 2015.
"The State of Diversity in Environmental Organizations: Mainstream NGOs, Foundations & Government Agencies." Green 2.0, 2014. www.diversegreen.org/wp-content/uploads/2015/10/FullReport_Green2.0_FINAL.pdf (accessed August 5, 2020).
Templeton, Christopher N., Erick Greene, and Kate Davis. "Allometry of Alarm Calls: Black-Capped Chickadees Encode Information about Predator Size." *Science* 308, 5730 (2005): 1934–37.
Thoreau, Henry David. *Letters to a Spiritual Seeker*, edited by Bradley P. Dean. New York and London: W. W. Norton & Company, 2005.

Walden: A Fully Annotated Edition, edited byJeffery S. Cramer. New Haven, CT: Yale University Press, 2004.
Walden, *Civil Disobedience, and Other Writings*, edited by William John Rossi, 3rd ed. New York: Norton, 2008.
"A Winter Walk." *The Dial*. October 1843.
Journal, Volume 1: *1837–1844*, edited by Elizabeth Hall Witherell, William L. Howarth, Robert Sattelmeyer, and Thomas Blanding. Princeton, NJ: Princeton University Press, 1981.
Journal, Volume 2: *1842–1848*, edited by Robert Sattelmeyer. Princeton, NJ: Princeton University Press, 1984.
Journal, Volume 3: *1848–1851*, edited by Robert Sattelmeyer, Mark R. Patterson, and William Rossi. Princeton, NJ: Princeton University Press, 1991.
Journal, Volume 5: *1852–1853*, edited by Patrick F. O'Connell. Princeton, NJ: Princeton University Press, 1997.
Thorson, Robert M. *The Boatman: Henry David Thoreau's River Years.* Cambridge, MA: Harvard University Press, 2017.
Tonstad, Linn Marie. *God and Difference: The Trinity, Sexuality, and the Transformation of Finitude.* New York: Routledge, 2016.
Tsing, Anna. "More-than-Human Sociality: A Call for Critical Description." In *Anthropology and Nature*, edited by Kristen Hastrup. New York: Routledge, 2013.
Tuck, Eve. "Suspending Damage: A Letter to Communities." *Harvard Educational Review* 79, 3 (September 1, 2009): 409–28.
Turner, Jack, ed. *A Political Companion to Henry David Thoreau.* Lexington, KY: The University Press of Kentucky, 2009.
Turner, Jack, *Awakening to Race: Individualism and Social Consciousness in America.* Chicago, IL: University of Chicago Press, 2012.
Van Anglen, K. P. "Transcendentalism and Religion: The State of Play." *Literature Compass* 5, 6 (November 1, 2008): 1010–24.
Van Yperen, Nathaniel J. "'The Fierce Urgency of Now': The Ecological Legacy of King's Social Ethics." *Journal of the Society of Christian Ethics* 36, 2 (September 2016): 159–72.
Vasalou, Sophia, ed. *Practices of Wonder: Cross-Disciplinary Perspectives.* Cambridge, UK: James Clarke & Co, 2013.
Wonder: A Grammar. Albany, NY: State University of New York Press, 2015.
Versluis, Arthur. *American Transcendentalism and Asian Religions.* New York: Oxford University Press, 1993.
Vinthagen, Stellan. *A Theory of Nonviolent Action: How Civil Resistance Works.* London: Zed Books, 2015.
Von Frank, Albert J. *The Trials of Anthony Burns: Freedom and Slavery in Emerson's Boston.* Cambridge, MA: Harvard University Press, 1998.

Waldron, Jeremy. *The Right to Private Property*. Oxford: Clarendon, 1988.

Wall, Diana diZerega, Nan A. Rothschild, and Cynthia Copeland. "Seneca Village and Little Africa: Two African American Communities in Antebellum New York City." *Historical Archaeology* 42, 1 (2008): 97–107.

Walls, Laura Dassow. *Henry David Thoreau: A Life*. Chicago: University of Chicago Press, 2017.

Seeing New Worlds: Henry David Thoreau and Nineteenth-Century Natural Science. Madison, WI: University of Wisconsin Press, 1995.

"'Walden As Feminist Manifesto.'" *ISLE: Interdisciplinary Studies in Literature and Environment* 1, 1 (March 1, 1993): 137–44.

Warner, Michael. "Thoreau's Bottom." *Raritan* 11, 3 (1992): 53.

Watson, Irene Margaret. *Aboriginal Peoples, Colonialism and International Law: Raw Law*. Abingdon: Routledge, 2015.

Weber, Max, *Economy and Society: An Outline of Interpretive Sociology*. Berkeley, CA: University of California Press, 1978.

West, Michael. *Transcendental Wordplay: America's Romantic Punsters and the Search for the Language of Nature*. Athens, GA: Ohio University Press, 2000.

Wetzel, James. *Augustine and the Limits of Virtue*. Cambridge: Cambridge University Press, 1992.

White, E. B. "Walden – 1954." In Walden, *Civil Disobedience, and Other Writings*, edited by William John Rossi, 3rd ed., 442–49. New York: Norton, 2008.

White, Lynn, Jr. "The Historical Roots of Our Ecologic Crisis." *Science, New Series*, 155, 3767 (March 10, 1967): 1203–7.

Wider, Sarah Ann. "'And What Became of Your Philosophy Then?' Women Reading *Walden*." *Nineteenth-Century Prose* 31, 2 (2004): 152–171.

Wiley, A. Terrance. *Angelic Troublemakers: Religion and Anarchism in America*. New York: Bloomsbury Academic, 2014.

Williams, Raymond. *The Country and the City*. New York: Oxford University Press, 1975.

Winters, Joseph R. *Hope Draped in Black: Race, Melancholy, and the Agony of Progress*. Durham, NC: Duke University Press Books, 2016.

Wittberg, Patricia. *The Rise and Fall of Catholic Religious Orders: A Social Movement Perspective*. Albany, NY: SUNY Press, 1994.

Wolf, William J. *Thoreau: Mystic, Prophet, Ecologist*. Philadelphia, PA: United Church Press, 1974.

Wollstonecraft, Mary. *A Vindication of the Rights of Woman and A Vindication of the Rights of Men*, edited by Janet Todd. Oxford: Oxford University Press, 1993.

Yale Program on Climate Change Communication. "Climate Change in the American Mind: March, 2016," http://climatecommunication.yale.edu/publications/climate-change-american-mind-march-2016/ (accessed August 20, 2020).

Young, Malcolm Clemens. *The Spiritual Journal of Henry David Thoreau.* Macon, GA: Mercer University Press, 2009.
Yunkaporta, Tyson. *Sand Talk: How Indigenous Thinking Can Save the World.* Melborne, Victoria: Text Publishing, 2019.
Zagzebski, Linda Trinkaus. *Exemplarist Moral Theory.* New York: Oxford University Press, 2017.
Žižek, Slavoj. "Notes towards a Politics of Bartleby: The Ignorance of Chicken." *Comparative American Studies: An International Journal* 4, 4 (December 1, 2006): 375–94.
Zwolinski, Matt, and David Schmidtz. "Environmental Virtue Ethics." In *The Cambridge Companion to Virtue Ethics*, edited by Daniel C. Russell, 221–39. Cambridge: Cambridge University Press, 2013.

Index

CPSIA information can be obtained
at www.ICGtesting.com
Printed in the USA
LVHW082142020821
694376LV00002B/88